HUMAN RIGHTS ISSUES IN THE 21ST CENTURY

HUMAN RIGHTS ISSUES IN THE 21ST CENTURY

MARIA S. BECKER
AND
JULIA N. SCHNEIDER
EDITORS

Nova Science Publishers, Inc.
New York

For permission to use material from this book please contact us:
Telephone 631-231-7269; Fax 631-231-8175
Web Site: http://www.novapublishers.com

LIBRARY OF CONGRESS CATALOGING-IN-PUBLICATION DATA

Human rights issues in the 21st century / Maria S. Becker and Julia N. Schneider, editors.
p. cm.
ISBN 978-1-60456-119-7 (hardcover)
1. Human rights. I. Becker, Maria S. II. Schneider, Julia N.
JC571.H76964 2007
323--dc22 2007047057

Published by Nova Science Publishers, Inc. ✦ New York

Contents

PREFACE

Human rights refers to "the basic rights and freedoms to which all humans are entitled, people sometimes take advantage of these, often held to include the right to life and liberty, freedom of thought and expression, and equality before the law." The United Nations Universal Declaration of Human Rights states, "All human beings are born free and equal in dignity and rights. They are endowed with reason and conscience and should act towards one another in a spirit of brotherhood."

The idea of human rights descended from the philosophical idea of natural rights that are provided by God; some recognize virtually no difference between the two and regard both as labels for the same thing while others choose to keep the terms separate to eliminate association with some features traditionally associated with natural rights. This book presents new ideas on human rights issues from an international standpoint.

Expert Commentary - Corporal punishment has become a very controversial issue to eliminate in African schools and even worldwide. The controversy appears to be due to the parallels between what happens at home and in schools. Some child–rearing practices within the home mandate parents to use corporal punishment when disciplining their own children but the laws and regulations within the schools bar teachers from using corporal punishment. In some cases parents believe that the African child cannot learn in the school without being beaten. As such, there is no doubt that teachers, parents and pupils hold various myths and beliefs on why teachers use corporal punishment in schools. If anything, the authors do not support the use of corporal punishment in African schools. It is against this background that this article sought to explore issues and challenges on why corporal punishment is still difficult to eliminate in African schools in the new millennium. Both local and international literature has been used to examine this issue.

Chapter 1 - This section of the book considers the movement of migrant workers. Discussions on migrants to the USA and Europe tend to focus on the need to keep such migrants away either to protect the existing workers or because of fear of large numbers of foreigners bringing crime or great demands on the resources of the host society. This paper discusses the severe suffering and absence of any human rights of those who move from poor to rich countries using the GCC as an example of the situation. The paper also discusses the contribution that the very poor temporary migrant workers make to making life easier for the rich inhabitants of the host countries.

This section considers the situation in the wealthy states of the GCC but similar circumstances are found in other parts of the world where extremes of poverty and wealth are found close together. It is often claimed that migrant workers do the tasks which others will not do but the reality is often that migrants are forced into undertaking tasks which no one should be required to do- working in dangerous circumstances or given insufficient food, rest, shelter, often physically and sexually abused and regularly not paid the promised amount for their labor. The tasks undertaken are performed to enable rich employers to save paying the 'going rate' so pocket greater profits or to enjoy a higher material standard of living by using the migrants to perform menial tasks which could be undertaken by machinery or improved ways of working. At a time when the British are commemorating the 200th anniversary of the slave trade in their empire the practice of what is very close to slavery is still found in many parts of the world—human beings exploited without any rights of redress or protection.

The author brings a managerial perspective, based on 30 years in commerce in Asia, rather than an academic or campaigning view but he has built up a great deal of knowledge of the mistreatment of migrant workers and the harm that this mistreatment does to individuals, societies and to businesses which attempt to work in an ethically just and humane manner.

Chapter 2 - The 21st century is already becoming one in which the human race will face competing rights to needs, resources and living conditions. In the west and western influenced nations, such as Japan, high living standards resulting from industrial and post industrial economic developments have led to calls for human rights such as democracy, freedom and individual wellbeing. In much of Asia these 'rights' are often not ones which are of primary concern in societies which value community cohesion, deeply felt religious conviction and trust in others. Many Asians desire to catch up with the material benefits of industrialization and are willing to forego many of the 'rights' sought in the west in return for prosperity.

The paper also discusses the western concern for written contracts, rules and laws while the Asian preference is to have mutual understanding and personal relationships to determine rights and obligations. These Asian preferences are challenged not only by the western governments, NGOs and pressure groups but by industrialization and urbanization. These challenges have often resulted in violent reactions and populist political movements against the west.

The authors bring their insights from Asia to help others understand why there is so much resistant to what are seen by westerners to be proper human rights. The insights are built upon their deep knowledge within Asia and within the west. The western author has worked in commerce in Asia for many decades while the Japanese author has worked in the west for most of her adult life. This paper is not an academic or a political treatise but offers insights into the practicalities of sharing the benefits of human progress with others in Asia whilst maintaining fundamental rights which should be accorded to all.

Chapter 3 - Terrorism is the threat of the age, or so we are told. The threat, at least as much as the reality, has ruined airline companies and tourist operators, thrown national economies into disarray and caused corporate collapse around the globe. The spectre of '9/11", Bali, Baghdad, Madrid, London, Glasgow and Gaza confronts us daily and nightly through our media. Reports from airlines tell us that it takes no more than a minor scare at an airport anywhere in the world to impel cancellations of seats and even flights. In the face of rational comment and any amount of evidence about the far greater threat to the world of AIDS, malaria, obesity and malnutrition, it is terrorism nonetheless that has the attention of the world and its media.

Behind the grip of terrorism lies the word, 'Islam'. The notion of the 'Muslim terrorist' has become a colloquialism in Western media. Interestingly, in all the history books and comment about the Second World War in Europe, the fascism and anti-Semitism on which the Nazi Third Reich was built is rarely if ever coupled with the word 'Christian', in spite of the fact that it made carefully constructed use of age-old Christian biases and pseudo-theologies, just as some modern terrorism employs Islamic equivalents. The same case could be made about the Ku Klux Clan, the South African apartheid advocates, or any number of other such instances where the perpetrators claimed their actions were based on their Christian beliefs.

Perhaps the reason that we do not do to Christians the same injustice that we do to Muslims relates to our being better educated about Christianity and its many complexities and differences. Through greater understanding, our facility to generalize and stereotype is slowed. Moreover, even in what is largely a post-church age, we seem to have too great a regard for Christianity and its principles than to allow its image to be polluted so easily by the claims of those whom we see clearly to be functioning outside of its norms and codes of conduct. Additionally, it could be that we are simply too sensitive to the feelings of those who align with Christianity to risk offending them. If these explanations come close to uncovering the reasons for the difference between the ways in which we ascribe a religious cause for terrorism to Christianity and Islam, then the challenge for restoring justice to Islam would seem to be for formal and informal education to take the goal of enhanced literacy about Islam more seriously (Lovat, 2005; 2006). We need to achieve the same understanding about Islam that seems implicit about Christianity, namely: that it is complex and different within itself, and so cannot be generalized about and stereotyped; that it has a set of principles, norms and a code of conduct that makes terrorism as incongruous to it as it is to the equivalent in Christianity; and, that its followers are as liable to be offended, hurt and confused as Christians would be if Christianity was routinely referred to as a cause of terrorism.

The purpose of this chapter is to uncover some of the lost story of Islam's remarkable achievements and contributions to civilization, including to everything that the 'West' has come to know and by which it is defined. It sets out therefore to restore justice to Islam by turning on their head conceptions that pit Islam against the West, such as connoted in the common phrase, 'Islam versus the West'. The authors' conception of the relationship between Islam and the West goes beyond even phrases like 'Islam and the West'. As much as anything, their story is about 'Islam within the West', a story of Islam's reforming power in the development of Western philosophy, science and self-understanding. It is a story that promotes Islam to take its rightful place as a leader of reform, dialogue and dealing with difference in equitable and charitable ways. It is a story about not only a sibling of the West's most powerful religions, Judaism and Christianity, but about a sibling that, with renewed understanding by Muslim and non-Muslim, could turn around radically its current popular image as a recalcitrant, separatist and violence-disposed ideology to being the obverse of this.

Of course, the authors do not retreat from the reality that Islam is regarded widely in very different terms and they will attempt to uncover the causes and the ensuing troubling theologies that threaten to turn Islam into the very thing that so many people fear about it. Above all, however, the authors want to paint a picture of Islam as an indispensable part of what most Westerners take for granted. Be it about modern medicine, science, education, social welfare, the role of women, of family, of human rights or of social justice, had there been no Islam, we quite likely would not be where we are today. The fact that so few Westerners recognize this is one of the tragic gaps in our education and self-understanding. The fact that, in all likelihood, so few Muslims understand this is also part of the problem we are attempting to rectify.

The chapter will take the form of an historical and documentary review aimed at recovering much of the positive story that has been lost, as well as understanding why so much of the positive potential in the story is being replaced by negative interpretations. Both aspects of this account are held to comprise justice issues in the West's perceptions of Islam. Finally, the article will provide a case study based on the experiences of one of the authors, Ibtihal Samarayi, an Iraqi who has been on the inside of detention owing to her own displacement. This Muslim woman has used artwork in her own attempt to restore justice to Islam and the many Muslims who have suffered from their own displacement owing to the struggle between cultures that underlies so many of the issues of the day.

Chapter 4 - During detention for re-education, the nature of labour seems to be compulsory. The prohibition of such labour has been recognised and codified into international human rights law, whereas there are some exceptions to this prohibition in some major human rights instruments. There remains the question of whether labour is a right or an obligation to perform. This study examines the nature of labour looking at the relevant provisions among international human rights standards and use of detention for re-education from the perspective of human rights. The right to work is fundamentally incompatible with a regime of forced labour. If compulsory work or service is permitted, it must be an implied exception to the right to work. China has the obligation to prohibit forced labour and protect the right to labour as one of basic human rights as a party to the International Covenant on Economic, Social and Cultural Rights (ICESCR), Equal Remuneration Convention (ILO100), Remuneration Policy Convention (ILO122) and Convention concerning the Prohibition and Immediate Action for the Elimination of the Worst Forms of Child Labour (ILO182). Any Chinese system in detention for re-education should be compatible with the nature of labour enshrined by these treaties.

Chapter 5 - Africa is at the epicentre of the child soldier phenomenon. Armed groups and forces using children cover the continent. In fact, children have been drawn into (whether through forced measures or 'voluntarily') nearly every one of its myriad wars. However, whilst the endemic link between children (and boys in particular) and armed conflict in Africa is generally becoming increasingly well documented, the specific correlation between girls and warfare in Africa remains under-researched and less well documented. Consequently this chapter focuses on "girl soldiers" and armed conflict in Africa. It is contended that girls, in their status firstly as females, and secondly as children, are markedly disadvantaged and discriminated against from a social and cultural point of view even in peacetime. Therefore arguably, they are in an even more vulnerable and susceptible position during conflict.

The first part of this chapter explores how girls in Africa become part of an armed conflict. Research denotes that whilst the majority are either abducted or forcibly recruited, some girls 'willingly' join armed groups to obtain things–inter alia protection, education and training, a sense of belonging/purpose, money, power–denied to them in civilian life. This in turn depicts that such girls are not passive victims but active agents with a strong sense of agency and ability to exercise choice.

The second part of this chapter examines the experiences of the girls once they are part (whether forcibly or 'voluntarily') of the armed group/force. Within the group, girls suffer from grave violations and abuses that have lasting mental, emotional, and physical repercussions. One such violation is sexual violence, (which also forms the focus of this section) as although not universal, it is a daily fare inside most armed groups in Africa and is even experienced by girls who joined without obvious coercion.

In the second part, the roles girls perform within armed groups are also analysed as they too have an important bearing on the experiences encountered. Research indicates that within an armed group, girls perform a wide variety of roles–roles that do not necessarily conform to simplistic gender stereotypes. Therefore some "girl soldiers" are fighters and take a direct part in hostilities, whereas others serve in a more supportive role such as cooks, porters, domestic labourers, spies, etc. However, it is important to note that the majority of the girls' roles are fluid, multiple, and overlapping.

Finally, in both parts of this chapter, the relevant international law (human rights law, international humanitarian law, and international criminal law in particular) pertaining to the issues is also considered. Fundamentally, international law makes it clear that the rights and dignity of girls must be protected at all times. However, such protection may recede when girls, exercising their agency, willingly participate in hostilities.

Chapter 6 - It is nearly twenty years since the UN General Assembly adopted the Convention on the Rights of the Child (UNCRC). Since then it has been ratified by more countries than any other international treaty – only Somalia and the United States have not yet done so. Lansdown (2002) suggests that 'during the last decade of the twentieth century the human rights of children finally became visible' (p.285). In the 21st Century the importance of children's rights and the commitments adopted by 192 countries under the UNCRC have been expanded and reaffirmed in The Millennium Declaration and A World Fit for Children (United Nations 2000, 2002). The ongoing challenge is in realising children's rights and promoting their well-being in practice. These challenges occur at a time when countries are seeking to respond to changes brought about by globalisation, technological advances and changes in the world of work (Hudson and Lowe, 2004). Local, national and international engagement is required to implement policies and practice that improve children and young people's life chances and promote their rights.

The first part of this chapter provides a brief overview of the rights enshrined in the UNCRC and its purpose. A number of human rights violations worldwide are identified within this discussion. In the second part of the chapter, the focus changes and attention turns to the progress that one Western society has made in realising children's rights, since they ratified the UNCRC. England has been selected for in-depth exploration. In a recent review of child well-being in developed economies the UK ranked the lowest country overall, closely followed by the United States (UNICEF, 2007a). A number of policy developments in England have been influenced by, or transferred from the United States (Dolowitz et al., 2000). This is of interest given that the former have ratified the UNCRC and the latter have not yet done so. The decision was also pragmatic, as the author's work aims to inform policy and practice and improve outcomes for vulnerable children and young people in England. The examination is not intended to comprehensively or systematically map the changes that have occurred in recent years, but rather to review certain developments to explore a range of factors that have contributed towards enhanced rights for children in England and those that have acted against this.

Chapter 7 - This chapter describes a test of a path model in which attitudes toward disability rights were predicted by religious fundamentalism, quest (religious) orientation, cultural conservatism, and belief in a dangerous world. Within the proposed model, dangerous world beliefs were expected to indirectly predict opposition to disability rights through several mediating variables: religious fundamentalism, quest orientation, and cultural conservatism. Additionally, the effects of fundamentalism and quest orientation on opposition to disability rights were expected to be mediated through cultural conservatism. Although quest orientation failed to mediate the relationship between dangerous world beliefs and cultural conservatism (or even to add incremental validity to the prediction of cultural conservatism) in the authors' study, the remaining proposed relationships were supported by the data. Following re-specification of our path model, religious fundamentalism was found to exert an indirect positive effect on opposition to disability rights through cultural conservatism while also exerting a negative direct effect on disability rights opposition.

Chapter 8 - One of the most pressing human rights issue in the beginning of the 21st century is the security and human rights nexus. On the forefront of the discussion is the impact of the global effort to counter terrorism on human rights.

September 11, 2001 signalled a new era in the chapter of the humanity's action against terrorism. Although the immediate response was that of a military nature, it is widely recognized that a prolonged counter terrorism action will be on the criminal justice front. A number of governments around the world started reforming their criminal justice systems to bring them up to date to face the challenge of international terrorism.

Recent developments show that the nature of terrorism is changing. Terrorism became indiscriminate and global in nature. If before terrorists targeted heads of states and governments and other VIP, nowadays, common civilians are targeted to produce an atmosphere of fear and panic among the population. Moreover, the international terrorism highlighted the 'dark side' of globalization. Today a leader of a terrorist organization could be coming from a state A, be radicalized in his believes in a state B, recruit members of his organization in a state C, get financing from a state D, fight for a 'cause' in a state E, while finding safe haven in a state F. Terrorists pay as much respect to national borders as swarms of locusts. The nations of the world and their criminal justice systems were slow to adapt to this new global 'modus operandi'. In my lectures, I often use the metaphor that it looks like we are using our bicycles trying to chase criminals that are driving fast modern vehicles.

Recognizing this problem, former UN Secretary-General Mr. Annan highlighted that ... terrorism is a threat to all states and to all peoples, which can strike anytime, anywhere. It is a direct attack on the core values the United Nations stands for: the rule of law; the protection of civilians; mutual respect between people of different faiths and cultures; and peaceful resolution of conflict... the United Nations must be at the forefront in fighting against it, and first of all in proclaiming, loud and clear, that terrorism can never be accepted or justified, in any cause whatsoever.

As the only truly global organization with the goals and means of preserving peace and security, the UN is naturally expected to be at the forefront of the global action against terrorism. Although having addressed terrorism prior to 9/11, the UN, because of the diversity of its membership, never had a comprehensive strategic approach how to fight it. On 8 September 2006, the UN General Assembly (GA), in unprecedented show of international solidarity agreed on the 'Global Counter-Terrorism Strategy'. The adoption of the United Nations Global Counter-Terrorism Strategy by the GA was a landmark event, as it was the first time that all countries agreed to a common strategic approach to fight terrorism. The Strategy forms the basis for a concrete plan of action, consisting of four key areas:

- Measures to address the conditions conducive to the spread of terrorism;
- Measures to prevent and combat terrorism;
- Measures to build the capacity of States and the United Nations to prevent and combat terrorism; and
- Measures to ensure respect for human rights for all and the rule of law as the fundamental basis of the fight against terrorism.

As you see, promotion of human rights while countering terrorism is considered so important that it is developed into a separate part of the strategy. The present article tries to challenge a common misconception that there has to be a certain trade off between new proactive counter terrorism legislation, on the one hand, and human rights on the other. We believe that since terrorism is a direct assault on the basic human right to life, any effort directed at countering this evil is also aimed at promoting human rights. A smartly designed criminal justice strategy aimed at preventing terrorist acts will only contribute to and promote establishing the rule of law.

The article is organized as following. First of all, the authors will tract the developments that led to the adoption of the Strategy. Secondly, they will see what actors are working in the field. Thirdly, the authors will see what issues are involved in a Counter-terrorism (CT)-Human Rights (HR) nexus. And finally, they will outline the role of the United Nations Office on Drugs and Crime in the global effort against terrorism.

Chapter 9 - This work considers the importance of ethics in the practice of psychology. Within this general framework, this paper takes into account the central role that human rights take in the main professional ethic codes of psychology in Argentina, like in many other ethic codes from other countries. The particular inclusion of these topics in Argentinean ethic codes of psychology is analyzed in this case not only as the inclusion of general ethical principles that guarantee personal and community welfare. It is specially considered that the permanent direct or indirect reference to human rights in those Codes is related to the '70 dictatorial government that, as in many other Latin-American countries, established a terror system, in which personal and social rights were seriously damaged, causing a deep wound in society.

In: Human Rights Issues in the 21st Century
Editors: M.S. Becker and J.N. Schneider, pp. 1-9
ISBN 978-1-60456-119-7

Expert Commentary

Corporal Punishment in Schools: Current Issues and Challenges in Africa in the New Millennium

Almon Shumba[1], Lily Cherian[2] and Douglas Mawere[3]

[1] School of Post Studies, Faculty of Education, University of Fort Hare, Main Campus, King William's Town Road, Private Bag X1314, Alice 5700. South Africa

[2] School of Education, Faculty of Education, University of Limpopo Turflop Campus, Private Bag X1106, Sovenga 0727. South Africa

[3] Department of Preclinical Veterinary Studies, Faculty of Veterinary Sciences University of Zimbabwe, P.O. Box MP 167, Mount Pleasant, Harare. Zimbabwe

Introduction

Corporal punishment has become a very controversial issue to eliminate in African schools and even worldwide. The controversy appears to be due to the parallels between what happens at home and in schools (Dubanoski, Inaba and Gerkewicz, 1983; Korbin, 1980; O'Brien and Lau, 1995; Shumba, 2003a and b; Zindi, 1995). Some child–rearing practices within the home mandate parents to use corporal punishment when disciplining their own children but the laws and regulations within the schools bar teachers from using corporal punishment. In some cases parents believe that the African child cannot learn in the school without being beaten. As such, there is no doubt that teachers, parents and pupils hold various myths and beliefs on why teachers use corporal punishment in schools. If anything, the authors do not support the use of corporal punishment in African schools. It is against this background that this article sought to explore issues and challenges on why corporal punishment is still difficult to eliminate in African schools in the new millennium. Both local and international literature has been used to examine this issue.

[1] Address all requests and correspondence to: Professor Almon Shumba, School of Post Graduate Studies, Faculty of Education, University of Fort Hare, Main Campus, King William's Town Road, Private Bag X1314, Alice 5700. South Africa. Tel: (+27) (040) 602 2493 (Work) and (+27) (0) 72 426 8036 (Cell). E–mail addresses: ashumba@ufh.ac.za and almonshumba@yahoo.com

Research on Corporal Punishment in African Schools and Implications

Corporal punishment refers to intentional application of physical pain as a method of changing behavior (Shumba, 2003a; Straus and Mouradian, 1998) and includes such methods as hitting, slapping, spanking, punching with fists, kicking, pinching, shaking or using various objects such as wooden paddles, belts, sticks, electric cords or others (Dubanoski, Inaba and Gerkewicz, 1983; Grossman, Rauh and Riveira, 1995; Shumba, 2001; 2003a and b; Zindi, 1995). Whilst there are worldwide frantic efforts to outlaw this practice through the United Nations Convention on the Rights of the Child (Jonsson, 2003; Rohner, 1975; Rohner and Rohner, 1980; Sebonego, 1994), it looks like the battle is still very far from being over especially in African schools (Dubanoski et al., 1983; Mutema, 1988; Newell, 1993; Ntshingila, 2004; Shumba, 2002; 2003a and b; Zindi, 1995).

Corporal punishment has been and is still a conventional method in disciplining children when at home still under parental care and in schools in some African countries. As such, it has now become a very controversial issue to eliminate in African schools and worldwide because of the parallels and contradictions between what happens at home and in schools (Newell, 1993; O'Brian and Lau, 1995; Shumba, 2003a and b; Zindi, 1995). For example, in some cultures, there are some child–rearing practices within the home that mandate parents to use corporal punishment when disciplining their own children (Dow and Mogwe, 1992; Dubanoski, Inaba and Gerkewicz, 1983; Korbin, 1980; O'Brien and Lau, 1995).

On the contrary, within the school, the government of Zimbabwe, for example, has enacted laws and regulations within the schools that forbid teachers from using corporal punishment on pupils (Statutory Instrument 65 of the Constitution of Zimbabwe, 1992; The Secretary of Education and Culture Circular P35, 1993). Under the current laws and regulations of Zimbabwe, only the school head is mandated and protected by the law to use corporal punishment on pupils within the school (Shumba, 2002; Shumba and Moorad, 2000). Teachers wishing to administer corporal punishment on misbehaving pupils are required by the law to first seek approval from the school head and should record in the school log book the name of the pupil and the nature of offence committed. Otherwise, any teachers who execute instance justice on pupils without approval by the school head are considered to have physically assaulted the pupil and are liable to be charged with assault or physical abuse (Statutory Instrument 65 of the Constitution of Zimbabwe, 1992; The Secretary of Education and Culture Circular P35, 1993).

In communities in which the school has developed as a recognizable social institution, corporal punishment has not only been tolerated but has been prescribed as an essential part of the pedagogue's function (Dow and Mogwe, 1992; O'Brian and Lau, 1995; Payne, 1989; Sebonego, 1994). The belief that corporal punishment is a necessary and effective in disciplining children has become engrained and uncritically accepted in most traditions. It is this belief that appears to have been used as a justification for the kind of disciplinary action in society and schools (Shumba, 2001 and 2003a). As such, it has now become very difficult to draw a line between what happens in the school and home since the school is an extension of the home (Shumba, 2001 and 2003a; Shumba and Moorad, 2000; Straus, 1994). It appears that it is the home culture or child–rearing practice that is extended to the school by some teachers in the name of discipline with teachers acting *in-loco-parentis* within the school

(Shumba, 2001 and 2002). Hence, teachers seem to view this as exercising their *loco-parentis* role within the school and not as a violation of any regulations (Dow and Mogwe, 1992; Magagula, 1992; Sebonego, 1994; Shumba, 2003a and b).

Current research notes that parents and teachers who were physically abused as children are more supportive of corporal punishment than those who were not (Climinillo, 1980; Hyman, 1988; Newell, 1993; Ntshingila, 2004; Poole, Ushokov and Nader, 2003; Shumba, 2003a; Straus, 1991, 1994 and 1996). This implies that violence is transferred from generation to generation and perhaps a suggestion why some teachers physically abuse pupils in schools. Some parents who were physically abused at home or school claim that they never suffered any negative consequences (Hyman, 1988; Ntshingila, 2004; Payne, 1989; Poole et al., 2003).

In a recent comprehensive study carried out by the South African Human Science Research Council (HSRC), parents admitted to hitting their children and nearly a third of parents said that they beat them severely (Ntshingila, 2004). The HSRC study found that: (1) a third of those who admitted to hitting their children said they beat them severely using a belt, stick or other objects; (2) divorced parents were more likely than married ones to smack their children; (3) African parents were most likely to beat their children severely, followed by white and Coloured parents, with Indian parents the least likely to do so; (4) children under three years were likely to be 'smacked' but from four up, were more likely to be 'beaten'; (5) parents aged 25 to 35 were most likely to smack their children, while those over 35 were more likely to beat their children; and (6) there was a link between parents who maltreated their children and those in physically abusive relationships with their partners (Ntshingila, 2004: 1). Despite the incidence of corporal punishment revealed by the study, current research shows that South Africans hit their children less than the Americans or Britons where similar studies show that 90 % of children will be smacked at this stage of development (Newell, 1993; Ntshingila, 2004; Payne, 1989; Poole et al., 2003; Shumba, 2001; Shumba and Moorad, 2000; Straus, 1991, 1994, 1996). Although most experts in South Africa have called for the banning of corporal punishment in the home, it appears a tall order to implement and control.

On the contrary, other studies assert that approximately one half of students who were subjected to severe punishment develop an illness called Educationally Induced

Post–Traumatic Stress Disorder (EIPTSD). Such a disorder is a symptomatology analogous to the Post-Traumatic Stress Disorder (PTSD) often characterized by depression and anxiety (Hyman, 1988; Hyman, Irwin and Laily, 1982). This mental health imbalance is induced by significant stress and with EIPSD, the stress is caused by the inflicted corporal punishment (Hyman, 1988). Hence, such physically abused students often have difficulty with sleeping, fatigue, feelings of sadness and worthlessness, suicidal thoughts, anxiety episodes, increased anger with feelings of resentment and outbursts of aggression, deteriorating peer relationships, difficulty with concentration, lowered school achievement, antisocial behavior, intense dislike of authority, a tendency for school avoidance and school dropout and other high risk adolescent behaviors (Dubanoski et al., 1983; Hyman, 1988; Hyman et al., 1982). This appears to be consistent with research that claims that physically abused children tend to become more rebellious and are more likely to demonstrate vindictive behaviors within the school or home (Poole et al., 2003).

Most studies available appear to suggest that African parents believe that corporal punishment is part of the African culture of child-rearing practices (Dow and Mogwe, 1992;

Sebonego, 1994; Shumba, 2001 and 2003a; Zindi, 1995). As such, it has now become common practice by most African parents to use corporal punishment to discipline their children at home and that some parents believe that corporal punishment makes pupils 'perform well' in school (Shumba, 2001; 2003aandb). As such, some of the parents seem to be completely and totally oblivious of the laws and regulations that govern the treatment of pupils by their teachers in schools because whatever teachers do is believed to be 'always right' (Dubanoski, Inaba and Gerkewicz, 1983; Shumba, 2003b).

CORPORAL PUNISHMENT AND IMPLICATIONS: THE ZIMBABWEAN SCHOOL CONTEXT

However, the practice within the school is different from that at home because there are stipulated procedures on how to discipline pupils in schools (Secretary of Education Circular P 35, 1993; Statutory Instrument 65 of the Constitution of Zimbabwe, 1992). In Zimbabwe, corporal punishment should be inflicted only by the school head or a teacher to whom authority has been delegated by the head, or any other teacher in the presence of the head, and should be inflicted on the buttocks with a suitable strap, cane or smooth light switch (Secretary for Education and Culture Circular P 35, 1993; Statutory Instrument 65 of the Constitution of Zimbabwe, 1992).

Current research shows that although the head is the only officer within the school with the authority to discipline pupils, it is now uncommon in Zimbabwe to find some school heads being charged for excessively canning pupils (Newell, 1993; Shumba, 2001; 2003a and b; Zindi, 1995). Other reasons why some teachers physically abuse their pupils from interviews conducted with Education Officers responsible for handling and processing all abuse cases by teachers in Zimbabwean schools appear to suggest that some of them tend to become too emotional when dealing with pupils and end up taking the law into their hands (Shumba, 2001; 2003a and b). When in such an emotional state, some school heads or teachers tend to by-pass the stipulated procedures by the Public Service Commission that teachers should obtain a mandate to use corporal punishment on their pupils from the school head (Secretary of Education Circular P 35, 1993; Statutory Instrument 65 of the Constitution of Zimbabwe, 1992). It appears that some of these perpetrators tend to become too emotional when dealing with pupils and end up taking the law into their hands. Under such an emotional state, the perpetrators do not follow the stipulated procedures by the Public Service Commission that they should obtain permission to use corporal punishment on their pupils from the school head (Statutory Instrument 65 of the Constitution of Zimbabwe, 1992). Other studies also shows that most cases of physical assault reported tend to involve injuries on pupils and such cases are handled and processed by the police before being handed over to the courts of law (Newell, 1993; Shumba, 2001 and 2003a).

Corporal Punishment and Implications: The International Context

Other studies on physical abuse of pupils by teachers in schools suggest that the violation of stipulated laws and regulations to be based on certain beliefs regarding the effectiveness of corporal punishment and on lack of knowledge concerning disciplinary alternatives to physical abuse or corporal punishment in schools (Newell, 1993; Payne, 1989; Zindi, 1995). For example, Dubanoski et al. (1983) found that both society and teachers in the Caribbean Islands hold four common myths about corporal punishment: the belief that corporal punishment builds character; the belief that corporal punishment teaches respect; the belief that corporal punishment is the only thing some children understand; and, the belief that without corporal punishment, behavioral problems increase. Similarly, in Turkish schools, both teachers and headmasters are encouraged to use corporal punishment on their students (Korbin, 1980; Rohner, 1975; Rohner and Rohner, 1980). This seems to imply that such practices are viewed as promoting and inculcating their cultural practices and not as child abuse.

Other studies found that some cultures view the deliberate infliction of pain on children 'as vital to the development of strength, endurance and cultural allegiance' (Anderson and Payne, 1994; O'Brian and Lau, 1995; Payne, 1989). Similarly, in some cultures, corporal punishment is viewed as an instrument used in teaching the child values and norms of the society during the parenting process (Benatar, 2004; Straus, 1991). However, Greven (1990) argues that while corporal punishment is viewed as a positive aspect of parenting that provides children with the necessary structure of personality growth, it involves inflicting pain partly for retribution, and teaches a child that those in power can force others to obey. If corporal punishment has effects on children, it is debatable that it promotes positive cultural values and norms of the society (Dow and Mogwe, 1992; Sebonego, 1994; Shumba, 2001, 2002 and 2003a). Similar research shows that those who believe in the use of corporal punishment in schools do not have proper classroom order and to them corporal punishment is the only technique left to preserve academic control (Dubanoski et al., 1983; Payne, 1989; Sebonego, 1994; Straus, 1994).

As such, it is such cultures that condone violence against children as acceptable and useful in society that have made physical abuse or corporal punishment a very controversial issue to eliminate in schools worldwide (Anderson and Payne, 1994; Dow and Mogwe, 1992; Dubanoski et al., 1983; Sebonego, 1994; Shumba, 2001; 2003a and b). This study seeks to determine: pupils' myths and beliefs on why teachers physically abuse them in schools; if pupils have knowledge of the laws and regulations that protect them against physical abuse in schools; and recommend possible alternatives that could be used by teachers to discipline pupils in schools.

Conclusions and Recommendations for Further Research

It appears very clear from the above findings that pupils hold a variety of myths about why some teachers physically abuse them in schools. The majority of pupils seem to suggest that teachers 'want to control pupils who do wrong things' and 'they want to be feared'.

Perhaps, the question that we must raise is that why should teachers resort to such strategies if they are capable of delivering their subject matter? Teachers who are conversant with their subject matter are likely to be able to create a positive atmosphere during the learning process and motivate pupils to play their part. Current research suggests that it is most often a headache for some teachers to maintain classroom control in schools because 'many teachers fail to foster an atmosphere of mutual respect between their pupils and themselves or as originating in failed pedagogical relationships' (Benatar, 2004; Mushoriwa and Shumba, 2002). This often results in compromising their positions within the classroom because such teachers appear to lack the ability or the inclination verbally to communicate expectations to children in a professional manner. It is unfortunate that some of the teachers seem not to believe in rewarding good behavior but in punishing the bad behavior (Benatar, 2004). It is also interesting to note that even in countries where corporal punishment has been abolished such as South Africa, there are some teachers who do not observe the stipulated laws. Some of these teachers appear to hold the belief that the African child can only learn by using corporal punishment (Magagula, 1992; Mutema, 1988; Ntshingila, 2004; Sebonego, 1994).

It is important for teachers to be able to motivate their students during the learning process. One way to do this is for teachers to be well versed with their subject matter and this makes them to be respected by their students than teachers with the 'Data Deficiency Syndrome' (Mushoriwa and Shumba, 2002). These are teachers who are less versed with their subject matter in their areas of specialization. Such teachers often have confrontations with their students because of ignorance about their subject matter and are not very comfortable to be asked challenging questions. Therefore, it is necessary for teachers to be not dogmatic and should be able to learn some new ideas from their students because students are not like a *tabula rasa* or empty vessels where one pours in knowledge (Anderson and Payne, 1994; Lefrancois, 1997; Mwamwenda, 1996).

It also appears from the findings of this study that the majority of pupils are familiar with the laws and regulations that protect them against physical abuse in Zimbabwean schools. It is very interesting to note that pupils cannot be taken for granted by some unscrupulous teachers in the new millennium because they seem to be aware of their rights within the school. This implies that pupils could possibly report any form of physical abuse to their parents and other authorities.

What appears clear from the above findings is that some teachers seem not to be aware of the alternatives that they could utilize in order to maintain classroom control in schools. This paper will also attempt to come up with some of the alternatives that teachers could utilize to maintain classroom control in schools. First and foremost, the teacher needs to display an attitude of respect for the students so that students can feel that they are loved and understood by their teacher. In other words, the teacher should be positive and not negative attitudes towards the students all the time. This makes the students feel loved and cared for by the teacher. It must be pointed out that there are some children who may have never been shown any love in their lives (Rohner, 1975; Rohner and Rohner, 1980; Shumba, 2001; 2003a and b). Therefore, it is important for teachers in their *loco–parentis* roles to develop a positive relationship with their students all the time (Shumba, 2001; 2003a and b).

There is also a need for both parents and students involvement in decision making about school issues that affect the students, including educational goals and disciplinary issues. Research suggests that lack of involvement in the education of their children often leads to classroom disciplinary problems in schools (Hyman and Wise, 1979; Kelly, 1983).

Inappropriate behavior can also be reduced by using a technique known as extinction (Benatar, 2004). This technique removes or eliminates the rein forcers that maintain the inappropriate actions. In this regard, the teacher or parent must use a calm voice when giving instructions and this normally eliminates problems. As such, teachers need to be trained in this aspect so that they can be handle children within the classroom. Other methods of handling inappropriate behavior are by holding teacher–parent conferences, revocation of privileges, after school detention and counseling. However, it must be pointed out that detaining the children equally indicates failure by the teacher to foster an atmosphere of mutual respect between their pupils and themselves (Benatar, 2004).

Another alternative is to develop a program to educate teachers, parents and school administrators on how to eliminate corporal punishment in schools and within the society. The negative effects of corporal punishment must be publicized and recognized by the public at large and this may result in a social atmosphere condemning it. Family therapists need to work with parents and students at home and in schools on the effects of corporal punishment on child development and educate them on alternatives that are available to eliminate it. It must be noted that corporal punishment is ineffective in producing durable behavior change of students in schools and at home.

In conclusion, it is clear from the above discussion that enacting a law to abolish corporal punishment does not mean that teachers stop using it in schools. This is because such teachers appear desperate for 'sensible' alternatives to corporal punishment in schools. As such, the use and non–use corporal remains a challenge to all teachers in Africa and worldwide.

References

Anderson, S. and Payne, M.A. (1994). Corporal Punishment in Elementary Education: Views of Barbadian School Children. *Child Abuse and Neglect*, 18 (4), 377 – 386.

Bell, J. (1996). *Doing Your Research Project: A Guide for First–Time Researchers in Education and Social Sciences*. Milton Keynes: Philadelphia, Open University Press.

Benatar, D. (2004). *Corporal Punishment: Philosophical Study*. http://www. corpun. Com /benatar.hmtl

Climinilo, L.M. (1980). Discipline: The School's Dilemma. *Adolescence*, 15, 1 – 12.

Dow, U. and Mogwe, A. (1992). *The Convention on the Rights of the Child and the Legal Status of Children in Botswana*. A Consultancy Report for UNICEF Botswana. Women and Law in Southern Africa Research Project (WLSA). Botswana.

Dubanoski, R.A., Inaba, M. and Gerkewicz, K. (1983). Corporal Punishment in Schools: Myths, Problems and Alternatives. *Child Abuse and Neglect*, 7, 271 – 278.

Grossman, D.C., Rauh, M.J. and Rivara, F.P. (1995). Prevalence of Corporal Punishment Among Students in Washington State Schools. *Archives of Paediatric of Adolescent Medicine*, 149, 529 – 532.

Hyman, I.A. (1996).. Using Research to Change Public Policy: Reflections on 20 years of Effort to Eliminate Corporal Punishment in Schools. *Pediatrics*, 98 (Supplementary), 818 – 821.

Hyman, I.A., Irwin, A. and Laily, D. (1982). Discipline in the 1980's: Some Alternatives to Corporal Punishment. *Children Today*, 11, 10 – 13.

Hyman, I.A., Zelikoff, W. and Clarke, J. (1988). Psychological and Physical Abuse in the Schools: A Paradigm for Understanding Post-Traumatic Stress Disorder in Children and Youth. *Journal of Traumatic Stress*, 1, 243 – 266.

Jonsson, U. (2003). *Human Rights Approach to Development Programming*. UNICEF: Kenya.

Kinard, E.M. (1985). Ethical Issues in Research with Abused Children. *Child Abuse and Neglect*, 9, 301 – 311.

Korbin, J.E. (1980). The Cultural Context of Child Abuse and Neglect. *Child Abuse and Neglect*, 4, 3 – 13.

Kurebwa, E.V. (1987). Corporal Punishment: Do Teachers Know Best? *Teachers' Forum*, 4, Harare: College Press. April.

Lefrancois, G.R. (1997). *Psychology for Teaching*, Belmont: CA, Wadsworth.

Magagula, C. (1992). To Flog or Not to Flog: A Literature Review. *BOLESWA Educational Research Journal*, 9, 1 – 17.

Mushoriwa, T.D. and Shumba, A. (2002). Self-Perceived and Measured Study Strategies Among College Students. *Southern Africa Review of Education Journal*, 2 (1), 46 – 49.

Mutema, M. (1988). *Issues in the Philosophy and Practice of 'Kurova' (Beating) as a Pillar Punishing Method in Schools*. Unpublished B.A. (Hons) degree dissertation. Department of Religious Studies, Classics and Philosophy, University of Zimbabwe.

Mwamwenda, T.S. (1996). *Educational Psychology: An African Perspective*, Second Edition. Durban, Butterworth.

Newell, P. (1993). *Protecting African Children From All Forms of Violence: The United Nations on the Rights of the Child*. Paper presented at the Second African Conference on Child Abuse and Neglect, Cape Town, SASPCAN. September.

Ntshingila, F. (2004). South Africa's Child–Beating Shock: Experts Call For A Ban on Corporal Punishment in the Home. *Sunday Times*, 24 October.

O'Brian, C. and Lau, L.S.W. (1995). Defining Child Abuse in Hong Kong. *Child Abuse Review*, 4, 38 – 46.

Payne, M.A. (1989). Use and Abuse of Corporal Punishment: A Caribbean View. *Child Abuse and Neglect*, 13, 389 – 401.

Poole, S.R., Ushokow, M.C. and Nader, P.R. (2003). Corporal Punishment in Schools: Position Paper of the Society for Adolescent Medicine. *Journal of Adolescent Health*, 32, 385 – 393.

Rohner, R. (1975). *They Love Me, They Love Me Not: A World Study of the Effects of Parental Acceptance and Rejection*. New Haven, CT: HRAF Press.

Rohner, R. and Rohner, E.C. (1980). Antecedents and Consequences of Parental Rejection: A Theory of Emotional Abuse. *Child Abuse and Neglect*, 4, 189 – 198.

Sebonego, M.M. (1994). *Report of A Case Study: Child Abuse and Neglect*. Unpublished B.Ed. Dissertation, Department of Sociology, University of Botswana, Gaborone.

Shumba, A. (2000). *The Epidemiology and Aetiology of Child Abuse by Teachers in Zimbabwean Primary Schools*. PhD Thesis, Faculty of Education, University of the Western Cape. South Africa.

Shumba, A. and Moorad, F. (2000). A Note on the Laws Against Child Abuse in Botswana. *PULA: Botswana Journal of African Studies*, 14 (2), 175 – 181.

Shumba, A. (2001). The Epidemiology and Aetiology of Reported Cases of Child Physical Abuse in Zimbabwean Primary Schools. *Child Abuse and Neglect: The International Journal*, 25, 265 – 277.

Shumba, A. (2002). Teacher Conceptualization of Child Abuse in Schools in the New Millennium. *Journal of Interpersonal Violence*, 17 (4), 403 – 415.

Shumba, A. (2003a). Pupil Physical Abuse by Secondary School Teachers in Zimbabwe: A Child–Rearing Practice or Cultural Dilemma? *Journal of Aggression, Maltreatment and Trauma*, 8 (4) (#18), 143 – 159.

Shumba, A. (2003b). Children's Rights in Schools: What Do Teachers Know? *Child Abuse Review*, 12, 251 – 260. John Wiley and Sons.

Statutory Instrument 65 of the Constitution of Zimbabwe (1992). *Public Service (Disciplinary) Regulations of 1992*, 423 – 448.

Straus, M.A. (1991). Discipline and Deviance: Physical Punishment of Children and Violence and Other Crimes in Adulthood. *Social Problems*, 38 (2), 133 – 154. May.

Straus, M.A. (1994). *Beating The Devil Out Of Them. Corporal Punishment in American Families*. New York: Lexington Books.

Straus, M.A. (1996). Spanking and the Making Of A Violent Society. *Pediatrics*, 98 (Supplement), 832 – 881.

The Secretary of Education and Culture (1993). *Circular Number P 35 of 3 May*.United Nations General Assembly (1989, November). *Adoption of a Convention on the Rights of the Child (U.N. Doc. A/Res/44/25)*. New York.

Zindi, F. (1995). An Analysis of the Arguments For and Against Corporal Punishment in Zimbabwe. *Zimbabwe Journal of Educational Research*, 7 (1), 69 – 83.

In: Human Rights Issues in the 21st Century
Editors: M.S. Becker and J.N. Schneider, pp. 11-18
ISBN 978-1-60456-119-7

Chapter 1

TEMPORARY MIGRANT WORKERS IN THE GULF CO-OPERATION COUNCIL STATES: POOR PEOPLE SUFFERING SO THE RICH CAN HAVE GREATER RICHES

Wes Harry
Lancashire Business School University of Central Lancashire and Cass Business School City University London, England

ABSTRACT

This section of the book considers the movement of migrant workers. Discussions on migrants to the USA and Europe tend to focus on the need to keep such migrants away either to protect the existing workers or because of fear of large numbers of foreigners bringing crime or great demands on the resources of the host society. This paper discusses the severe suffering and absence of any human rights of those who move from poor to rich countries using the GCC as an example of the situation. The paper also discusses the contribution that the very poor temporary migrant workers make to making life easier for the rich inhabitants of the host countries.

This section considers the situation in the wealthy states of the GCC but similar circumstances are found in other parts of the world where extremes of poverty and wealth are found close together. It is often claimed that migrant workers do the tasks which others will not do but the reality is often that migrants are forced into undertaking tasks which no one should be required to do- working in dangerous circumstances or given insufficient food, rest, shelter, often physically and sexually abused and regularly not paid the promised amount for their labor. The tasks undertaken are performed to enable rich employers to save paying the 'going rate' so pocket greater profits or to enjoy a higher material standard of living by using the migrants to perform menial tasks which could be undertaken by machinery or improved ways of working. At a time when the British are commemorating the 200th anniversary of the slave trade in their empire the practice of what is very close slavery is still found in many parts of the world- human beings exploited without any rights of redress or protection.

The author brings a managerial perspective, based on 30 years in commerce in Asia, rather than an academic or campaigning view but he has built up a great deal of knowledge of the mistreatment of migrant workers and the harm that this mistreatment does to individuals, societies and to businesses which attempt to work in an ethically just and humane manner.

Introduction

For probably as long as mankind has existed poverty at home and potential riches elsewhere have tempted people to move. This has generally been a slow and steady process often linked to seasonal changes in the home and host environment. People moved for months at a time to nearby locations. With the increase in the world's population, the availability of mass transport and with more obvious inequalities in income and capital temporary and permanent migration has increased so that now millions of people move to places where they hope to have better opportunities for survival and relative prosperity. Europe and the USA have experienced recent increases in mass migration but these places have not absorbed the proportion of migrants which the countries of the Gulf Cooperation Council (GCC) countries have handled. This section of the book discusses migration in the GCC but many of the issues can apply in countries of Asia, Africa, and South America as well as in Europe and North America.

GCC

The countries of the GCC are the Bahrain, Kuwait, Qatar, Oman, Saudi Arabia and the United Arab Emirates all of which were sparsely populated desert areas until oil wealth, mainly in the 1970s, brought the technology and riches to sustain cities and higher population. The oil industry required technical and professional workers able to undertake specialist work which the host population did not possess. The wealth also resulted in large scale infrastructure projects which also required specialist foreign workers. These expatriate workers joined small numbers of Arabs, Iranians and south Asians who had worked in public sector and trading jobs for many decades before oil wealth transformed the region. It was expected that most of those working in the major oil and infrastructure projects would return to their home countries when construction was completed leaving only a few maintenance staff and instructors who would pass skills on to the host country nationals. But the expected reduction in expatriates did not happen and now the proportion of foreigners in the GCC workforce is now between 55% and 90%- with the UAE having the highest percentage. Few of these workers have specialist skills and most are employed in manual, low skilled service work or as domestic helpers. These foreigners are all temporary migrants because the residence conditions in the GCC require that non-citizens either be resident on the basis of a work permit or be the dependent of someone with a work permit.

The citizens of the GCC had few of the skills needed in the oil sector, construction or public service but were happy to take managerial or supervisory positions and to establish agencies to employ needed foreign workers. Many of those holding managerial and supervisory positions relied solely on their citizenship to gain and hold a job- capability and dedication were not required criteria. These citizens were almost impossible to discipline or to dismiss. As there were few citizens, in relation to the needed jobs, those who were in work could command high salaries and benefit packages far exceeding the value of the jobs they held. Therefore employers sought cheaper than usual foreign workers (to make up for the non performance of many citizens and the high cost of these citizens). As employers could not discipline host country nationals they made sure that the foreigners employed would obey all instructions with out complaint and that they would not demand rights in employment or in residence. The labor agents are often public servants working outside (or even during) normal working hours and who use their connections to circumvent regulations on employment rights (even the very limited rights which are supposed to exist).

POOR TO RICH COUNTRIES

The GCC countries are fortune in having very poor countries close by. Most Arab states have lots of unemployed people, many of whom are well educated, and few employment opportunities. At first the GCC states welcomed fellow Arabs as teachers, public servant, shopkeepers as well as skilled and unskilled laborers. These workers often brought their families and looked to settle in the 'wider Arab lands'. However the citizens of the GCC and their governments did not wish to share their wealth and did not wish to be hosts to potential many millions who could lay claim to citizenship and share in the wealth. So the governments slowed the recruitment of Arabs and sought workers from other poor countries who would not feel that they had rights in the region.

Among the other close by poor countries are those of south Asia and at first workers were brought in millions from Pakistan, India and Sri Lanka. The people from these poor countries were willing to work for low wages (US$100 a month is not an uncommon wage) and put up with difficult working and living conditions because they could earn and save much more than they could at home. These south Asians, usually from the poorest sections of poor countries, had little expectation of rights in the GCC- as they had little expectation of rights at home. As we will see later many workers suffered and continue to suffer not just an absence of rights but serious abuse.

The countries of south Asia, particularly Pakistan, Sri Lanka and Nepal suffered breakdown in civil order so an extra impetus for a move to the GCC was the expectation of being in a civil society where law and order would give them some measure of security. The Muslim migrants especially thought that they would have some welcome in the Arabian peninsula which was the origin of Islam and the location of the two holist places in that religion.

Once again the hosts started to worry that fellow Muslims would like to settle in the region and claim rights through religious affinity. With membership of the United Nations GCC states discovered that they were expected to abide by conventions allowing those resident in the countries concerned for more than 20 years to have the right to citizenship. A number of long resident migrants sought to take advantage of these rights but most found that their residence permits were quickly cancelled and they were sent 'home'. When the GCC states felt that the traditional sources of south Asian workers were bringing in potential trouble makers and when these same south Asians started to ask for higher wages the employers in the region turned to cheaper sources and ones which either had non Muslims or else Muslims who would not demand equality or rights so workers from Muslim Bangladesh and Indonesia and mainly non Muslim Philippines, China and Nepal were encouraged to take up jobs.

At each stage the GCC countries and citizens wished to have migrant workers who would be cheap to employ and who would not be in a position to claim rights. There are millions of very poor people in Asia who have been drawn to the GCC for low wages even despite the publicity which is given in their home countries about the level of abuse and lack of rights to be found in these countries. The desperately poor know that many other regions have as may malpractices as the GCC and in any case human faith in 'bad things happen to others not oneself' ensures a continuing supply of migrant labor.

Temporary Migration

Mention was made above of Arab workers in the 1970s bringing their families to the GCC. Since that time governments have generally made it difficult for the average worker to bring families to the region. Even if a husband and wife both find jobs they have to earn a fairly high (very high in average foreign worker wages) before they can live together. Babies born of mothers who are not legally in the country sponsored by their husband are likely to be taken from the mother at birth (it is assumed the baby is illegitimate) and the mother expelled from the country after a period in jail. Dependents taken ill will be expelled from the country if they cannot meet medical bills.

So workers, with exceptions such as those employed in well paid jobs, expect to leave their families behind and have a temporary residence in the region. Home visits would typically be for 2 months each two or three years. Some low paid workers still want to bring their families to the region and would like to settle. Apart from Arabs who feel an attachment (and believe they have rights in these Arab lands) there are devote Muslims who expect to be treated as fellow believers and be welcomed on the Arabian Peninsula. But rarely are Arabs or Muslims without strong connections to those in power able to settle in the region. Even long term residents such as those from south Asia and Iran who settled in these states before they became wealthy are generally restricted to temporary residence dependent on a local business partner or sponsor to allow them to remain in the country. So most foreigners accept that their time in the GCC will be very limited and will endeavor to make as much money as they can and will hope that when it is time to go their employer will honor agreements to provide transport home and final pay which has been retained to ensure good behavior. If the employer does not pay the worker's dues (normally up to 2 years' pay) there is little the worker can do. Often the employer will make a complaint about the worker just before they are due to leave alleging fraud or theft or indiscipline so that payment can be withheld. Or else it is claimed that the worker took out a loan against the salary so is not entitled to their money. Many domestic helpers who resign or are about to go on leave find that they are accused (sometimes correctly) of stealing from their employer and then find themselves in jail and sent home destitute. It is normal practice for employers hold the passports of workers (even senior staff) and leaving the country requires the employer's permission- some employers charge fees from the worker for giving permission.

Attraction of Rich Places

Those in the wealthy west will wonder why people will work in the conditions found in the GCC and in other rich countries. But the very poor are usually desperate and will take any job which promises a better life and many labor agents are very persuasive at assuring the candidates that their employer will be honest and respect their rights. It is not just rich places which attract the poor- even poor countries such as India or Pakistan are attractive to Sri Lankan domestic helpers or to Nepali laborers among others. Although these host nations are poor there are rich people within them who prefer to employ a foreigner without rights or support than to employ a fellow citizen.

The migrant workers go to the rich and relatively rich countries to earn enough for their survival and the survival of their families. The poorest do not expect a wage but only hope for food and shelter and many employers are happy to offer little beyond basic food and shelter. Those a little above the survival level will hope to save enough to pay off family debts, pay for marriages (their siblings first and then maybe their own) and if they are very fortunate acquire a little capital for a small business or a house. A large proportion of these migrant workers do succeed in achieving their modest aims. But first they have to pay off the labor agent who got them the job and the amounts to be paid are substantial with 6-12 months wages being the norm. This cost of paying the agent plus the difficulty of acquiring a job at home means that many temporary migrants have no option but to stay as long as they can once they have moved to the GCC.

Advantages to Migrant

There are undoubtedly some advantages to the migrant from leaving home and moving to the GCC. They have the means of survival (food and shelter) have the prospect of income and savings. They have the hope of modest accumulation of resources. And they have the means to satisfy at least some of the demands of relations at home (who will write asking for more money not thanking for money already sent).

No matter how bad some employers are within the GCC most foreign workers know that there are even worse employers at home. Although there are severe restrictions on foreign workers, it has to be admitted, that many do enjoy the independence that they gain from being away from family and day-to day commitments.

However the major advantages to the migrants are the potential savings they can make from jobs which should pay 3-10 times as much as they would get at home. For most people that increase in pay is worth the risk of abuse. But if the pay is not given or if the agents take a very large slice (more than the 25% expected) then the abuse and absence of rights are not with risking.

Advantages of Migrants to Hosts

Many host employers (especially of domestic labor) do genuinely welcome the migrants to work for them. In the spirit of generosity and hospitality, in which Arabs take pride, they will treat them as part of the extended family but will expect obedience and a control over their lives which would be exercised on family members in Arabia. It is now the norm for most citizen families in the GCC to have at least one domestic helper and often even a family of modest means will have two female helpers and a male driver. The paternalistic control can be, and often is, abused but the migrant cannot complain for fear not only of expulsion but also from being disloyal to the 'family' or feel guilt that they have deserved the abuse because they have not been good to the family.

For most employers in the GCC it is, however, not generosity which governs the relationship with migrant workers but meanness. Employers mainly look for the cheapest employees and even then will often renege on promised wages. One example known to this writer took place in a GCC country concerned Bangladeshi 'tea-boys' employed by a well connected contractor to a major company. The contractor was obliged by the company to pay the tea-boys US$400 a month (his profit was on top of the $400) but actually only paid $150. The employees were also entitled to $15 a month for food. During the Ramadan fasting month the company continued to pay the contractor although no tea or refreshments were to be served by his employees. So the contractor told the employees that there was no work for that month so they would not be paid. And they would not receive the food money because the mosques distribute free food after the day of fasting. So not only was the contractor getting his monthly profit and his extra $150 which had been with held each month but in Ramadan he had the whole of the employee's wages plus the food money. Any worker who complained would be shipped straight to Bangladesh with out even the small amounts of money they were entitled to.

It is this absence of the right to complain and to have contracts and laws enforced which makes foreign workers so attractive to unscrupulous employers. The migrant workers are treated as disposable, cheap resources whose only role is to make more money for the employer. The GCC governments prevent workers (except a few in top managerial and professional jobs) from transferring from one employer to another so the workers have no right to move from an abusive employer to a more reasonable one. Even if the worker is so badly treated that they wish to go home they will be prevented from returning to the country for 2 or 3 years – to avoid job hopping from bad to good employers. So the worker is stuck in whatever situation they find themselves in.

ABUSES

As was discussed in the example above the agents and contractors can make much more money from exploiting workers than they can from honest business practices. Most honest people are soon driven out of the business of labor supply and recruitment agencies because of the practices of the unscrupulous. Officials in the home and host countries are bribed to ignore illegal activity or are themselves agents. Such officials make business difficult for those who do not pay bribes or who practice ethical working.

A major problem, as illustrated earlier, is the non-payment or underpayment of money due to migrant workers. Occasionally some businessmen (invariably men in this region,) for reasons of morality, ethics or because they do not want unscrupulous businesses to prosper, suggest to governments that all pay should be through bank accounts (so that there is a record of amounts paid) but these initiatives have always failed. The employers you abuse the relationship with the migrant workers get the staff to sign documents (in languages which are often not understood by those who sign) saying that they have had loans or received full payment. Or else the employer says that the cash (or a large proportion) will be saved for end of service and at that time the employer will find an excuse not to pay.

In such circumstances with less money coming in than expected and cries from home for higher remittances the migrant workers are under severe stress. The stress leads to illness and often leads to suicide. Sometimes the suicide takes the form of deliberately initiating an accident- particularly a road accident when the car driver involved will be obliged to pay the family of the deceased 'diyya' or blood money (around US$15,000- but the amount can vary depending on the victim's sex and religion in Saudi Arabia for a Muslim male it is around US$25,000 and a Hindu female under US$1,000). Strictly diyya should be paid in the case of industrial accidents but few employers will report an industrial accident.

With the potentially large amounts of money to be made from abusing migrant workers criminals are attracted to the trade. Some make money through the hwala system of transferring the workers money from host to home countries. The hwala system works by one person handing over cash- say $100 in the GCC and an equivalent amount is handed over in local currency in south Asia. The south Asian cash came from crime and could be difficult to launder (turned from 'black' money to 'white' money). But through hwala the criminal now has apparently legitimate money in the GCC- which can be invested in property, trade or crime. Banks and western law enforcement agencies try to prevent the hwala system operating especially since it is alleged to be a means of transferring funds to terrorists. The system however is cheap to use (the transferee usually has a much better rate of exchange than they would get from a bank and there are no bank transfer costs which typically are a major portion of the small amounts remitted by temporary migrants).

An example of the system of abusing temporary migrants was that practiced by criminals from the former Soviet Union during the 1990s. Prostitutes (often young women duped into prostitution when they expected well paid legal jobs) were flown from former Soviet states to the GCC. The prostitutes then earned money for the criminal organizers who purchased high value goods in the region and shipped them back to their home state and sold at a high profit. The system is very reminiscent, in many ways, of the 'triangular' trade taking slaves from Africa to America where raw materials were purchased and taken to Europe from where manufactured goods were taken to Africa to buy slaves. Not least of the similarities is the complete disregard of morality but also making money out of the suffering of fellow human beings. Governments and religious leaders were able to ignore the suffering of the slave trade and are usually able to ignore the modern slavery practiced on many migrant workers.

Apart from being forced into prostitution female workers, especially in domestic service, are often subject to sexual assault, rape and torture. Having non family females in an Arab household was not normal situation prior to the importation of large numbers of migrant workers. Males within the household often take advantage of the situation and the worker cannot complain without being accused of seducing the 'innocent' male and/or being deported without any money. The female members of the family either ignore the sexual and other physical assaults or else say that it is expected that the domestic helper provide sexual 'services' as part of her duties. One must not imagine that the Arab/ host households are the only ones which abuse of domestic helpers takes place. Such abuse also takes place in the households of fellow expatriates, including fellow countrymen and including those from western countries. The abusers are invariably not punished.

What can be Done to Meet Human Rights of Migrant Workers in the GCC?

Home and third country governments, NGOs and campaigning groups can put pressure on GCC authorities to grant at least minimal rights to migrant workers. It is not reasonable to expect the GCC to award citizenship or rights of residency or even to form trade unions- which could abuse their role to threaten the host states. But the most serious abuses can be dealt with. The judicial system could be even a little more fair to the migrant so that claims of serious abuse (especially rape and torture) can be dealt with- the embassies of countries such as Indonesia and the Philippines have hundreds of rape victims seeking refuge each year- these are not all seductresses or women who make false claims. The labor departments could move away from their close relationship with employers and labor agents and have some concern for the minimal rights of workers- as members of the United Nations the GCC states should abide by the UN Human Rights requirements and those of the International Labor Organization.

Tourists and business visitors to the region must be aware that the gleaning buildings and well stocked shopping malls depend on cheap, often abused, migrant labor. Will the visitors be prepared to pay more for their goods and services to give a decent way of life to the laborers or will they turn a blind eye.

Finally we must recognize that at least the countries of the GCC do offer employment to very poor people from poor countries whereas the rich countries such as the USA and those in the European Union try hard to keep out the poor migrants. The migrants are kept out of these rich developed countries because of fear that they might become permanent residents or might take the jobs of host country nationals or might bring crime with them- exactly the same sentiments, about migrants, expressed by many in the GCC.

In: Human Rights Issues in the 21st Century
Editors: M.S. Becker and J.N. Schneider, pp. 19-25
ISBN 978-1-60456-119-7

Chapter 2

HUMAN RIGHTS IN THE 21ST CENTURY: SOME VIEWS IN ASIA

***Wes Harry*[1] *and Chizu Nakajima*[2]**
[1]Lancashire Business School University of Central Lancashire and Cass Business School City University London, United Kingdom
[2]Cass Business School City University London, United Kingdom

The 21st century is already becoming one in which the human race will face competing rights to needs, resources and living conditions. In the west and western influenced nations, such as Japan, high living standards resulting from industrial and post industrial economic developments have led to calls for human rights such as democracy, freedom and individual wellbeing. In much of Asia these 'rights' are often not ones which are of primary concern in societies which value community cohesion, deeply felt religious conviction and trust in others. Many Asians desire to catch up with the material benefits of industrialization and are willing to forego many of the 'rights' sought in the west in return for prosperity.

The paper also discusses the western concern for written contracts, rules and laws while the Asian preference is to have mutual understanding and personal relationships to determine rights and obligations. These Asian preferences are challenged not only by the western governments, NGOs and pressure groups but by industrialization and urbanization. These challenges have often resulted in violent reactions and populist political movements against the west.

The authors bring their insights from Asia to help others understand why there is so much resistant to what are seen by westerners to be proper human rights. The insights are built upon their deep knowledge within Asia and within the west. The western author has worked in commerce in Asia for many decades while the Japanese author has worked in the west for most of her adult life. This paper is not an academic or a political treatise but offers insights into the practicalities of sharing the benefits of human progress with others in Asia whilst maintaining fundamental rights which should be accorded to all.

HUMAN RIGHTS

The UN Charter on Human Rights and the European Union convention maintain that Human Rights are fundamental principles and standards that enable *individuals* everywhere to have freedom to live in dignity. These organizations believe that all human rights are universal, interrelated, interdependent and indivisible. For many people in Asia, who are struggling for survival, such Human Rights seem a distant prospect and a prospect which many do not seek. For long term prosperity rights of people in Asia are essential but Asian writers such as Ong (1999) and Chua (2003) have demonstrated how politicians, among others, divert people from realizing the link between the absence of their rights and the maintenance of poverty. Politicians and community leaders claim that demands for Human Rights are a means of damaging communities and the more extreme populist politicians use supposed demands rights to attack minority groups and deny them even the basic right to life.

ASIA

This brief discussion gives views on Human Rights from Asia but Asia is a very large area with the highest number of human inhabitants of any continent so we will offer a selection of views which are not objectively gathered but do give opinions and beliefs shared by many within this vast continent which contains over half of humanity. The continent contains a wide variety of societies and communities and includes the world's largest democracy (India), country with the highest population (the People's Republic of China- which we will refer to as China), the only Hindu kingdom (Nepal), only Jewish state (Israel), Buddhist kingdoms (Bhutan and Thailand), seat of Islam (Saudi Arabia) and country with the highest number of Muslims (Indonesia) as well as communist regimes including China and North Korea. Asia has a high percentage of rich -5 of the 20 richest people are in Asia but so are more than 60% of the world's poorest (of which half are in South Asia- the home region of 3 of these richest people). According to Oxfam (Oxfam.org) Asia has the widest gap between rich and poor of any continent.

So it is quite understandable that in Asia there are views held by many which are contrary to those of the westerners who have been prime movers in drive for Human Rights. Although there are many Human Rights Activists in Asia their voices are muted compared to those in the west.

Westerners tend to be concerned with individual Human Rights while most Asians consider that individuals' obligations to others (within the family, clan, community, religious group and within the nation State) far exceed their individual rights. Most Asians while admiring or jealous of the material prosperity are surprised or shocked at the apparent laxity within society (supposedly highlighted by crime, pornography, family breakdown and isolation of individuals) which seems to result from an emphasis on Human Rights. Certainly Asian societies share many of the social ills which are experienced within the west and there is as much hypocrisy in the east as in the west but many Asian believe their way of life is under threat from imported 'rights' but with few benefits arising from gaining these rights..

Westerners' individual focus is demonstrated by the popularity of Maslow's (1970) hierarchy of needs culminating in 'self actualization'. However anthropologists studying in

Asia, such as Shweder (2003) find that among people of this continent realizing their religious duty or having a respectable role in the family or community is the height of the individual's needs- these duties and roles are not Human Rights found in any UN or EC declarations.

Maslow's hierarchy is usually shown as a pyramid with 'basic' needs of food, shelter etc at the base of the pyramid. These basic needs are rarely matters of concern in the west. People might worry about mortgage payments or whether the price of unseasonal fresh fruit is too high but few are at risk of starving or being destitute. In most of Asia the 'basic' needs are precarious with no expectation that the state or government will meet these and the only source of help in time of need is the family or community. Thus ties to these bodies are strong and the consequences of breaking, or attempting to break them, for individual Human Rights are serious. If the extended family breaks down into nuclear families or individuals the literal 'life line' in times of trouble will not exist.

Differences Between Asia and the West

As we have discussed above in Asia the community and family is far more important than the individual. In, often crowded, communities relying on few natural resources and with little faith in rulers or state institutions people have had to rely on self help groups and have been willing to forgo individual short term benefits for long term survival of themselves and their relations. In such situations obligations and duties are much more important than individual rights. Asians feel that much of the family and relationship breakdowns seen in the West are due to individuals believing that they are more important than the group.

Unlike Western nations which were created in the 18th and 19th century most Asian countries are recent creations (most were parts of colonial empires, engaged in civil war or occupied by other countries until the 1940s or later) and many are still unstable with various ethnic and religious groups combined into one nation. There is much fear amongst rulers and citizens that minority claims for Human Rights by minority groups will lead to civil strife and even civil war. So emphasis is placed on duties and responsibilities and individual rights are attacked for being western imported ideas designed to weaken the community and the state. We can cite examples of the duties being used to suppress minorities such as in Malaysia and Indonesia where the Bumipurtas (sons of the soil) have advantages over minorities and generally the minorities accept the situation. Another example is Pakistan (which was established as a home land for Muslims) where attempts to claim to be victims of discrimination by Muslim sects (and other religious groups) leads to violence against the claimants.

Within the past 20 years the majority of the population in Asia subsisted on the equivalent of US$2 or less and in some countries, such as Cambodia, and for many even within relatively wealthy states such as China and India many still survive on less than 50 US cents a day.

To most Asians (outside the wealthy, liberal and often foreign educated elites) struggling to survive and create a better life for their children the western countries and the Human Rights of the 21st century are seen to have an unacceptable emphasis on rights for special interest groups- criminals, welfare recipients, single parents, those with unconventional lifestyles and offer no support to those who have family and community welfare at their heart. It seems that in the West money is spent on the relatively poor in the rich countries but that the desperately poor in poor countries are neglected. The rights of the poorest are unseen or ignored.

Legal Rights

From Asians perspectives it seems that the USA is a society highly regulated by criminal and civil laws and enforced by strangers wielding power on behalf of society- often in the name of freedom and liberty. The USA has 20 times more lawyers per head of population than Japan (the most westernized of Asian countries) - while there may be explanations for some differences such as most defendants brought before Japanese criminal courts pleading guilty the magnitude of the difference is based on contrary views on rights and obligations. In Asia was little need for laws and lawyers as tradition, culture and religion provided the guidance for conduct in society. Obviously these Asian norms of rights can be seriously misused e.g. imposition of an interpretation of Sharia law or 'honor' killing where young women (it is rare that men are punished) are considered to have offended the family's 'honor'. However for most Asians rights are linked with mutual obligations and duties so that the community, clan or family share in the necessary means of survival and, with good fortune, stability and a measure of prosperity. The individual subsumes their rights to the wider benefits of the group.

In the West individualism extends to copy right laws and intellectual property where it is considered that the inventor or copyright holder can reap most of the advantages of new (or newly patented) ideas, systems of features. In Asia, with exceptions, there is a much more recognition that advances should be shared. Even if patents and rights of intellectual property are accepted in Asia the vast profits being made by Western organizations at the expense of poorer people, such as those needing treatment for Aids, encourage piracy of such property. Customers of such pirated property include wealthy western tourists and business visitors to Asia.

While the Western organizations, and those strongly influenced by the West including the World Bank, United Nations and other institution, encourage trade and exports from the West to Asia there are severe restrictions, often in the form of onerous 'quality standards' placed on Asian exporter but Western businesses are allowed to export to Asia, and other parts of the developing world produce which could not be sold in the West or not sold at the below market price at which it is made available in Asia. While Asian countries are regularly taken to task by the World Trade Organization and international and domestic courts there are virtually no cases against the European Union or the USA for dumping agricultural produce in Asia at below cost so driving local agricultural producers out of business.

Disparity in Access to Resources

West has had benefits of 'progress' in political and material wellbeing and now that Asian countries are catching up it seems that attention is now paid to Human Rights within these countries but when the countries were ruled by western oriented rulers (such as the Shah of Iran) or powerful states (such as Russia/ Soviet Union in Central Asia) the Human Rights of the citizens were rarely mentioned within the western countries which saw no advantage in helping the weak in Asia. To Asians it seems that international political processes lead to sanctions (and worse, in the case of Iraq) on those who dare to select (or accept) a political way different from the Western power(s). Western politicians may claim that such processes are part of the realism of politics but to Asians this seems like hypocrisy.

The material wellbeing of Asian is being held back by claims by westerners of damage to the environment or economic damage from increasing prices of raw materials (oil, rice, etc) but the same westerners have harmed, and continue to harm, the environment at rates at least similar to the Asians with little sign of wishing to take drastic action at home. It seems that the westerners complain about the high cost of raw material and 'cheap' labor but are unwilling to make their products available to Asia at prices which these poorer nations can afford. This is part of a fundamental difference in approach to pricing and selling between Asia and the west. In Asia price depends on what the seller considers the buyer can afford (price is not made apparent at first) hence apparent haggling/ bargaining which western tourists become familiar with while in the west the seller fixes the price which can be lower than the prospective buyer can afford- so the buyer gets a bargain- or higher than they can afford- so prospective buyer does not purchase.

The tourists, and academic researcher, journalists and other westerners, interacting with Asians are usually either with the poor hawkers, service workers or members of the elite but rarely do they come in contact with factory or office workers or rural poor who make up the vast majority of the population. So the westerner has limited access to information on the Asians' views on resources and rights. The opinions which are shared are, mainly, from these who wish to humor the visitor, or who do not wish to give a negative opinion to a foreigner or who share many of the values of the westerner.

Kept Poor to Service the Rich

Most westerners enjoy material benefits which are denied to Asians because the western countries have periods of stability, have access to cheap natural resources and state support of individual rights such as intellectual property rights. This denial to Asians is seen as part of a move to keep Asians poor to prevent them rivaling the westerners. It is seen that western nations such as the USA and Australians became rich because they usurped the rights of the indigenous people- USA took the land of native Americans and Australians have occupied land which belonged to the original people- whose Human Rights (to survival) were ignored and continue to be ignored. Force, albeit mainly applied one to two hundred years ago has created prosperity for such western nations.

Even if western governments no longer colonize Asian countries through military might but it seems that they use economic might to displace local producers in the same way as they previously displaced land holders. Asian labor is undervalued to give western consumers cheap goods, and the polluting industries are 'exported' to Asia so that the clean, healthy jobs are kept in the west. The capitalism practiced in Asia is of a type which local employers, institutions and governments find difficult dealing with. Jobs, such as those engaged in manufacturing clothes and shoes for the West, are moved from China to Vietnam to Cambodia etc chasing the cheapest

Sources of labor with no concern for the Human Rights of the workers or their families.

It is argued that Asians accept low wages so take jobs from the richer countries – but western consumers are unwilling to pay reasonable rates for the Asian's work and the shareholders of the companies which import the goods to the west are unwilling to reduce their profits in exchange for recognizing the rights of the workers to a 'living wage'. There is a belief in the west that the Asians are only able to produce cheap goods because their labor is low skilled and low value. But Asians, as well as westerners, are capable of working in high skilled, high added value occupations and will usually work harder and enjoy working harder than those in the leisure focused societies of west.

Rights Asians Want

The rights that most Asians seek are those of security and stability within their family and community. They seek long and happy lives for their children within an extended family. Asians do recognize that access to health, education, and a role in the political process is essential to the long term wellbeing of their families and communities and would wish to have these Human Rights but they fear that rights will result in insecurity and instability.

In many parts of Asia (mainly East Asia) access to material benefits are seen as more important than access to Human Rights. Undoubtedly powerful political groups in countries such as China have placed emphasis on increasing material wealth rather than rights in order to maintain their own privileges but with the recent memories of broken communities and strife most people are willing to accede to this emphasis. In some parts of Asia, Saudi Arabia is an example, religious responsibilities are much more important to rulers and ruled than Human Rights. Attempts by the USA and allies to give 'freedom' to the citizens in Iraq are among many instances cited as leading to disastrous states of instability and insecurity.

Want most Asians (and most poor people in the world) seek is to have strong families and communities in which rights are secondary to responsibilities and duties of the individuals within these groups.

Final Thoughts

The, sometimes provocative, stance we have taken in this paper is intended to give the readers insights and points to consider before imposing, or seeking to impose, western ideas of Human Rights in Asia. Asians have as much right to their beliefs and ways of life as those in the west. Certainly there is much wrong in the way individuals and groups are treated in Asia. So called 'honor' killings which place family pride above the right to life or indentured labor where individuals are enslaved to pay off family debts are among the practices which should be condemned. But before assuming that other Asian ways of dealing with rights and obligations are to be criticized the western governments, NGOs and individuals should consider whether they have right to impose their views of Human Rights on others.

The Asian view of the west is a mixture of jealousy of the western affluence and fear of the apparent decadence. Few Asians realize that it is the chaos, uncertainty and flexibility (even on rights) which gives strength to the western social models while rigidity, tradition and faith weaken Asia. Both Asia and the west have much to offer each other but through understanding and communications not through imposing rights and laws on the others.

References

Chua A (2003) '*World on Fire*' London Heinemann

Ong A H (1999) '*Flexible Citizenship*' London Duke University Press

Maslow A H (1970) *Motivation and Personality* Harper Row New York

Shweder R A (2003) '*Why do men barbecue?*' Cambridge Massachusetts Harvard University Press

www.Oxfam.org accessed 25/07/2007

In: Human Rights Issues in the 21st Century
Editors: M.S. Becker and J.N. Schneider, pp. 27-72
ISBN 978-1-60456-119-7

Chapter 3

Restoring Justice to Islam: An Historical, Theological and Artistic Exploration

Terence Lovat and Ibtihal Samarayi
Research Institute of Advanced Study for Humanity (RIASH)
The University of Newcastle, Australia

Introduction

Terrorism is the threat of the age, or so we are told. The threat, at least as much as the reality, has ruined airline companies and tourist operators, thrown national economies into disarray and caused corporate collapse around the globe. The spectre of '9/11", Bali, Baghdad, Madrid, London, Glasgow and Gaza confronts us daily and nightly through our media. Reports from airlines tell us that it takes no more than a minor scare at an airport anywhere in the world to impel cancellations of seats and even flights. In the face of rational comment and any amount of evidence about the far greater threat to the world of AIDS, malaria, obesity and malnutrition, it is terrorism nonetheless that has the attention of the world and its media.

Behind the grip of terrorism lies the word, 'Islam'. The notion of the 'Muslim terrorist' has become a colloquialism in Western media. Interestingly, in all the history books and comment about the Second World War in Europe, the fascism and anti-Semitism on which the Nazi Third Reich was built is rarely if ever coupled with the word 'Christian', in spite of the fact that it made carefully constructed use of age-old Christian biases and pseudo-theologies, just as some modern terrorism employs Islamic equivalents. The same case could be made about the Ku Klux Clan, the South African apartheid advocates, or any number of other such instances where the perpetrators claimed their actions were based on their Christian beliefs.

Perhaps the reason that we do not do to Christians the same injustice that we do to Muslims relates to our being better educated about Christianity and its many complexities and differences. Through greater understanding, our facility to generalize and stereotype is slowed. Moreover, even in what is largely a post-church age, we seem to have too great a regard for Christianity and its principles than to allow its image to be polluted so easily by the claims of those whom we see clearly to be functioning outside of its norms and codes of conduct. Additionally, it could be that we are simply too sensitive to the feelings of those who align with Christianity to risk offending them. If these explanations come close to uncovering the reasons for the difference between the ways in which we ascribe a religious cause for terrorism to Christianity and Islam, then the challenge for restoring justice to Islam would seem to be for formal and informal education to take the goal of enhanced literacy about Islam more seriously (Lovat, 2005; 2006). We need to achieve the same understanding about Islam that seems implicit about Christianity, namely: that it is complex and different within itself, and so cannot be generalized about and stereotyped; that it has a set of principles, norms and a code of conduct that makes terrorism as incongruous to it as it is to the equivalent in Christianity; and, that its followers are as liable to be offended, hurt and confused as Christians would be if Christianity was routinely referred to as a cause of terrorism.

The purpose of this chapter is to uncover some of the lost story of Islam's remarkable achievements and contributions to civilization, including to everything that the 'West' has come to know and by which it is defined. It sets out therefore to restore justice to Islam by turning on their head conceptions that pit Islam against the West, such as connoted in the common phrase, 'Islam versus the West'. Our conception of the relationship between Islam and the West goes beyond even phrases like 'Islam and the West'. As much as anything, our story is about 'Islam within the West', a story of Islam's reforming power in the development of Western philosophy, science and self-understanding. It is a story that promotes Islam to take its rightful place as a leader of reform, dialogue and dealing with difference in equitable and charitable ways. It is a story about not only a sibling of the West's most powerful religions, Judaism and Christianity, but about a sibling that, with renewed understanding by Muslim and non-Muslim, could turn around radically its current popular image as a recalcitrant, separatist and violence-disposed ideology to being the obverse of this.

Of course, we do not retreat from the reality that Islam is regarded widely in very different terms and we will attempt to uncover the causes and the ensuing troubling theologies that threaten to turn Islam into the very thing that so many people fear about it. Above all, however, we want to paint a picture of Islam as an indispensable part of what most Westerners take for granted. Be it about modern medicine, science, education, social welfare, the role of women, of family, of human rights or of social justice, had there been no Islam, we quite likely would not be where we are today. The fact that so few Westerners recognize this is one of the tragic gaps in our education and self-understanding. The fact that, in all likelihood, so few Muslims understand this is also part of the problem we are attempting to rectify.

The chapter will take the form of an historical and documentary review aimed at recovering much of the positive story that has been lost, as well as understanding why so much of the positive potential in the story is being replaced by negative interpretations. Both aspects of this account are held to comprise justice issues in the West's perceptions of Islam. Finally, the article will provide a case study based on the experiences of one of the authors, Ibtihal Samarayi, an Iraqi who has been on the inside of detention owing to her own displacement. This Muslim woman has used artwork in her own attempt to restore justice to

Islam and the many Muslims who have suffered from their own displacement owing to the struggle between cultures that underlies so many of the issues of the day.

Early Principles and Reforms

Even a scant reading of the tradition would convince one that there is no religion less appropriately used to justify intolerance, much less violence, than Islam. There is no religion that has such strong and explicit tenets towards tolerance in its sacred text, and no religion with such a strong track record of dealing with other religions and minority communities within its jurisdictions in an equitable and charitable way. In the early Middle Ages, when such tolerance was far from the norm, Islam built model civilizations based on multi-culture and multi-belief. By and large, a Jew, Christian or Hindu was better protected in most Islamic princedoms than in any other foreign state including, in many cases, living in their own princedoms if the prince happened to belong to a different persuasion of their religion.

This tolerance was not accidental nor was it part and parcel of ancient Arabic culture for that culture had been as faction-ridden as any other in pre-Islamic times (Hoyland, 2001). The tolerance was practiced because of the Muslim's strong belief that Islam truly was the fulfillment of God's ancient Promise (to Abraham initially) that He would establish a model community in the midst of the nations. This would be a community that would reflect God's deep desire that humankind should live in peace and practice all forms of personal integrity and social justice. This would be the community that would show the rest of the world how to live well and under God. In many ways, Islam can claim to be one of the world's great experiments as a welfare state and democracy, a claim which an important if unheralded portion of today's Muslim population sees as Islam's way out of the mire of its association with terrorism (Eickelman, 1998).

Talbi (1995) highlights the clarity with which the Qur'an promotes the sibling relationship between Muslims, Jews and Christians. Because they share in the Promise made to Abraham, they were to be respected and accommodated by the new Islamic community. However, while the heartfelt Jew or Christian might share in the Promise, the institutions of Judaism and Christianity had both failed to do justice to it.

Hence, for Muhammad, it was Islam that submitted to the terms of the Promise most authentically and so fashioned itself around the concept that it was the nation that God had promised, the true 'People of God', or '*Ummah* of *Allah*'. Inspired by Moses and Jesus, Muhammad went on to establish the religion that he believed both Moses and Jesus had striven to erect, albeit in vain. He therefore saw no contradiction in praising their efforts while showing up the failure of their followers to follow authentically the terms of the Promise. In his own mind, Muhammad seemed quite clear that Moses, Jesus and he were at one in their vision and their adherence to the Promise. They were all prophets of God and he declared himself to be 'the last and greatest' only because he finally established the model community *(Ummah)* in the form of Islam. As far as Muhammad was concerned, Moses and Jesus were Muslims (submitters to God) in the true sense, as was Abraham, the ancient prophets, John the Baptist and Mary, all of whom strove to do God's will. So too, any Jew who lived by the Ten Commandments or any Christian who followed Jesus' Great Commandment (to love God and neighbor), was a Muslim, and so to be respected and accommodated as such in

Islamic communities. By inference, the authentic followers of any religion could also be accommodated as being 'anonymous Muslims'.

Importantly, Muhammad seemed bent on giving the benefit of the doubt to those who followed other religions, especially Jews and Christians. As fellow 'People of the Book' (fellow believers in the true God), they should be assumed to be genuine in their beliefs and so to be respected. For the era, this could be interpreted as a quite remarkable gesture of multicultural largesse. Within the great Islamic Civilization that went on to capture the hearts and minds of most of the Middle East and much of Europe, Africa and India, the concept of the *dhimmi* (important minority group) communities was unique. The *dhimmi* communities were those minority groups that lived within a Muslim society that followed another religion yet were tolerated, respected and indeed often regarded as an indispensable contributor to the richness of the Islamic *Ummah*. For hundreds of years, generations of Jewish and Christian communities lived, and even prospered in some cases, within Muslim worlds as *dhimmi* communities.

There is much debate in the scholarly world about the merits and de-merits of '*dhimmitude*' in Islam (Bat Ye'or, 2002; Lewis, 2002). Some of the views one will find are more clearly based on a pure interpretation of the historical source material, while others are more clearly influenced by recent events. Our own interpretation is that, human frailty notwithstanding, *dhimmi* in Islam deserves its reputation as a ground-breaking social attitude and practice, relative to its times. The important thing to note about this Muslim social ethic was that it came directly from the early Muslim community's understanding of the will of Muhammad about matters of dealing with difference and especially minority communities. As such, the injunction towards tolerance was seen to have come directly from God and to be a defining feature of the model community that was established in God's name. It was part and parcel of being the *Ummah* that it should respect difference in this way. To be Muslim was to be fair and to be just, in the way enjoined by God and interpreted by the prophets, finally by the last and greatest of these, Muhammad.

Hence, we are bold in the assertion that no religion is more inappropriately used as an instrument of intolerance, least of all violent intolerance, than Islam. One of the challenges for modern Islamic scholarship is the re-capturing of the story of Islam as one of social reform. In this spirit, in the foreword to Yahya (2002), we read:

> Muslims must recapture the true spirit of Islam, and reclaim it from those who have harmed its integrity and honour .... (Yahya) illustrates by using the core text of all Muslims—the holy Qur'an, that true Islam cannot in any way, shape or form be associated with terrorism. (p. 13)

Similarly, Talbi's (1995) view of Islam as being most properly a leader of interfaith dialogue and reform, and of an interpretation of the spirit of the Qur'an in impelling Islam in this direction, is clear:

> ...the dialogue with all men of all kinds of faiths and ideologies is from now and onwards strictly and irreversibly unavoidable, Man has never lived in isolation, and man's history may be considered as an irreversible process of an unceasingly extending communication. Man's fulfillment is in community and relationship. And this is written in the Qur'an! "0 mankind! We created you from a single (pair) of a male and a female, and made you into nations and tribes, that ye may know (be friendly towards) each other ..."

> ...it is not impossible to admit the plurality of the paths of salvation, both in and outside the Islamic tradition providing people are both sincere and righteous. If this can be admitted ... we can think of the whole of mankind as a brotherly 'community of communities' — or God's Family as the Hadith states — in which everyone has the right to be different, to be accepted, and fully respected in his chosen differences. To respect others in their chosen and assumed differences — not just to tolerate them on point of pain — is finally to respect God's Will Who willingly created man free to choose what he likes to be and to build with true liberty his own destiny... (And this is written in the Qur'an): "Thou wilt not guide the one whom thou lovest; but God guides those whom He will. And He knows best those who are truly guided."
>
> ... For me, Dialogue is above all a mood, a spirit of openness, a disinteresting collaboration that does not challenge the presuppositions of the respective partners. We have to focus on cooperation in real and urgent issues confronting our human family, and the first step toward peaceful co-existence and cooperation among communities of different faiths and ideologies is to shy away from thinking in nationalistic or exclusive terms to believing in global and universal ones. We are, all of us, embarked on the same frail boat and, from now onwards, we can have only an interdependent future. (pages 61-67)

Nettler (1999), in commenting on Talbi, says:

> The Qur'an, as basis and foundation of the whole structure, is Talbi's ultimate source. He sees in his theory of pluralism a 'modern' idea from the depths of revelation. Despite his obvious debt to modern thought, Talbi's point of departure is from within the sacred text and its early historical context. His approach to that text and history presupposes there is a humanistic message of the Golden Rule and an empirical validity in historical sources such as the constitution of Medina which support that message. (page 106).

Nettler's reference to the Constitution of Medina is about the kind of community that Islam first established around the belief that it was the model community that God had envisioned. As suggested above, this community, together with most Islamic civilizations of the early Middle Ages, was remarkable for its ethnic and religious tolerance. Similarly, other features that one associates with the modern welfare state and democracy, rather than with the modern stereotype of Islam, were in fact to be found in early Islamic civilizations. Among these features were those concerned with social welfare systems, education and healthcare schemes, and many issues designed to promote the status of women. Almost a thousand years before the so-called Enlightenment in the West began the move towards these features, they were part and parcel of early Islamic civilization (Lewis, 1987).

As with ethnic and religious tolerance, these features were not there merely by chance. Muhammad had taken to heart the message of the ancient prophets that God did not want sacrifice and ritual but justice and mercy to flow like a river, and that his people should act justly, love tenderly and walk humbly (submissively) with their God. So, he wrote into the 'Five Pillars of Islam' (for him, the completion and fulfillment of the ethic of the Ten Commandments/Great Commandment), a practical social welfare scheme of tithing that saw everyone giving a percentage of their goods to the community. This was symptomatic that the supreme ethic of the Muslim put as much store on practical charity, welfare and wellbeing as on obligations around prayer. For Muhammad, this would ensure that Islam could never stray into the mere platitudinous in the way that Muhammad believed both Judaism and Christianity had strayed.

In contrast to what he saw as the structural weaknesses of Judaism and Christianity, the fact of tithing within Islam being constructed as a religious requirement guaranteed that, from the earliest days, healthcare and social support were made available to all, including in most cases to the *dhimmi* communities. Similarly, education was considered crucial as a religious as well as a social duty. It is not surprising then that the first 'modern' university was an Islamic university, generally regarded as the one established in Cairo in the eleventh century. Finally, the issue of women's rights in Islam is predictably the most controversial of the many features of modern revisionist scholarship in and about Islam (cf. Ahmed, 1992; Haddad and Esposito, 1998; Armstrong, 2001). What is probably less debatable is that the issue was taken up more seriously in early Islam than in any religious establishment before its time and that early crafting of *Shari'a* (Islamic law) reflected this priority. The debate is more about the directionality of the attention that was given to the issue. Again, we side with essentially though not exclusively feminist Muslim scholarship that suggests that Islam represents a positive moment in the liberation and equality of women and that, as with its many other reforms, this came centuries before, and no doubt influenced, similar reforms in the West.

Medieval Reforms and Scholarship

The essential reforming nature of Islam is not restricted to its earliest communities in the Middle East and Northern Africa. In many ways, the more decisive moments for Islam's reforming power over the West came in the form of its European settlements and followers. Cultural relations between the Muslims and Christian Europe were established in two ways, first, via Spain and, second, by way of Sicily and the Kingdom of Naples. The translation of Arabic works into Latin was completed by the Christian Archbishop of Toledo in the mid-1100sCE. In Toledo, at this time, Muslims and Christians lived side by side in what was essentially an Islamic caliphate. The Archbishop, Raymond, perceived the overwhelming benefits of Islamic thought and culture and so encouraged his flock to take an active interest in and dialogue with the intellectual life of the Muslims. In so doing, he established a translation bureau with the specific task of translating key Islamic texts into the language of the church. In this way, the thought of great Muslim scholars like al-Farabi, Ibn Sina [Avicenna], and Ibn Rushd [Averroes] were conveyed to the West. Ironically, the same bureau translated the almost lost works of Aristotle which had been translated in earlier times from their original Greek into Arabic. All of this work, including most crucially the work of Aristotle, was the work that influenced the ground-breaking thought of arguably the West's greatest thinker of the era, Thomas Aquinas (Van Den Burgh, 1954).

This translating work revealed the advanced scholarship of Islam as well as giving Westerners a sense of its enlightened social theory and practice. As a result, the perception by Western thinkers about Islam was broadened and Islamic thought acquired a newfound reverence. One key translation was around the work of al-Farabi. He had been influenced by the Arabic translations of Greek philosophers by Nestorian Christians in Syria and Baghdad in earlier times. Among these translations were the crucial works of Aristotle which, without al-Farabi's revival of them, might well have been lost to future generations. It was because of his grasp of Aristotle that he developed renewed forms of Aristotelian logic, which would go on to form the basis of later Western philosophy's development of Formal Logic as a foundational sub-discipline of philosophy (Netton, 1989). Furthermore, al-Farabi placed emphasis on the ability of each person to discern and discriminate between good and evil on the basis of logic. The combination of this facility to discern the rights and wrongs of any human action, together with each person's free will, became the basis of a new form of moral thought that, through Aquinas, would go on to challenge the old, less-empowering basis of morality underpinned by the features of Augustinian conscience. Aquinas's concept of *synderesis* was of an inborn facility planted in each person by God that provided the facility to know the good and the capacity to pursue it (Aquinas, 1936).

Aquinas's conception amounted to a classic example of medieval neo-Aristotelianism (Aristotle, 1985) and his debt to al-Farabi is palpable. Justifiably, al-Farabi earned the nickname, *Mallim-e-thani*, understood as "second master", or teacher, after Aristotle who was considered the first master and teacher. His book, *Isha' al-'Ulum*, was adopted in Christian schools, just as it had been in Islamic schools, as an indispensable reference in a range of academic disciplines. Roger Bacon [1214-1280 CE], the Franciscan scientist, made use of it in his attempt to reconcile religious and scientific thought and to pioneer a distinctively Christian approach to science (Amin, 2007). Moreover, it seems that al-Farabi's book led a revival in Arabic music in the very cosmopolitan atmosphere of Islamic Spain, as well as exercising great influence on Hebrew thinkers who translated his works into Hebrew (Randel, 1976).

Another crucial translated work was that of Ibn Sina, known in the West as Avicenna. Gundisalivus translated *al-Shifa* [The Book of Cure] into Latin while Gerard of Cremona translated *al-Qanun*, which became a text-book for medicine in European colleges of medicine from the thirteenth to the seventeenth centuries. It was because of this latter book, mainly, that Ibn Sina achieved fame in the West, so much so that Dante put him on a level between Hippocrates and Galenus, while Scalinger went as far as to place him in the same category as Galenus in medicine, but on an even higher plane in philosophy.

The first Christian thinker to be influenced by Ibn Sina was Gundisalivus, the head of the translation bureau in Spain. He wrote his book, *The Soul*, in which he started with Ibn Sina and ended with Augustine. He adopted Ibn Sina's proofs of the existence of the soul, indicating that it was a substance and not an accident, immortal and spiritual. He also adopted from Ibn Sina his famous symbol known as 'the man suspended in space' with no relation with the outside world, and yet his mind revealing to him that he is a thinking being who exists. That symbol was mentioned by many authors of the Christian Middle Ages, and so it is thought that Descartes in the seventeenth century most likely received it from them, going on to express the same thought in his famous assertion, *cogito ergo sum*, deemed to have heralded the birth of modern science in the West (Butterworth and Blake, 1993).

Evidence of Ibn Sina's influence on the Christian Middle Ages can perhaps be revealed best in the strong attack launched by Guillaume d'Auvergne [d.1249CE] against Aristotle and his 'disciples' [al-Farabi, Ibn Sina and al-Ghazzali]. This theologian mentioned Ibn Sina about forty times in his books, sometimes opposing his ideas, while at other times citing his definitions and examples. He adopted Ibn Sina's definition of truth as 'what corresponds in the mind to what is outside it'. He also adopted Ibn Sina's distinction between 'essence' and 'existence', as well as his inference that the soul can be conscious of itself without resorting to the body. This is the proof mentioned by al-Shifa and al-Isharat as the 'symbol of the suspended man' (Amin, 2007)

In mid-centuries Islamic Spain, the philosophy of Ibn Rushd, known in the West as Averroes, would inspire and direct the thoughts of the West in ways that led directly to the Renaissance, Reformation and Enlightenment. It was Averroes (cf. Kogan, 1985) who ultimately influenced Aquinas's most crucial works, including his central thinking on natural law. It was the stark clarity and purposeful intention of Averroes's rationalistic account of religious belief that so impressed Aquinas and, in turn, provided theological and religious belief with the philosophical buttressing that it needed in a world faced with the advance of science. On Ibn Rushd, Landau (1962) has the following to say:

> The western philosophers could have never reached the level we see today unless they had obtained the results of Ibn Rushd's research in philosophy. Muslim Spain has produced some of the brightest intellectual luminaries of the Middle Ages. One of them was Ibn Rushd … who is universally acknowledged as the great philosopher of Islam and one of the greatest of all times. George Sarton in his introduction of history of science said that "Averroes was great because of the tremendous stir he made in the minds of men for centuries. A history of Averroism would include up to the end of the sixteenth-century, a period of four centuries which would perhaps deserve as much as any other to be called the Middle Ages, for it was the real transition between ancient and modern methods." (page 32)

In turn, of course, Averroes was himself inspired and partly mentored by the other great Muslim philosopher of the day, Ibn Tufayl, yet another native of Spain. Averroes reacted to what he saw as the over-reliance on the mystical thought of the likes of al-Ghazzalli, the much revered Muslim mystic, and was intent on demonstrating that the heart of Islam could be justified in rationalistic terms. It was Ibn Tufayl's philosophy, especially as expressed in his most famous work, *Hayy Ibn Yaqzan* [Walk on], that convinced him of the potential for this rationalism and it was his capacity to convey his philosophical tenets in poetic, allegorical and other highly accessible forms that built into Averroes the surety and passion for common sense that he demonstrated throughout his life and for which he is so revered in Islam and in Western scholarship (Hawi, 1973).

Lastly, we must refer to the debt which Jewish philosophy owes to Muslim philosophy. Suffice it to say that Aristotle's works were not translated into Hebrew, but Jewish philosophers were content with what the Muslims wrote as summaries and commentaries. It was discovered by Western scholars that Jewish theologians followed in the steps of Muslim philosophers, and that thinkers before Maimonides owed their methods and ideas in religion to them. They also discovered that the work of the great Maimonides revealed beyond doubt the importance of Muslim influence on Jewish thought (Kasher, 1995; Kramer, 1999).

Al-Farabi, Ibn Sinr, Ibn Rushd and Ibn Tufayl represent a coherent, assured and persistent intellectual force in medieval times that went beyond anything the West could muster at the time. A great Western thinker of the ilk of Aquinas relied on this Islamic force to forge the reforms of Western intellectual life that represented his quest in life and his great contribution. He relied on them as much as on their Aristotelian underpinnings, for these Muslims were the ones who had taken Aristotle and applied him to new and urgent circumstances. There is little doubt that Judaeo-Christian understanding of itself, and the entire West's self-understanding, would somehow be very different had these remarkable characters and their impelling ideology not existed. If one truly understands the intensely sibling relationship between Islam and Judaeo-Christianity, then the inspirational work of these medieval Muslim scholars on the West was entirely consistent with the origins and purpose of Islam in the minds of the early Muslims.

Islam and the Judaeo-Christian Tradition

If one were a Jew or Christian wishing to truly understand Islam in a way that did justice to the tradition, then one would attempt to study it from the Islamic rather than the more familiar Judaeo-Christian perspective. One would attempt, in so far as it is possible, to put on Islamic 'spectacles', to walk in Islamic 'shoes'. One might begin with the common story of Abraham but temper the premise of Genesis, Chapter 17, that Isaac was the heir to the promise, with the Qur'anic view that Ishmael was the true heir. Once one opened one's mind to this line of thought, one might well be challenged by the consistency of this view with Genesis, Chapter 16, wherein it is clear that Ishmael was in fact the first-born and in circumstances that, relative to the mores of the day, would likely have seen him as unchallengingly the rightful heir to any Abrahamic heritage. This is the view endorsed in Islamic belief when Abraham returns to his 'first family' in Mecca and, together with Ishmael, establishes Islam's most sacred site, the Ka'aba, on the very spot where Allah's creative work began (Hoyland, 2001; Rogerson, 2003).

Once one takes this line, rather than the more familiar Judaeo-Christian line on the origins of the tradition, one is put on a different track altogether in interpreting the rest of the story. One might begin, for instance, to be more sympathetic to the Islamic view that Moses was the direct descendant of the 'Arabic' Ishmael, and that his separation from the Pharaoh's house was essentially that of an insider, rather than an outsider, and mainly about a rejection of the institution and institutional religions of the pharaohs in favor of re-discovering the ancient Promise made to Abraham and Ishmael. Furthermore, one might begin to contemplate the wisdom of the Islamic position that the people who finally entered the Promised Land, be they regarded in modern conceptions as Arabic or Hebrew, had rejected the spiritual interpretation of the Promise provided by Moses after Sinai, in favor of the more tantalizing institutional interpretation. By this latter, the ancient 'Zionist' state was effected, complete with king, priesthood, army and, above all, the physical Temple, this latter being the supreme symbol of earthly statehood.

It is a dominant Islamic view that the ancient kingdoms of Judah and Israel were established around a misreading of the nature of the Promise. The Promise was about establishing a people within a people, a people imbued with godly vision and godly ways, a people who would live and establish communities in ways distinctive of their beliefs. According to this Islamic view, Moses foresaw the rejection of the spiritual interpretation of the Promise, especially after the people's reaction to his Sinai message. The ancient prophets, whose constant cry was against the institutional interpretation, also understood the Promise in this way. Amos said the Lord does not want sacrifice and ritual but justice and mercy that flow like a river. Jeremiah said the Lord does not want the Temple on the hill but the Temple built in the hearts of his people. Micah said that the proof of being God's Chosen was in acting justly, loving tenderly and walking humbly with their God. According to both the

Christian and Islamic views, John the Baptist and Jesus held the same prophetic view, and suffered violent deaths for conforming their own actions to their prophetic knowledge.

Interestingly, the Qur'an offers a picture of Mary, Jesus' mother, as a prophetic type as well. It is yet another illustration of the richness that Christians can uncover in studying Islam that the Qur'anic Mary is so much more powerful and substantial a figure than to be found in the canonical gospels of the New Testament (Rogerson, 2003). Of course, there could well be a reason for this. Many of the Christian forms and sources suppressed around the time of the Council of Nicaea (325CE) were of the more human Jesus to which many of the apocryphal sources were committed. The ideology that dominated thereafter was more heavily of the divine Jesus, about which having an earthly mother was clearly somewhat enigmatic. Again, one of the great benefits of understanding Islam is that it has kept alive many of these earlier forms and their sources. As Christianity itself continues to mature and become less defensive, one would hope that Islamic sources of this type will prove to be of inestimable value in Christianity's own self-understanding.

The above Old Testament and New Testament characters are all prophetic heroes in Islamic folklore and, of course, the supreme prophetic hero is Muhammad who, understanding keenly the spirituality that drove Judaeo-Christianity, established the perfect religion to restore its essential spirituality while eschewing the institutional forms in which it was wrapped. For Muhammad, the Five Pillars of Islam were a dramatic re-statement of both the Ten Commandments and Jesus' Great Commandment, but were in the kind of practical form that could never be ignored by his followers in the way that Moses' and Jesus' followers had ignored their central tenets. In Islamic folklore, living by the Five Pillars truly did impel the kind of communal living to which the Promise to Abraham, Moses and Jesus had been directed. This was the Islamic *Ummah,* that community that lived by the rule of God *(Hakkimiyah Allah),* wherein social living was characterized by the prophetic virtues of the Promise, namely, justice, mercy and tolerance, as well as scholarship and spirituality.

Among those Muslims who know and understand their own broader tradition, one would find huge amounts of confidence that they know, understand and relate more closely with both Moses and Jesus than does the average Jew or Christian, respectively. For most Jews and Christians, their faith and culture is wrapped up and bound by their status as citizens of the so-called 'West'. For the devout Muslim, the features of this are the non-Promise, non-prophetic features of secularism, wealth, opulence and imperialism. This stands in contrast to their understanding of Islam as being 'of the Promise', namely, God-centred, poor and humble, and, for many, especially those of the Shi'a tradition, inherently and most properly, victims, just like the prophets before them.

For the devout Muslim, the armament that maintains the fortification of Islam against all opposition is *Jihad. Jihad* is not the violent entity of folklore about Islam, although it must he said that there was, from the earliest days, a potential for *Jihad* to develop this way. Essentially, however, *Jihad* is best defined as the personal and corporate striving for submission to Allah, captured best by the Five Pillars of Islam. By conforming their lives to the Five Pillars, the veritable conjunction between the Ten Commandments and the Great Commandment, the Muslim becomes the heir to the Promise, one of the Chosen People of God. Within moderate Islam, by far the most dominant Islamic force, this is a Promise shared with Jews and Christians, and with others of authentic religious belief. Among less moderate Muslims, still a minority but growing in recent times, the Promise is exclusively the heritage of Muslims, and only those Muslims who hold to their own fundamentalist interpretation of Islam (cf. Nusse, 1993).

Of particular interest for those Christians who might wish to deepen understanding of their own tradition, the texts of the Muslim Jesus would seem to be drawn from a knowledge and understanding of Jesus that both pre-dates and post-dates the establishment of Islam. Some of them are no doubt remnants from those earlier traditions of Christianity often expelled from the Christian canon as much for political as for doctrinal reasons. Adang (1996) confirms the likelihood that the Jesus who inspired Muhammad was an 'apocryphal Jesus', rather than the 'canonical Jesus', when she verifies that ".... on the whole, the biblical narratives in the Qur'an reflect the influence of apocrypha, pseudepigrapha, and midrashim, rather than canonical scripture." (page 3) Such narratives contain high potential, therefore, for offering insights into strands of Christianity lost for the most part to the mainstream tradition. For those interested in self-reflection about the true origins of Christianity, beyond the politically correct versions of these origins, the texts of the Muslim Jesus being available to us in translated form for the first time ever is a major advance (Khalidi, 2001).

Additionally, the texts of the Muslim Jesus provide insight into the central role played by the Jesus hero in the early development of Islam, including during a period when, by almost any impartial account, Islamic scholarship and spirituality were as open and vibrant as those of Christianity were closed. These were the dark ages of intellectual endeavor in the West, where virtually the only Christian scholarship was happening in the reclusive environment of the monastery, while at the same time Islam was busy establishing universities with a measured charter of universal education. Similarly, Christian spirituality was static and controlled by the papacy where Islamic spirituality was alive and very much in the market place. The Muslim Jesus of the early Islamic establishment period, therefore, is likely to contain some strands of the Jesus tradition lost, ignored or expelled from the mainstream Christian tradition. This fact alone presents a compelling reason for those Westerners interested to understand their own history, including those Christians who wish to understand their own faith, to make a study of this aspect of Islam. This is quite apart from what they might learn about Islam itself.

So, what is there to be learned from Islam about Jesus? Who is the Muslim Jesus, in contrast to the Jesus affirmed through the political events of the early church? From the Qur'an itself, we find much with which we are familiar, like stories of a virgin birth and other miraculous events surrounding the birth. We also find elements in these birth stories that are partly familiar, like the infant Jesus engaging in conversation with those who came to see him. Interestingly, many Christians will recall being told stories like this in their own infants' religious education and Sunday Schools, even though there is nothing in the Christian canon to confirm them. They too belong to the apocryphal tradition, that which was discarded along the way, not always for the best theological reasons, but which has been preserved in part through the texts of the Muslim Jesus.

We also find perspectives which might be quite challenging for many Christians, but which deserve some pondering, granted they probably reflect the kind of Christian thought about Jesus that was most influential on Muhammad. While there is talk of Jesus' resurrection after his death, there is a very explicit rejection of Jesus' divinity: "Allah forbid that he himself should beget a son!" The Christianity that most influenced Muhammad would seem at odds with the divinizing of Jesus that was one of the central events of the Council of

Nicaea in 325 CE. In contrast to the supreme heresy of suggesting that there could be another God, the Qur'an makes it clear precisely who Jesus was, purportedly in Jesus' own words:

> I am the servant of Allah. He has given me the gospel and ordained me a prophet. ...He has commanded me to be steadfast in prayer and to give alms to the poor . . . He has exhorted me to honor my mother and has purged me of vanity and wickedness.
>
> Such was Jesus, we are told, he was the son of Mary and that is the entire truth.

So it is that we find the Muslim Jesus to be what Khalidi (2001) describes as a 'controversial prophet'. While the Qur'an's depiction of any of the other Judaeo-Christian prophets, including John the Baptist, is fairly much as we would expect from our biblical knowledge, the Muslim Jesus spends much time contradicting what many of his followers (ie. the canonical church) believe about him. The Qur'anic account, and those of the entire Muslim Gospel, amount to what the Qur'an describes as a 'cleansing' from the perverted beliefs of his followers. The Muslim Jesus engages in polemic, sets the record straight and is an active agent in his own 'cleansing' from heresy. The combination of this cleansing role with the demonstrably revered status of Jesus leaves one in little doubt that, at the heart of this heartfelt belief about Jesus' true nature, lies a strong Christian stream of thought, no doubt the form of Christianity most influential on Muhammad. For Muhammad, this was the authentic version, one that justified his own belief in Jesus as a prophet in the line of the Old Testament prophets. Like ancient Zionism, Roman Christianity was held to be in error, including about Jesus. Through the Qur'an and the broader texts of the Muslim Gospel, Jesus is given a voice again and, of course, we find him saying much of what can be found in the largely unknown apocryphal gospels, except that he says it more strenuously. The intention to distance himself from the triumphalist Roman interpretation of his role is quite explicit. The texts of the Muslim Jesus serve the purpose of giving Jesus the last word, and the authenticity of the triumphalist church of the early Middle Ages is called into question by this word.

There is much substance for self-reflection in the texts of the Muslim Jesus for the Westerner brought up to assume certain truths. This applies not only to religious truths, but the many truths about the entire Western tradition that have flowed from the religious assumptions of Judaeo-Christianity. The Jesus to be found in Islam stands as religious, historical and cultural critic of much that we take for granted. The challenge is to reject the critique or to be moved to a new knowing of one's cultural heritage and so find oneself in a different place, including in a different relationship with Islam. We would suggest that restoring justice to Islam in a world that has lost touch with its rightful heritage demands the latter approach.

The Rightful Heritage of Islam: A Story of Loss

Of what happened to begin the destruction of the *Ummah* of the Golden Age of Islam, suffice it to say that, while Muslims were generally well-educated about their common ancestry with Jews and Christians, and the majority of Jews and Christians who lived within the Islamic world had come to appreciate their shared heritage, the Christian world generally held no such sentiments. Again, it is important to note that education was scarce in the West at the time, and that the old empire was held together through a combination of fear and mutilation of Christian spirituality to fortify that fear. Knowledge about Islam was restricted to age-old fears of their own, dating back to the successful Islamic incursion into much of the former Christian world, including as far north as Spain. For all the reality of it, Islamic civilization was believed to be godless and corrupt. The overlay onto beliefs about Islam of fundamental Western Christian conceptions of superiority, 'salvation only within the church' and 'right to rule' could not be overstated. Add to this base conception the need of Western rulers, including bishops, to distract their subjects from the growing calls for reform in areas of human rights, education and the role of the laity in the church, and we have the formula for the series of partly random events that went on to comprise the Crusades. The fact that the Muslim world held effective control of what Jews and Christians referred to as 'the Holy Land' provided the apparent legitimation and religious purpose essential to any effective crusade.

Over two centuries and eight Crusades, the original Islam was effectively destroyed. Along with it went much of the credibility about Christianity (and to some extent Judaism) that Muhammad had extended to it. Whole generations of Muslims came to see Christians in much the same way that many Westerners today would regard Al Qa'eda, as artisans of mindless terror. Against their live experience of the worst kinds of barbarity that Christian civilization could heap upon them, the kindly and equable sentiments of Muhammad in the Qur'an became less and less believable. There are two points of immediate relevance to be made about the destruction of the original Islam.

First, there were consequences to the destruction of Islam that relate to its material prosperity. Beyond any religious considerations, the original Islam turned a part of the world that had been for the most part a backwater into one of the world's most prosperous areas. Islam served as a glue to pull together especially the Arabic portion of its civilization. Out of the disparate and largely warring tribes of the pre-Islamic world, came a focus and a unity that not only spawned tolerance, social justice and creativity, but also wealth. Furthermore, it was a wealth that was largely shared among the people, courtesy of the Pillar about tithing, in a way that would not characterize Western societies until well after the revolutions of the eighteenth and nineteenth centuries. Because Islamic civilization was prosperous in this distributed sense, it became powerful in a way that only wealth distribution can achieve. For the most part, Muslims believed in their world for reasons of both religious and social ideology (Lewis, 1987; 2002). While Muslim re-constructionists like Ali as-Sulami and Nur ad-Din (cf. Shatzmiller, 1993) remind us that there was also an element of complacency in Islam that might be blamed for the disintegration of the original *Ummah,* the dominant Islamic interpretation nonetheless is that it was the external incursion of the Crusades that destroyed the Golden Age of Islam.

Second, the bloody treatment meted out to Islam, with its associated long-term experience of being the 'victim' released a minority seed that had been in the roots of Islam from the beginning but had been relatively marginalized by the majority. The seed is particularly though not exclusively represented in Shi'a Islamic spirituality. Shi'ites make up less than 10% of Muslims in the world today, although it is much of Shi'a Islam that has become so well known in the West, especially through the revolution in Iran impelled by the 1979 return from exile of Ayatollah Khomeini. For many Westerners, it was the spectre of the Iranian revolution that represented the beginning of the anger in Islam that culminated in 9/11. The Iranian Revolution turned what had been the most Westernized of all Muslim countries into the most dramatically anti-Western Islamic theocracy. The venom towards the

USA and the disregard for all Western convention that became obvious, best captured in the 1981 storming of the US Embassy and hostage-taking of its diplomats, came as a shock to most Westerners who had been led to believe that Westernization was something that most Iranians desired. Little did they know that the seeds of this anger and disregard had been growing for a thousand years, well fuelled by the deep suspicion of all things Judaeo-Christian and the associated 'victim' mentality of the Shi'ite Muslim. Central to this suspicion and growing conspiracy theory were events that came to a head in the re-establishment of Israel as an independent nation in May, 1948, an event that many Muslims regard as an aberration, a violent act of injustice and as further proof that the medieval Crusades by the West persist, this time taking the form of the installation of Zionism.

Re-Establishing Israel: A Zionist Crusade?

Amidst the deep and long-standing suspicion by a portion of the Muslim population that the medieval Crusades represented a persistent conspiracy on the part of the West to destroy Islam, the decision on the part of the international community, essentially driven by the most powerful Western nations, to re-establish a nation called 'Israel' in the years immediately after the Second World War was a watershed event. At the time, the full meaning of the event was masked by an overwhelming sense of guilt and compassion towards the events of the Holocaust and the Jewish people. The (largely Christian) West stood guilty. While disowned and condemned through the likes of the Nuremberg Trials, it was nonetheless one of their own (in the broader sense) who had perpetrated the horrors of the Holocaust. The Third Reich had functioned largely in a Christian regime, with a demonstrable level of complicity by the Christian churches and, at best, much in the way of turning a blind eye to some of the Reich's grosser remedies. The decimated Jewish people had to be atoned and re-establishing their nationhood was seen as the ultimate political way of achieving this. The role of the USA and the UK in achieving this could not be overstated.

It was not the first time in 2,000 years that such a solution had been proposed, including with much enthusiasm in the period between the two world wars. Even earlier on, in the later parts of the nineteenth century, there had been heavy migration of Jews to Palestine, especially coming out of Europe. This was a fairly direct result of growing European nationalism that had two effects on European Jews. One effect amounted to an early marginalizing, such as would boil over into anti-Semitism some decades later. The other effect was seen in the renewed sense of the need for Jews to be reassembled in their own nation. Moreover, there had always been a powerful lobby within American Jewry that had interpreted its religious heritage as necessitating the 're-building of the Temple' in the Holy Land of old.

At the same time, there was a growing concern in the Arabic world that the desire on the part of the West to restore the old Jewish state had potential to revive much of the odiousness of the Crusades of old. Interestingly, the Jewish people were always divided among themselves about the desirability of re-establishing the physical nation. Many held that, religiously, the worst thing that had ever happened was the establishment of the physical kingdom in ancient times. The Natarei Karta is a Jewish movement associated strongly with resistance to the re-establishment of a physical state for Jewish people. As Muhammad had come to believe, so the Natarei Karta believe that the Promise to become God's Chosen People was not referring in any way to the establishment of a physical kingdom. It was to be a people among other people, showing others by the way they lived what God's ways were about. While even within the USA there was opposition to the notion of re-establishing the new nation, opposition was even more prominent in the Jewish communities of the Middle East.

As suggested above, most Jewish communities living in what was largely a Muslim world were living reasonably well. The *dhimmi* Jewish communities of Islam were treated far better than Jews had been treated in most of Europe. By and large, they were respected and, in many cases, even revered for the special part they had played in inspiring the original Islam. Many of these Jews had no desire to displace themselves from their ancestral homes to live together as Jews in what, for them, would be inevitably a difficult situation. These Jews were far more aware and foresaw the realities of the inevitable tensions than those coming from far away places like the USA, Canada and Australia, for instance. It was knowledge of these tensions and mixed feelings, together with the practical concerns over who would be displaced to make way for such a nation, which had led to a customary caution on the part of the international community towards any such solution. It was with the events of the Holocaust that the need to atone for the situation and to provide maximum protection for the Jewish people became an international imperative. At this time, the momentum for establishing an Israeli state became overwhelming.

There is rarely a solution to any problem that does not unveil another problem, and the case of the re-establishment of the Israeli state was no exception. It was not just the Palestinian Muslims whose claims were overturned and whose lives were disrupted. The entire Arabic world had the balance accrued over 1400 years upset by this event. The single biggest upset was, of course, the displacement of the Arabic (largely Muslim) people known as Palestinians from a land that even parts of the Bible refer to as 'Palestine'. The people known as Palestinians had ancestral and historical claims on this land that dated back thousands of years. In their place, and seen as invaders, came a largely foreign people drawn from the four corners of the earth, very few of them with claims on the land other than spiritual ones that were held by those being usurped as having no legitimacy. From an apparent solution, came at least one huge new problem.

In fact, the problems multiplied. As suggested, the concept of 'Jew' had been relatively unproblematic throughout the history of Islam (Nevo, 1995). Unlike the cataclysmic confrontations with the Christians throughout the Crusades and down through the ages, there had been no such violent confrontation between Jews and Muslims beyond a few skirmishes recorded in the very earliest Muslim settlements. By and large, Jews were experienced as a minority group wherever Islam had developed, and the strong tenets towards tolerance from the Qur'an had ensured a mainly compatible, largely protective relationship on the part of Islam towards the Jews. There is little evidence through history of major tensions or bigotry. In a word, there was nothing threatening about the Jews as far as the Muslim was concerned, and much to feel grateful for among those Muslims who knew their history. At best, the Jew was revered, at worst seen as quaint.

With the founding of the modern state of Israel, this all changed. For a start, 'Jew' quickly came to connote invader, foreigner, well-backed with powerful friends in the dubious West. Additionally, because of the friends they were keeping, the Jews became associated with a Christian alliance in a far sharper way than would have been seen by the average

Muslim in the past. The history of Jewish-Christian relations had been at least as strained as those between Muslims and Christians. Where Jews and Muslims experienced Christianity as a powerbase, the Jews and Muslims invariably found themselves on the same side as the victims. Most recently, of course, Muslims had witnessed the attempted extermination of the Jews, largely at the hands of pseudo Christian-related followers and their anti-Semitist ideologies. If anything, this event had increased the sense of protectiveness of the Muslim towards the Jew. To have the alleged Christian West now championing the cause of the Jew and, in so doing, imposing what they could only see as a foreign Jewish state at the expense of the displacement of their own Muslim siblings was bound to change the perception of the Jew by the Muslim in a way that we are probably still coming to terms with half a century on.

As if the situation was not challenging enough, the establishment of the Jewish state had a marked de-stabilizing effect on the Jewish *dhimmi* communities. Some of the members of such communities naturally felt attracted to the new state of Israel for a variety of reasons, including the opportunity to be part of a majority, to share their faith with a wider group, or just to take advantage of the opportunity afforded for greater power and prosperity. The loss of what was often the younger and more active sections of a community naturally weakened the *dhimmi* communities living within a Muslim state, at times making it less viable as a healthy minority in a society. Moreover, those who were left often became the victims of the kind of vilification and acts of revenge that resulted from the Muslim's growing resentment and anger at the way events were transpiring. In turn, this often forced an even greater level of immigration to the new state of Israel and the eventual collapse of the powerful symbol of Islamic tolerance represented by the *dhimmi* community.

For the most part, the Jewish-Islamic dynamic that had functioned with balance and equanimity for a millennium and a half regressed into an internecine stand-off and occasional warfare. To complicate matters further, the glue that had been represented by cultural affinity was weakened when, for instance, a Syrian Jew found him or herself caught in the middle. On the one hand, this person was of Syrian origin yet was religiously a Jew and so basically was pleasing to neither side, was forced to leave the ancestral home yet remained an object of suspicion in their new one. This situation was no doubt even worse for the Palestinian Jew whose country folk and religious folk, so to speak, were each other's prime enemies. To the Palestinians, these people were once a protected minority but were now seen to represent the hated majority. On the other hand, to many Israeli Jews, they could never be fully accepted as Jews. For these former members of a revered and fairly stable and secure *dhimmi* community, life could be particularly lonely.

The establishment of the modern state of Israel did more than disrupt the current state of affairs in the Middle East. It also re-kindled ugly memories of the past, both the medieval and ancient past. Moreover, it had the effect of generating a whole new interpretation of the Abrahamic heritage and the positioning of Islam against, rather than as an allied part of, the Judaeo-Christian contribution to this heritage.

First, to the medieval history: especially because of the unhappy history between Islam and Christianity, the imposition by the (Christian) West of the Jewish state, complete with Western armies as part of the set-up phase, was altogether too reminiscent of the medieval Crusades. The festering resentment that was never far from the surface of Middle-Eastern Muslim consciousness was released. Especially for those caught up in the Palestinian cause, it became an imperative that memories of this ugly moment in Islamic-Christian relations be revived. As a consequence, there has been a growing awareness instilled in many Arabic

Muslims over the past 50 years about the destruction wrought by the Crusades and the 'Western conspiracy' contained therein. The Crusades (and therefore the Christian West) have come to be blamed in renewed and strident fashion for the poverty, low levels of health-care, education and social services that now afflict so much of the Middle Eastern Muslim world where, prior to the Crusades, the 'Golden Age of Islam' saw the opposite.

The Christian West, but especially the West represented by the USA and UK (most heavily involved in the setting up of Israel), came to be seen as a demon all over again. The Crusades were characterized as an attempt to destroy Islam but, having merely weakened it, the establishment of the new state of Israel was seen as a renewed attempt to destroy it, only this time under the camouflage of atoning for the horrors of the Holocaust. The more buttressed Israel became owing to the weight of financial and military support from the West, the more this scenario became plausible. By the time of the 1967 War when the Israeli military all but destroyed the allied Arabic forces (largely Islamic), the myth about 'the establishment of Israel amounting to a Western conspiracy to destroy Islam' had become a truth with any amount of evidence attached. In the decades since, the evidence has simply continued to mount, if one is inclined to see things this way, with clear policy preference towards Israel's claims and against the Palestinian claims, on the part of most Western states (especially the USA and UK), and with countless violent interchanges that, for instance, have pitted a well-trained and supported Westernized Israeli military against stone-throwing Palestinians. In time, the futility of stone-throwing, together with the impossibility of assembling their own military, has led to new forms of aggression, such as kidnapping, hijacking and suicide-bombing. Most recently, the invasions of Afghanistan and Iraq, however justified, have added another layer of evidence (to those who choose to see it this way) that, one way or another, the West is intent on destroying Islam. In turn, the phenomenon represented by the suicide-bomber has expanded and been universalized well beyond the borders of the troubled Middle East. Acts of terrorism in New York, London, Bali and Madrid are representative of the expansion.

As suggested above, the re-interpretation of past events does not stop with the Crusades. For some Islamic scholars and agitators, the entire history of the tradition dating back to Abraham is re-interpreted in light of recent events. The effect, intentional or not, is to ramp up the conspiracy theory. So, even the account in the Old Testament of Abraham's choice of Isaac (the Jew) over his older son Ishmael (the Arab and, by implication, de facto Muslim) is seen as a piece of literary piracy by the Jews to deliberately distort the record regarding the Promise and its proper heritage. The fact that the Christians have incorporated this 'piracy' into their own bible makes them co-conspirators in this distortion of the truth. Moreover, the institutional interpretation of the Promise that issued in the ancient twin kingdoms of Judah and Israel is seen as being at fundamental odds with the true (Islamic) interpretation represented perfectly by the warnings of the ancient prophets. These prophets were Muslims (submitters to God, literally) and the fact that they were rejected and often killed is regarded as further evidence that the Jews and Christians belong to a line of anti-Muslim crusaders and warriors.

In all of this potted history, one version of the conspiracy theory is contained in the notion of 'Zion', 'Zionism' or 'Zionist'. In modern terms, the notion of Zionism was one of the products of European nationalism of the nineteenth century. One of the titles associated with the Jews' renewed sense of needing their own nation was 'Zionism'. The European Jews who migrated to Palestine in the later part of the nineteenth century used the title freely. The title therefore became associated with invasion and ideological threat to Islam. It therefore became an appropriate way in which to label earlier empire-building on the part of the Jews (and Christians) (Nevo, 1995). There were therefore seen to be three Zionist establishments.

The first episode of Zionism was represented by the ancient kingdoms of Judah and Israel, complete with kings, armies, priests and temples. It was built on the back of invasion and hostility and, more importantly, set up in opposition to the warnings of the (Muslim) prophets. It represents the beginnings of the blight of Judaism and its false witness to the Promise, a blight that continues to plague the Islamic world.

The second Zionism was seen in the events of the Crusades and the plundering of Islamic civilization and spirituality. Having replaced the ancient Zionist state with the *Ummah,* the great civilization of Islam, the Muslims (like their ancient prophetic forebears) were set upon again in a further episode of the grand conspiracy to destroy Islam. While the Christians were the obvious perpetrators this time, nonetheless the Jews were implicated as part of the grand Judaeo-Christian Conspiracy. The fact that the Crusaders tended often not to discriminate between Jews and Muslims in their raging is a fact conveniently forgotten.

The third Zionist episode then becomes the establishment of the modern state of Israel on May 14, 1948. This was done in the face of explicit failure to appease the Arab (largely Muslim) majority in Palestine. It was finally forced by a British resolution to drive home the agenda for Israel. It was done with strong support from the Western nations, but most especially the USA. Even the role of Australia, a current US/UK ally in Afghanistan and Iraq, was quite prominent in that the United Nations Special Committee set up to deal with the issue was chaired by Dr H.V. Evatt, the then Australian Minister for Foreign Affairs and later Opposition Leader while Leader of the Australian Labor Party. Against events like this, one can easily imagine how one with a conspiracy theory of the sort described is likely to interpret the events of the Iraq invasion of 2003. The fact that the invaders with troops on the ground were the USA, Britain and Australia, largely Christian countries, and that those being invaded were largely Muslim, does nothing to soften the conspiracy theory.

Finally, it must he said that, for those Muslims who hold to the conspiracy theory about the Western alliance and its being intent on Islam's destruction, there are excerpts from the Qur'an that give credence to their views. The Qur'anic account of Muhammad's establishment of Islam in Medina contains several references to the hostility of the Jewish clans already living there. This is fairly normal stuff, of course, when someone new comes to town, however, in the context of the conspiracy theory and in the absence of a balanced education about these things, these texts can be used to give the impression that, from the beginning and in a profound way, Judaism (and, by inference, Christianity) and Islam were in fundamental opposition to each other.

Moreover, there is an ongoing more scholarly debate in Islam about the role of the so-called *Isra'iliyyat* literature. This largely Jewish (but also partly Christian) literature had considerable influence on the corpus of Islam's sacred source material. For most of its history, Islam has had this presented as a positive influence, as a way in which part of the Abrahamic heritage was communicated and the prophetic influence (including of Jesus) was fortified. With the conspiracy theory, however, has come more negative re-considerations of *Isra'iliyyat.* For some scholars, this influence is now construed as an insidious way in which Judaism and Christianity infiltrated the purity of Islam and infected it with a disease that has eventually weakened it. So, *Isra'ilyyat* and, by inference, Judaeo-Christianity are blamed for everything that has gone wrong for Islam and its people, including the destruction at the hands of the Crusaders, its subsequent regression into poverty and political weakness and the loss of Palestine to the modern state of Israel. *Isra'iliyyat* is constructed as what went wrong at the foundation of Islam, namely that it was too accommodating of outsiders, especially Jews and Christians, and this is what has to change (Nettler, 1999). For the radical Islamist, the vehicle of change is an equally radical form of *Jihad,* interpreted as being synonymous with *Da'wa* (or holy war). *Jihad* as *Da'wa* has become so associated with the violence-oriented end of radical Islamism that it is often referred to colloquially as Jihadism, and its devotees as Jihadists.

JIHAD

'*Jihad*' is a notion largely misunderstood because it also has been manipulated as part of the conspiracy theory. As we have seen, for Muhammad, being a Muslim was literally about submission to Allah (God) and Allah's plan. This faith was not to be just a cerebral thing, but had to take the form of practical action, a '*Jihad*' (or striving) to live the kind of life that Allah had revealed in the Qur'an. *Jihad* is then an essential aspect of Islam.

Jihad centres on the Five Pillars of Faith, the cornerstones of the religion. Beyond the spiritual duties of prayer and the once-in-a-lifetime pilgrimage to the Holy City of Mecca, the Pillars are built around some very practical duties. These include the tithing of a portion of one's personal income to be used to support those in less fortunate economic circumstances. Like many prophets before him, Muhammad had noted that the pious sentiments of religions do not always translate into action. So, he attached to the 'care for neighbor' principle a practical cost, as if to sort out the sheep from the goats among his followers.

As we have seen, it was this strong sense of social justice that was one of the defining features of the first few hundred years of Islam. Among other things, it was to issue in a status and respect for women that would rarely have been found in the Christianity of the day. Similarly, in early Islamic civilization, there was a tolerance towards the followers of other religions which defied the norm to be found elsewhere. This was all, in a sense, the result of *Jihad*, an individual and corporate striving to live as Allah had commanded.

It was the so-called Christian Crusades that wrecked this civilization. For the average Muslim of the time, the Crusades would have appeared as nothing better than abominable acts of terror committed in the name of religion. Through this event, a seed was sown in Islam which would have seemed quite unfamiliar to most Muslims of this period. While there had always been a minority view in Islam that *Jihad* could include 'violent striving' for one's faith, the specter of seeing their largely peaceful and enlightened civilization desolated in such a brutal way, and in the name of religion, added weight to the view.

While *Jihad* has nothing in and of itself to do with warfare, it has been used periodically in the past 1,000 years to stir up religious fervor in order to wage war against purported 'enemies of Islam'. There have been and are today those in Islam who are able to wrap a theology around their history and so re-establish that the ongoing supreme enemy is the 'Western Crusader'. Currently, no 'enemy' would represent this better than the largely Christian, wealthy and supposedly imperialistic USA, with Israel, its puppet, playing the role of a surrogate US nation established right in the middle of the heart of Islam. In this religious context, Osama Bin Laden is just one piece of the puzzle. More crucial is the belief, buttressed by a very cogent and socio-historically grounded theology, that suggests that the establishment of Israel had nothing to do with compassion for a displaced people or atonement for the sins of the Third Reich. According to this particular Islamist belief, it was, and remains, a conniving scheme by which the old Crusaders could plant a fortress in the middle of Muslim territory and so, bit by bit, wear out and finally eradicate Islam.

While there was always an element of Islam rather disposed to the violent interpretation of *Jihad* (including especially the Shi'a faction in Islam's early history), the interpretation intensified with the Crusades. As illustrated above, the Crusades feature heavily in any interpretation of Islamic reaction and, over the issue of *Jihad*, it is no different. Shatzmiller (1993), in introducing the work of Elisseeff in the former's edited volume, speaks of the rise of the concept of *Jihad* after the fall of Jerusalem to the Crusaders in 1099CE. Nur ad-Din was the first person to organize a Muslim counter-attack. There, the notion of *Jihad* became the embodiment of Muslim devotion, and Nur ad-Din spoke of himself as the truly holy warrior and martyr in the cause of Islam. Shatzmiller (1993) says:

> Under the Crusaders' impact, Muslim society had to discard many outlooks, and new attitudes had to be adopted. The Muslims needed to put their house in order, but that process implied more than merely military and political unification; it also required an inner rejuvenation. A new belligerence was inspired by the old Jihad ideology, which received new faces and new applications. (p. x)

Elisseeff (1993) seems actually to imply that the notion of a violent or warrior-like *Jihad* was initiated in the West, thanks to the Christian Crusaders. The Crusades therefore became known as the 'Western Jihad', when Muslims saw the similarity between the notion of *Jihad* (striving for religion), as they had understood it, and the religiously-motivated striving that seemed to underpin the Crusades. Nur ad-Din, the Muslim to dub the Crusades as a Western *Jihad*, actually used the Christians' devotion to their bloody cause to try to inspire Muslims to do the same. In an ironic way, while classing them as infidels, he seemed actually to admire the Christians for being so dedicated to re-capturing Jerusalem and coming to 'free their fellow Christians from Muslim domination' (as they were told). He used this to contrast the relative slackness of Muslim spirituality, as he saw it. Muslims had become too complacent with their cosy civilization and the Christians had taken advantage of that. He asserted that Muslims had been lured into a weak form of *Jihad* by overly liberal and spiritual forms of Sufism (cf. al-Ghazzali, 1991). As it had been practiced in the early Islamic communities, therefore, *Jihad* was seen to be part of the complacency that allowed the Crusaders to wreak so much damage. Muslims had been 'asleep at the wheel' and their conceptions of *Jihad* were part of the problem. The true *Jihad* was said to be warlike; it was a case of fighting even to the death for one's faith. Nur ad-Din actually exploited a Christian spirituality of martyrdom to make this point, a point he saw expressed perfectly in the Christian Crusader's dedication to the cause, even unto death. He urged that Muslims should get away from their soft spirituality, obsession with scholarship and cosy communal living and be similarly devoted to holy war in the way of the Christians. Thus began in earnest the era of *Da'wa, Jihad* as 'holy war'.

From this time, it has become difficult to distinguish between the more spiritually oriented *Jihad* and the warlike one. Even some of the former great characters, like al-Ghazzali, was quoted as having been critical of the laxness of Islamic civilization prior to the

Crusades. While al-Ghazzali was clearly more concerned with spiritual laxness and urged the people to remember their call to the great Promise (expressed as *Jihad al-akbar* = the major striving), he nonetheless also spoke of *Jihad al-asghar* (=the minor striving), which was the struggle against the infidel. From everything we know of al-Ghazzali, it is hard to imagine he would ever have sanctioned violence except in self-defence, however, his name became partly associated with legitimating the *Da'wa.*

Apart from his concern with spiritual laxness, al-Ghazzali, together with many other prominent Muslims in the period prior to the Crusades, expressed concern at the many divisions that had developed in Islamic civilization. This fact also came to be blamed for the destruction of this civilization at the hands of the Christians. As well as implying holy war, *Jihad* therefore came to imply something about the unity of Islam. Part of the re--establishment of Islam as an assemblage of holy warriors implied the need for the various factions to forget their differences and fight together in the common cause against the infidel, being prepared for martyrdom in the course of this holy war. In short, the concept of *Jihad* became a major tool in the campaign to re-unite and re-ignite Islam after the destruction wrought by the Crusades. Eliseeff (1993) writes:

> Ali as-Sulami saw only one solution which could save the Muslim provinces, the call to Jihad. Two preliminary phases were necessary. The first phase consisted of a 'moral rearmament' designed to end the 'spiritual decline' which had reduced the Muslims to their current situation... The second phase consisted of regrouping the Islamic forces by putting an end to the disaffection which had enabled the Crusaders to become so firmly established in the Orient ... Only when this psychological climate had been created, could the military Jihad commence ... (p. 164)

> The twenty-eight years of Nur ad-Din's reign, 1146-1174, constitute a decisive phase in the evolution of the Jihad conscience in Syria ... The classical ideology of the Jihad appeared in all its strength during the course of his reign. Among the fundamental ideas which as-Sulami originally expressed in the first part of the 12th century and Nur ad-Din further emphasized, was the re-glorification of the Talab ash-Shahada - the search for martyrdom — which became the most important element of his propaganda. This talab turned the Muslim who died fighting a shahad into a martyr who had fallen on the battlefield, thus securing access to Paradise. The second and third objectives were new and instilled a certain vigor into the movement. The first was to ensure the Holiness of Jerusalem and of Palestine, an objective implying the extermination of the rulers of the Latin orient ... The second was the re-establishment of the political unity of Islam in the Near East. (pp. 167-168)

Taji-Farouki (1995) offers the case of the Islamic Liberation Party (ILP) as a modern and extreme example of how the concept of *Jihad* continues to be used as a tool for warlike zeal. It is part of the revolutionary Islamic Jihad-Palestine movement, proposing that a united caliphate should be established representing one worldwide Islamic state. It is merciless in its opposition to the West, in particular to Israel and the USA. It uses Qur'an 3:28 as proof that it is forbidden for any Muslim to maintain so much as friendly relations with unbelievers (= non-Muslims):

> An unbeliever (Kafir) is anyone who follows a religion other than Islam ... Idolators, Jews, Buddhists, Christians and communists are exactly the same in this respect — all will be consigned eternally to Hellfire on the Day of Judgement. (page 40).

It ignores entirely other references from the Qur'an that endorse Jews and Christians as '(fellow) People of the Book'.

Taji-Farouki (1995) continues:

> ...the party sees Israel as a 'Colonialist bridgehead'. It holds that the American and European unbelievers created it as a base through which to perpetuate their control and economic exploitation of Muslim lands. Israel also allegedly safeguards their vital interests there in the longer term, by guaranteeing the failure of any attempt to reunify these lands within an Islamic framework. Accordingly, it condemns Israel as a 'cancer' in the heart of the Muslim world, and a 'poisoned dagger plunged deep into its breast'. ...
>
> The creation of Israel allegedly represented the consummation of a plan devised some two centuries previously. However, the inspiration behind it derived from a much earlier period - that of the Crusades. The episode of the Crusades occupies an important place in popular Muslim consciousness, and has assumed paradigmatic proportions in contemporary Islamic ideologies. The Palestinian Islamist groups find it particularly relevant to their circumstances: they uphold it as the epitome of unbeliefdom's unprovoked aggression against Islam, and the ultimate Muslim triumph. ...
>
> ... the Crusaders' malice remained concealed in their hearts, till they disclosed it when they succeeded in doing away with the Ottoman Caliphal state and then establishing a Jewish state in Palestine....
>
> According to this, a line of continuity is posited between the historical Crusades and European Colonialism which is construed as a strategy for tearing up the Muslim world as revenge for the ultimate failure of the Crusades. The party finds evidence of the continuing American and European 'Crusader mentality' in remarks... attributed to Generals Allenby and Gouraud during the period of the First World War, and in recent comments in the world press to the effect that Islam is the West's primary enemy, following the demise of Communism. ...
>
> The Christian motive for the creation of Israel can thus be traced back to the Crusader wars. (pages 40-41)

The ILP urges Muslims to destroy Israel through *Jihad*, described in its literature as the 'Islamic option', a holy war option sanctioned by God:

> Israel, then, is a doomed nation: the Jews' fate is sealed, for no reason other than their Jewishness. Nothing can repel this destiny or avert God's wrath from them. Presently, it brands all Jews as 'enemies of God' who are contaminating Palestine' it makes no attempt to differentiate between... Zionist and non Zionist Jews... As frustration with the slow pace of the peace process mounts, Palestinian Muslims are increasingly willing to place their confidence in the Islamic option. (Taji-Farouki, 1995: 53)

In similar vein, Nusse (1993) takes us inside the mind of HAMAS, another Islamist group, this time with a powerful political front as well as a sophisticated and quite convincing theological apparatus. The HAMAS ideology is a particularly potent form of Jihadic fundamentalism, apparently endorsed by a majority of Palestinians in open elections held in 2005. Central to its ideology is the destruction of Israel, held to be the supreme symbol of the West's avowed intention to destroy Islam. Any moderate Muslim, including among the Palestinian brotherhood, who associates with Jews or Christians is complicit in the West's grand intention and so becomes an enemy of 'true Islam' and able to be targeted along with their Western friends. This accounts for much of the tension in the Middle East and within

Islam generally. As troublesome as its opposition to the West is the oppositional difference to be found within Islam. This became particularly obvious in the ten year Iran/ Iraq war, where Iran, employing a revived Shi'a Islamism pitted itself against Iraq which, at the time, was essentially a Western ally, propped up by the USA. Ironically, Saddam Hussein, the US-backed leader of Iraq would, of course, go on to become the most hated object of US sentiments a few years later. In a further irony, it is the destruction of the essentially Westernized buffer state of Iraq that has spawned a newfound anti-US bridgehead in Iran. The tensions within Islam are also apparent in the oppositional difference between HAMAS and the other main Palestinian front, FATAH, the political movement that sits behind the Palestinian Liberation Organization. Unrest at the prolonged state of seemingly futile negotiations over the Palestinian question has led an increasing number of Palestinians to throw their support behind the more radical option in HAMAS, with an ideology designed to bring about a return to 'True Islam', including the restoration of a Palestinian state at any cost including wholesale destruction of any opposition, Muslim or non-Muslim.

'True Islam' is what all Muslims must return to, according to HAMAS. It is conceived to be that rule of God *(Hakimiyyah Allah)* that characterized the original Muslim communities. Gone are any sentiments about these early communities being sites of tolerance, peace and interfaith acceptance. Gone are the conceptions of *Shari'a Law* as being directed to human rights and social justice. The original Islam is held to be a place where Muslims ruled with an iron fist, where other faiths were not accommodated and where women knew their place of subservience and held to it. *Shari'a* was the law that ensured the rule of God was maintained. Where alternative forms of early Islam are acknowledged, they are roundly criticized for not being true to Islam and being responsible for the deterioration of Islam that occurred via the Crusades. HAMAS's unapologetic goal of restoring true Islam justifies the obliteration of Israel and the West and any Muslim leadership considered *Jahili* (not based on the Qur'an). Exacerbated by the defeat in the Six-Day War of 1967, the complete focus on the establishment of the *Hakimiyyah Allah* was then on the successful imposition of a Palestinian state in Israel, an event known as the *Intifadah*:

> ...the Jews (are) 'the people upon whom God's anger came (= in the Qur'an). ... God's anger came upon them because they did not follow properly the religion He had sent them, but killed his prophets and distorted the original godly Jewish religion. They have, especially tried to harm and dominate the Islamic Ummah because this Ummah is the 'new international force bringing an authentic civilizing and godly programme to mankind,'
>
> ...Muslims are warned not to take Jews or Christians as friends because such people are 'friends only for each other' (Qur'an 5,51) ... they seek corruption in the land ... Jews tried to harm the Muslim community and its leader (Muhammad) ... Jewish rabbis strove to introduce confusion among Muslims by pretending to be converted to Islam, without having done so 'in their hearts' (= those who brought the Isra'iliyat to Islam). ...All these allegations are presented in the framework of the struggle of Jewish tribes against the (original and pure) Muslim community in Medina.
>
> The evolution of these accounts into an international conspiracy theory was only possible in the context of 20th century world-wide communication. Nevertheless, these developments do not explain fully the major departure from the traditional Islamic stereotype of the Jews. The image of wretchedness amid humiliation which used to characterize the Jews in traditional Islamic thought, based on the strength and confidence of Islamic civilization until at least the 15th century, has been superceded in many modern Islamic writings on Zionism,

> Israel and Jewry by that of the powerful Jew, seriously threatening both the Muslim community and the rest of the world.. In terms different from the traditional descriptions, Jews are described as the 'Jewish Satan', the 'bloodsucker of mankind', 'racists', 'criminals of the tribe of Zion' and 'Nazis' ... This change in conceptions of Jews reflects modern European anti-Semitism. (Nusse, 1993: 102-104)

According to Nusse (1993), HAMAS claims to distinguish between 'Zionism' and 'Judaism'. Judaism is considered to be a 'religion that stipulates racism and hostility towards others in its books and incites falsely to take away Palestine under the slogan of the Holy Land'. (page 105) Zionism, on the other hand, 'represents the entity of the enemy' (Israel) and is 'responsible for the transformation of Jewish thought into a reality that is perceptible today in Palestine.' (page 105) Zionists are those Jews who want to realize their religious thought on Muslim soil. The theology that sits behind HAMAS Islamicizes history, assuming that Abraham was the first Muslim and, together with Ishmael, built the first mosque. This effectively subverts any Israeli claim to be the descendants of those with historical claim. The uncompromising goal is the establishment of an Islamic state in Palestine. Here, HAMAS departs from an Islamic tradition that has not been strong on physical land; indeed, this has more regularly been seen as part of the Islamic critique of Zionism. HAMAS, however, has borrowed the land theology from the Jews in the notion of an Islamic state being fundamental to the fulfillment of the Promise:

> For the Islamists, the question of Palestine is a/so pro-eminent in shaping the future of the Islamic Ummah: the Palestinian Jihad has had positive consequences for the Islamic awakening. Control over Palestine announces control over the whole world.
>
> ...Islamists reject the legitimacy of any decisions taken by the existing international organizations and do not expect not expect any support from them ... not only is the whole world order allied against Islam, but the Ummah itself is fragmented and does not play an active part in shaping the current world order. ...Arab countries fail to see that Jewish mass migration threatens them as well by the extent to which it strengthens Israel. Palestinians alone have to pay the price for fighting the common enemy and attempting the transformation of the international order. ... Confronted with this perceived isolation of their struggle on all levels, the only means to reach the proclaimed goal ... is Jihad.
>
> Any alternative way of finding a solution, such as an international peace conference, is rejected: 'such a conference would merely place unbelievers in the position of arbiters over Islamic territory. The Qur'anic verse quoted in support makes evident the ease with which certain texts and ideas can be used to express contemporary problems and feelings: 'but neither the Jews nor the Christians will be p/eased with you until you follow their religion. Say: God's guidance is the real guidance. And if you follow their desires, after what has come to you as knowledge, you will not have God as either helper or protector.' The warning of the Qur'an against the tricks amid errors of enemies is easily transplanted to the present defensive situation of the Arab-Islamic world. Any Palestinian concession to the interests of the Israeli state is equated with apostasy through time acceptance of Western (Jewish and Christian) standards,...The Intifadah, then, is the only truly Islamic way of winning back Palestine.
>
> The link between Jihad and the purification of Muslim society is founded in the necessity of Islamic consciousness, and widens the notion of Jihad beyond simply military conflict. Intellectual elites are cal/ed to contribute ... by writing books and article. ... The role of women is emphasized as they give birth to new Muslims and prepare them for the Jihad. (Nusse, 1993: 109-113).

In this context, one of the key intellectual contributors to Islamism is Muhammad al-Ashmawi, Professor of Letters at Alexandria University. His work (cf. Nettler 1995), on the surface seemingly more moderate than many of his peers, could actually have potential to do more long-term harm to the sibling relationship between Islam, Judaism and Christianity than most. He appears to base his case on the need for Islam to rid itself of its political face and return to its true spiritual roots. While blaming Judaeo-Christian influence, and specifically the *Isra'iliyat,* for infecting Islam with its current political agenda, he appears to exonerate Jews and Christians on the basis that they do not have the benefit of the final manifestation that God revealed to Muhammad, a manifestation that clarified once and for all that the Promise was always to be understood in spiritual rather than political terms.

Because Jews and Christians do not have the benefit of this manifestation, they can be forgiven for clinging to their more primitive interpretations. He draws a heavy line between Islam and Judaism, in particular, in declaring that the latter was never intended to be more than the legislative and institutional force that many Muslims see today. While not blaming Jews and, by inference, Christians personally, he nonetheless relegates their religions to such an inferior status that it becomes inconceivable that they could have anything positive to offer to Islam. Hence, the entire history of Jewish and Christian influence on Islam is re-interpreted as being regrettable and in need of urgent redressing.

In trying to explain what has gone wrong with Islam and why it is imperative that Muslims unite to return Islam to its true roots, al-Ashmawi is quoted as saying:

> Isra'iliyat is ... the 'Israelite thought' which entered Islam in spite of its being completely alien to Islam ... Islamic thought has most certainly followed in the footsteps of Judaism, without being aware of the differences between the essence of Moses's mission and the essence of Muhammad's mission ... and that the former is a legislating mission and the latter a mission of mercy and ethics ... Confusing the foundation of the two missions and directing Islam in the way of Judaism is to alter the basis and nature of (the Islamic) mission, to corrupt it, and to repudiate it in order to make it adopt the colouration of the Isra'iliyat and the forms of Judaism. (Nettler 1995: 179-181)

The problem with Islam is, therefore, its 'Judaization', a problem that goes back to Islam's foundations when it allowed the foreign influences of Judaism and Christianity to sully its mission. While one does not find the kind of vilification in al-Ashmawi that one finds in so much revisionist Islamic scholarship of the day, nonetheless there are none who revise the orthodox history more dramatically. Under al-Ashmawi, even some of Islam's own traditional sacred heroes are effectively written out of the script. The inevitable logic would seem to be that neither Moses nor Jesus can be seen any longer as Muslims in any sense, nor should they be allowed any influence. They become little more than unwitting functionaries responsible for wholly imperfect religious forms. One could only conclude that they, along with their imperfect traditions, must be expunged from Islamic thought and tradition if Islam is to return to its allegedly 'true roots'. Under the guise of an apparently moderate and non-punitive re-assessment of the history, al-Ashmawi has actually provided the theological rationale for the obliteration of Islam's long-held-to-be siblings, be it in terms of revisionist history or political solutions for today. For those who want to take it so far, he provides the perfect justification for the extermination of the modern state of Israel and for wholesale *Jihad* against the West.

Such Islamist views are naturally challenging to Westerners whose identity is wrapped around one of the traditions within Judaeo-Christianity. No less are they challenging to the average Muslim, however, who would find them unacceptably revisionist to the point of inventing a history and theology that has simply never existed. These views, however, are held by an increasing portion of those who describe themselves as Muslim, no doubt many of them with sincerity. Returning to the theme of education being the way through the morass created by this revisionist Islamism, it must be said that an education that took its charter of personal development and social education seriously would deal with these views, sensitively with their commonalities but robustly and boldly with their differences. Indeed, one is inclined to say that grappling seriously with the knowledge, insights and claims of Islam could well impel a more profound understanding of their tradition than the Judaeo-Christian Westerner would find anywhere else. As an important ancillary objective, it might well instil a greater appreciation of and sympathy towards Islam and its followers, and towards the huge contribution that Islam has made to the Judaeo-Christian West.

The fact that a religion of the import of Islam should employ the key heroes of Judaeo-Christianity to challenge its own institutional tenets is not to be rejected lightly. Especially when one considers that much of the critique provided by Islam is to be found within the Judaeo-Christian tradition itself (eg. Natarei Karta within Judaism, the Reformation within Christianity), the Islamic critique might well be taken as an opportunity for Judaeo-Christian Westerners to ponder on the integrity and authenticity of many of their own claims. This would be a noble and mighty contribution of education, not only in fostering an appreciation of an important alternative set of views in multi-faith societies and so fostering enhanced dialogue, but also in deepening understanding of their own broader faith and cultural tradition. This would be the kind of education bound to make a difference.

Sound education cannot be merely intellectual and conceptual, however, no matter how historically and theologically validated. Part of adequate education about Islam and the West must engage people's emotions, communicative capacities and their artistic and expressive selves. Only in this way can we truly enter into the minds and experiences of the other. It is in this light that we offer the following case study of one of the author team, Ibtihal Samarayi, an Iraqi Sunni Muslim who escaped the horrors of Saddam Hussein's Iraq, suffered as a refugee in Iran and Turkey and finally found her way to Australia where she went on to complete her education, including through a doctorate in fine art. Her knowledge of Islam, in conjunction with her unique experiences and her expertise as an artist, has allowed her to capture and express the unusual circumstances of her life and of those many other Muslims caught up in similar circumstances. In particular, her artistic sense and expressive capacity has allowed her to analyze the experiences of young children caught up in the displacement that is the fate of many young Muslims today. Her work offers rare insight into the mind of the young Muslim faced with the trauma of detention and refugee status. One can see through the artwork that emanates from such trauma how easily current Western solutions to the problems of displaced Muslim populations could facilitate rather than stem the cause of Islamism and create in fact an expanded problem that will haunt the West for generations to come. The following kernel of her doctoral work will be told in Dr Samarayi's own words in the form of a case study.

USING ART TO RESTORE JUSTICE TO ISLAM

Case Study of Ibtihal Samarayi

I was born in the town of Ba'quba, 60 kilometres north of the city of Baghdad in Iraq. I was the youngest in a family of ten children, having eight brothers and only one sister. My father was a successful businessman, owning a chain of large department stores around Baghdad. This made it possible for me, as well as for all my siblings, to complete my university studies. My chosen study was Cinematography, in which I received a degree from the University of Baghdad in 1990, just a few months before the commencement of the Iraqi Gulf War in 1991. In achieving first place in the Department of Cinematography, June 1990, I was offered the position of tutor to the first year students in the course, while pursuing the Masters Course in Cinematography. The Gulf War changed everything.

I was three years old when, in 1967, Israel achieved its independence from Palestinian occupation. This was considered a black day in the annals of Arabic History. In Iraq, this was presented as an unlawful seizure of Palestinian land. It sparked a renewed determination by the Palestinian forces to re-capture their land. The streets of Iraq rumbled to the sound of tanks on their way to Jordan. The television monitors brought to Iraq by the British in 1956 screened unending scenes of warfare and exhortations by the Iraqi military to join the fight for justice and the honour of the Palestinian people.

In 1980, a few months into the Iraqi-Iranian war, my brother, just seventeen years of age, was reported "lost in action". Later, we were to learn that he had been taken prisoner in Iran, where he was held in prison for eight years. Shortly after this, my father was arrested, being accused of political agitation, and thrown into prison. Within months of his release, he died, partly as a result of his treatment in jail.

Another incident, throwing light on the sham surrounding Hussein's much publicised birthday celebrations, occurred at about this time. It was Saddam Hussein's birthday in 1988. I was an eighteen-year-old University student and, as such, was obligated to attend the public function. The entire student body was marched to Baghdad's *Celebration Square*, along with all students from other schools in the city and indeed the entire civilian population, to honour the "Great Leader". A friend and I decided not to join in the celebration and made our way to the bus stop. Here we were confronted by a group of Hussein's personal guards who forced us into a security van and drove us away to a place of detention inside one of Hussein's palaces, where we were given a tongue-lashing, interrogated, and held for eight hours.

During my time at high school, I was obliged to include some aspect of the Israeli-Palestinian war in every piece of artwork. Always, the work had to depict the Palestinians as victorious, even when they were being defeated. European art was studied at art colleges at university level and was generally held up as an example to be prized and emulated.

War influenced every aspect of my teenage years, especially through the Iraqi-Iranian war that was at its height between 1980 and 1988. During this time, the media ran endless pro-Iraqi propaganda relating to the war. Cinemas rarely showed anything other than war films designed to stir the population to fight for Iraq. All Iraqi youths, upon completion of high-school, were conscripted to fight against the Iranian forces. I was fourteen years of age when my brother, Bassim, then seventeen years of age, and having just completed high school, was confronted in the street near my home by a group of uniformed officers and conscripted on the spot to join the Iraqi Army.

There was no escape. To refuse military service in Iraq would mean instant imprisonment. My brother had strong feelings about the moral justification of Iraq's involvement and refused to serve in it. So desperate was my brother to avoid participating in this war that he attempted to kill himself rather than siding with the government. Discovering him bleeding and nearly unconscious, my family rushed him to hospital. Police guards at the hospital removed him to another section of the building reserved for those attempting to avoid military conscription. The gash in his chest had been deep and the doctor reported that he had come within a centimetre of his life. Barely had Bassim's wound healed, when army officers on duty at the hospital rushed him off immediately to fight in the front line at the Iraqi-Iranian border, where fighting was at its height. Our family was informed that he had been 'lost in action'. Some months later, we received notice that he had been taken prisoner in Iran. With the end-of-war political agreement between Iraq and Iran for the mutual release of war prisoners, eight years from the commencement of the war, Bassim was finally released. He was then twenty-six years of age.

Another incident, which deeply shocked my family, occurred when another brother, Kassim, a practicing medical doctor, was confronted in his clinic by officers who ordered him to serve at the front line as a medical doctor. He was also ordered to fight against the Iranians in the North of Iraq towards the end of the Iraqi-Iranian War in 1987. He refused. At 1am the morning after his refusal, army officers arrived at his home and began shouting and kicking noisily on the door. When Kassim answered the door, he was grabbed and kicked about the stomach and dragged to a waiting jeep, in front of the entire family. My father rushed to his assistance shouting abuse at the government officers and threatening them with his gun. Almost immediately, the house was surrounded by army personnel. My father was called, marched off to the jeep, blindfolded, and taken to the army headquarters where he was interrogated and thrown into jail. Here, he was short-listed to be tried by the military court and, almost certainly, hanged. He remained in prison for eighteen months and was released only through bribes of money offered by my brothers to avoid my father's case reaching the high court of the Iraqi military. The corrupt senior officers of the Iraqi Intelligence Department were quick to receive the bribe. Nevertheless, my father remained in the prison. He was then seventy years of age. Broken in spirit and health, he died within a few months of his release from prison in 1988.

However, it was the second Iraqi war, the Gulf War of 1991, to which my artwork principally relates. Circumstances relating to my personal safety as well as that of my husband, Sadraddin, precipitated our escape from Iraq. Since he, too, had refused to fight in the Gulf War, Sadraddin was immediately blacklisted by government agencies as a deserter, the punishment for which was summary execution. As his wife, I would have shared a similar fate. We had no choice but to escape from Iraq. This meant, for us, having to cross the snow-covered North Iraqi mountains. There was no transport available, which meant we had to go by the most unfrequented passages known only to a few merchants who also acted as 'people movers' that is, paid 'people smugglers'. For people, such as we, whose lives were in jeopardy by reason of involvement in some form of anti-government protest, these so-called smugglers attained an almost hero status in Iraq, since they also put their own lives in danger. The arranged passage was through the most rugged and difficult terrain, much of it covered in snow, and had to be negotiated on foot. Only the most basic items could be carried on our backs. Sleeping in freezing conditions, and surviving on the most minimal food supplies, some days eating only some small edible plants growing through the snow or even on some old left over scraps of bread found on the mountain trail, we finally arrived some days later, bedraggled and exhausted, at the small village of Shnoya in Iran. It was February, 1991. Friendly village people assisted us on the second leg of the journey. Disguised in local Iranian dress and mixing with local townfolk, we were taken on board a large passenger van and driven right to the Chashma Gul Refugee Camp in Iran, situated close to the Iraqi boarder. However, we were not permitted to enter the camp, which had been set-up by the United Nations in 1991. First, we had to get permission from the Iranian government. This meant a further two month wait, accommodated at the small camp at Zeally village, especially set up by the local village people, to accommodate families and solders escaping from Iraq during the war.

Once permission was given, thousands of refugees from Iraq, especially Kurdish people from North Iraq, poured into the camps. Conditions here were basic. There were no showers or hot water. Even cold water for drinking or washing was at a premium. For us inmates, it meant a daily trek, walking for miles on foot to carry water in jugs drawn from wells in the mountains, back to the camp. Long queues for canned food were an everyday experience. Sleeping conditions on the hard ground were difficult and uncomfortable. We had only a few folded garments between us in the hard ground underneath us. Only one blanket was issued to each adult. One of the most difficult aspects of the refugee experience was that of having to share a very limited space with other people. We had been obliged to share our very small tent with another couple, together with their two small children. Sleeping in these conditions was well nigh impossible.

After a year in Chashma Gul Camp, at the end of the Gulf War, the Iranian government announced that all Iraqi refugees should return home. However, we all suspected that our return to Iraq would mean execution for every one of us, being refugees despised as 'deserters and traitors'. None of us trusted Saddam Hussein, so that when the Iranian trucks arrived at the camp to return us to Iraq, and forced us all in, my husband and I planned to jump out on the way back. Arriving at a crowded village market, we both jumped out of the truck, and went into hiding. When it was all clear, we were able to contact an old family acquaintance, a merchant, who was able to arrange for a guide to take us on foot across the hazardous passage through the rugged mountain ranges of south-west Turkey. In negotiating the difficult terrain, we were confronted by armed border guards who immediately opened fire on us. Diving for cover behind rocks, we were able to escape from their view and proceed with great caution along the mountain trail. To enter Turkey, we needed permission from the government. The merchant sent us on to his merchant friend in a Turkish village, where it was thought we would be most unlikely to encounter Turkish police, who would have had to deport us, as illegal entrants, back to Iraq. The merchant, accepting my gold necklace for payment, helped us to go to Ankara. From there, we heard that the United Nations (UN) was no longer accepting Iraqi refugees. The UN had been told by Hussein's Government that the Iraqi refugees would be able to return safely to Baghdad. Coming from Hussein, we were naturally suspicious of this offer, so we tried once again to hide in Ankara, in Turkey, for a few months. We heard later, as we had suspected, that Saddam had hanged those refugees who had chosen to return to Iraq. After that, the UN re-opened its doors to Iraqi refugees. Finally, after waiting in the camps for five years, we were accepted as refugees and allowed to enter Australia. This, then, is the backdrop of my own personal experience and the source of all my subsequent artwork, an analysis of which will form the major part of this section of the article.

CAPTURING AN ELEMENT OF THE CONTEMPORARY MUSLIM EXPERIENCE THROUGH ART

My hope, in expressing myself through my art, is two-fold. In the first place, I felt I needed to get my whole war experience out of my system, particularly my time as a refugee, held at limbo, in sometimes inhumane conditions at the Zeally and Chashma Gul camps. The former camp was located on the Iraqi-Iranian border, the latter, several hundred miles inside the Iranian border. To accomplish this, I decided to physically involve myself in reconstructing a representation of those same dwelling places, which had been my homes for over five years. I have also included representations of other refugee camps such as the one at Rafha in Saudi Arabia in which Ali Al-Uboodi (one of the refugees I interviewed), was held for five years.

This physical involvement in the construction of the camp Installations, I am arguing, contributed quite substantially to my own healing process, eliminating the worst aspects of my personal trauma, a constant fear of deportation back to Iraq and certain execution. I have felt that, in revisiting scenes of terror and horror through my art, I have, to a large extent, been able to lessen their pernicious hold on my conscious and unconscious mind.

Figure 1. Ibtihal Samarayi-Installation -Refugee Camp:, *These Were My Homes*, Mud, rope, canvas, 2001.

My second reason for choosing to interpret the impact of the wars in Iraq, as experienced by me and my family, was to shed light upon the situation for refugees in Iraq as it affected me personally, and to tell some of the untold stories of suffering and tragedy experienced by my fellow countrymen and women.

Before I begin to describe the installations, I should explain that the final work consists of five separate dwellings, representing the five different types of accommodation, which were the wartime homes of many of the refugees of Iraq. Related to my Installation work, is the separate installation, *These were my Homes.*

My work attempts to express and document my passage through war trauma. The sudden jolting and abrupt change of lifestyle that was thrust upon me, was perhaps the most difficult aspect of the war to deal with. For me, it meant the complete and absolute severance from my family and friends and from the generally happy life I had been used to in Iraq. To be thrown in with strangers of many different backgrounds, in sometimes appalling conditions, necessitated an enormous personal adjustment. I have not seen or heard from my family since 1991 and, as blacklisted persons, my husband and I will never be able to return to Iraq as long as the present situation persists.

Figure 2. Ibtihal Samarayi-Manipulated digital image, *The Military Boot*, 2001,2mx1.5m.

The Military Boot, is set against a quotation from the Qur'an, the Muslim holy book. The large boot in the centre of the picture, representing the power of war and also the military dictatorship of Saddam Hussein, smashes down indiscriminately, crushing the flattened image of the Iraqi family underneath it. The flames leaping from the ground represent what seemed to be an attempt by the forces of war to destroy Iraqi culture. The Muslim quotation in Arabic which forms the backdrop to the image is "*Allah we depend on you, to you we return. Our destiny is in your hands*". The creation of this image was my way of coming to terms with the trauma which resulted in the destruction of my family. It helped me to clarify the cynical nature of politically motivated war and to place the burden of guilt on those governments which can find no other solution to their problems than a military one. Instinctively, I chose to "open the box and inspect the content for what it really is." This confrontation therapy has helped me to talk about events which initially I was unable to face.

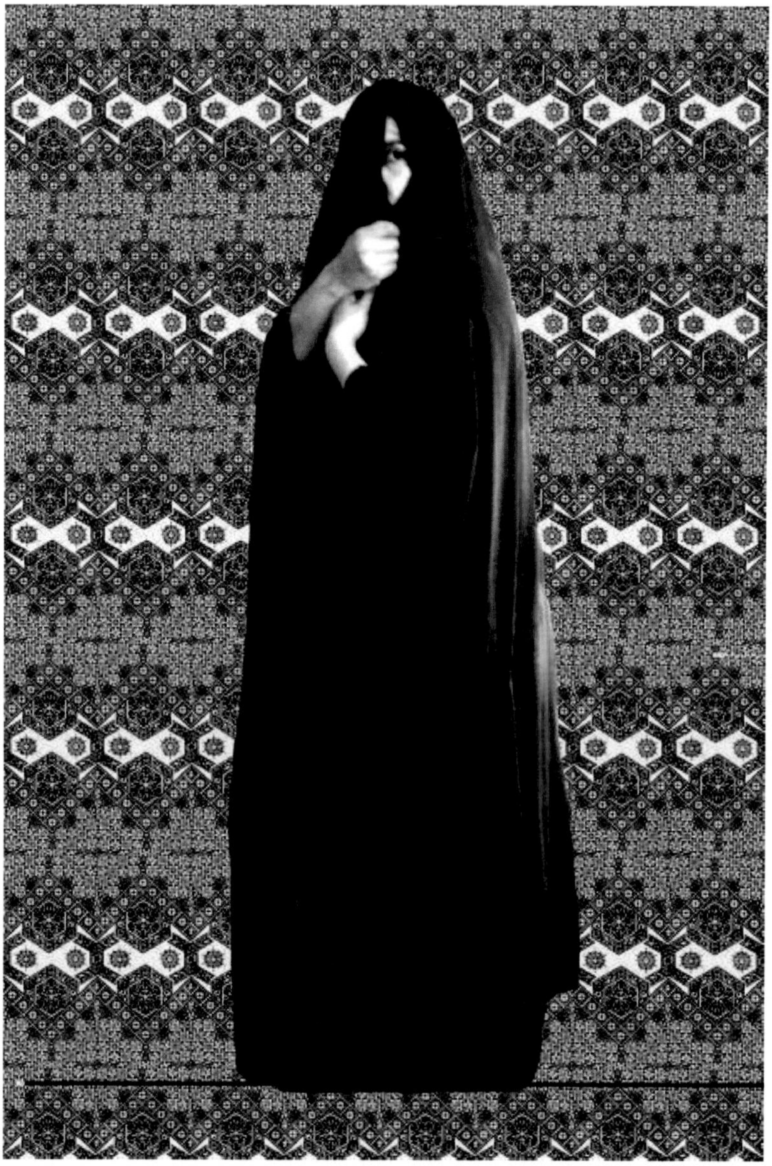

Figure 3. Ibtihal Samarayi-Manipulated digital image, *Retreat into the Past*, 1999 2mx1.5m.

The Gulf War of 1991 changed Iraqi society. Before the war, almost all younger Iraqi women were wearing Western fashions and were seen moving freely about the cities of Iraq, mixing with the opposite sex and, for those who wished to attend University, competing equally with male students for academic places. From the time the war began until now, it is as if time has moved backwards several decades to the 1940s when most women were obliged to wear the traditional top-to-toe black Abaya. Immediately after the close of the Gulf War, women returned to the old style covering and were segregated from the male population in most social situations. The reasons for this are many. Psychologically, there was a widely felt need to seek protection from the unpredictable and frightening world they had experienced through the war. There was also a widespread sense of guilt, that they were being punished for some lapse in their religious duties and that they must make a special effort to try to purge themselves of their sins and return to their traditional God. There is also the factor of 'existential guilt', when many would be asking themselves, for example, "Why should I be alive when so many young people, even children, were killed?" My image attempts to illustrate the present status of the Iraqi woman. Fear has made her socially anonymous. For her personal security, she clings to what seems to be the comparative safety of tradition represented here by the Islamic patterned backdrop behind her.

Figure 4. Ibtihal Samarayi-Manipulated digital image, *Requiem for Three Sisters*,2001, 160x200 m.

The US trade embargo on Iraq had tragic consequences for the Iraqi family during this time. Although it was widely reported in the Western press that the embargo was for the specific purpose of preventing goods which could be used in building ammunition from reaching Iraq, the fact was that the real impact was on the Iraqi family through the effective ban on basic foods such as flour, rice, sugar, and cooking oil. It was also extremely difficult to get enough petrol to run the family car. Car tyres were simply not available as it was assumed that the materials used in their manufacture could be used in the making of chemical weapons. Food and medical supplies to Iraq were also drastically cut. Many families were unable to feed their children adequately and thousands of them were forced to remove their young children from school, even at primary level, to assist in augmenting the family income. Many children were consequently malnourished and many others, deprived of essential medicines, were dying.

This image has special meaning for both Australians and Iraqis, as it concerns the plight of many of the world's asylum seekers. The image of the three little girls, drowning in the sea is a reference to the three little sisters who lost their lives in October 2001 when the crowded refugee boat, in which they were travelling, sank in rough seas off the Australian coast.

Figure 5. Ibtihal Samarayi-Manipulated digital image, *Letter from a child*, 2002, 160x2 m.

I have related the image to an aboriginal story surrounding the 'Three Sisters' of the Blue Mountains to the west of Sydney, Australia. The legend tells of the father's attempt to save his 3 daughters from a monster, by turning them into stone. Likewise, the father of the 3 girls who lost their lives had hoped to save them from the tragic situation in Iraq (a figurative monster of war) in order to give them the chance of a better life in Australia. The story was well-publicized in the Australian media. The father, a hard-working baker, living in Sydney, had received a phone-call from his wife and children the night before they set off and warned them strongly against attempting the dangerous journey from Indonesia. However, the family, being desperate to join their father after five years of separation, decided to risk the journey. The rest is history.

I created this image as a personal protest against the treatment of children, many of whom have been themselves victims of war trauma in their own countries. At the time of writing, many children are still being held in detention centres in Australia. I have selected a desert-like backdrop to symbolise the sterile and barren nature of life within the confines of these camps.

Figure 6. Ibtihal Samarayi-Manipulated digital image, *From the Other Side*, 2002, 160x2 m.

The image here expresses the tragedy of war from the Iraqi child's point of view. The faded image of the child, his leg held in a chain, peers out from his hiding place. He does not understand the meanings of the destruction around him or of the various political interpretations placed upon it. He only knows that his home is being destroyed, together with everything dear and familiar to him. This is represented by the traditional Islamic backdrop which seems to be threatened by the terrifying juggernaut of war. The flames of destruction have also swallowed up his right to a normal childhood. Survival of the family, or what remained of it, was the only consideration. He would be pulled out of the school, and set to work to augment the family income, whether selling seeds, beans, items of clothing, used furniture or even prized family heirlooms; these would all be sacrificed in a desperate fight for survival. A child in this situation would have to grow up very quickly. He might be only seven or eight years of age but, with his father killed in the war, he could be promoted instantly to family bread winner. In some cases, a child thrown into a demanding and difficult situation such as this might respond positively, quickly gaining confidence in his ability to handle anything that fate might throw his way. Indeed, a high percentage of people undergoing traumatic experiences reported that, having survived an enormous challenge, they felt they were better off for the experience. While this might have been the experience of some of the more emotionally mature children, it would be impossible to calculate the psychological damage visited upon many of the more vulnerable children experiencing the horrors of wartime Iraq and of detention if their parents were successful in escaping the war.

At another level, this image represents my own reaction to the wars that seemed to dominate my childhood. I was the trapped child caught up in the tragic results of almost unceasing warfare in my own country. Like many children in my situation I was deeply troubled and confused about the reasons why this calamity should have come upon me. What had I done wrong to deserve this punishment? Feelings of irrational guilt followed me through my childhood and caused endless nightmares and restless nights.

The following artwork will explore my artistic response to the psychological and physical impact of long periods of incarceration in refugee detention centers. In particular, it will examine the resultant behaviors of war trauma, the loss of basic human rights and the imposition of constraints upon freedom of expression experienced by three male detainees in the Woomera Detention Center in South Australia, another male detainee in Port Hedland in Western Australia and three children detained with their parents, also at Woomera in South Australia.

Figure 7. Ibtihal Samarayi-*Locked Inside 1*, 2003, Wood, Foam, Digital Image, 1.6m x 2m.

Figure 8. Ibtihal Samarayi, *Locked Inside 2*, 2003, Wood, Foam, Digital Image, 1.6m x 2m.

The circle of the huge padlocks is already symbolic. When the viewer inside the circle, the single eye depicted as if looking through each keyhole, for which the key itself is for ever just out of reach, powerfully evoked a feeling of empathy with the detainees. But in what seemed to the viewer a piece of imaginative montage, these eyes become the eyes of the watchers, the guards watching the inmates of the centres, and these locks become also a Benthamite Panopticon. And this multi-layered representation of eyes raises the more open question in the viewers minds as they watch – who is it who sees? The circle of the watchers and the watched remains held inside the locks, and does not emerge to be seen by the eyes of, for example, the Australian public. No one knows what is happening.

"*Locked Inside 1*" is my first padlock of the Installation. It represents a child locked inside the detention centre. You can see his eye watching you, begging you for help. It is the psychological feeling of the prison for both the actual prisoner and the audience.

This symbolic image represents the emotions of any child kept away from playing on the beach like normal children. The dove represents a child kept inside a cage. The background presents a contrast between the normal life and the abnormal, like that between the desert and the beautiful beach.

Figure 9. Ibtihal Samarayi, *The Out of Reach Key*, 2003, tin pipe, wood, patina liquid, Iron Powder, 1m.

The installation's signifiers, metaphors and symbols acknowledge and reinforce this anxiety of detention as a perplexing state or space of anticipation, hostility, rupture and affirmation the refugee's state of non-being. The installation engages and references the modality of space mediated through temporality – where the refugees are caught or suspended in time and space, in a state of an in between ness that defies cultural logic, international law and the respect for human dignity where the already traumatized are further detained in a state of disenfranchisement and exist in condition that is never fully constituted. As with the *Out of Reach Key,* the suggestions are confined within political contingency that is bureaucratically policed and articulated from outside their gasp. In the Installation, there is no shared history, no past, but a schizophrenic present dislocated in difference displacement. The padlocks I constructed are big; bigger than the viewer and bigger than internee. They are monumental in scale and unequivocally state the determined function of authority that enables their forced in closure deprivation and alienation. The circle of padlocks are representative of both a psychological and political prison – either way the padlocks are an expression of suffering and traumatic isolation , they are also a representation of the political and military power of the nation. However, when I surrounds the padlocks with emblematic images of guards, fences, razor wire and 'big fire' produced by children from detention centre reflects clearly the enormity of the psychological problems and distress that impacts upon the delicate innocence children caught in the delirium of war or detention.

Figure 10. Ibtihal samarayi-The complete work of Locked Inside Installation with the out of reach key, 2005, tin pipe, wood, patina liquid, Iron Powder, Wood, Foam, Digital Image.

Figure 11. Ibtihal Samarayi-Image of the installation, photograph by Sadraddin Ahmed-Aziz, *Locked Inside* , 2003, Wood, Foam, Digital Image, 1.6m x 2m.

Art as a Release from Trauma: (Refugees - Interviewed by Ibtihal Samarayi)

Islam in Arabic means "submission" and derives from a word meaning "peace," for it is in submitting to God's Will that human beings gain peace in their lives in this world and the hereafter. Islam is a universal message revealed in the sacred book, the Qur'an, through the Prophet Muhammad. It shares with the other Abrahamic religions, Judaism and Christianity, their ethical teachings and the belief in the One God. Islam is both a religion and a way of life.

For Muslims, the Qur'an is the actual Word of God revealed through the archangel Gabrielle to the Prophet of Islam during the twenty-three year period of his prophetic mission. It was revealed in the Arabic language, which became therefore the language of Islam even for non-Arab Muslims.

Figure 12.Hameed Aqbaly, *Islamic Calligraphy*, 1m. x 1.5m. Acrylic on Paper, Liverpool, NSW, 2003.

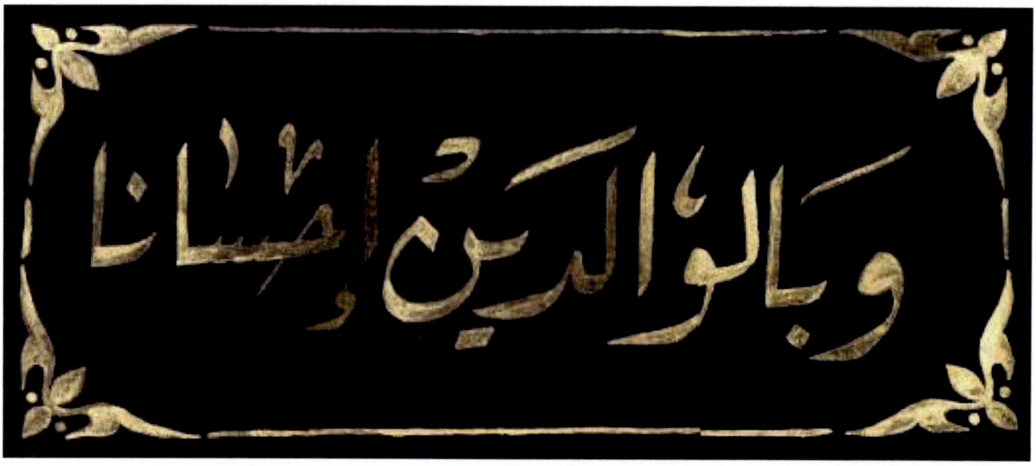

Figure 13. Hameed Aqbaly, *Islamic Calligraphy*, 1m. x 1.5m. Acrylic on Paper, Liverpool ,NSW, 2003.

From the Qur'an: "*All that happens to us is ordained by God*". It is entirely traditional to surround sacred texts with decorative design.

This artwork dramatically describes the panic felt amongst the forces for hope, symbolised in the meaning of the words as a prayer to Allah, circling red flowers, panicking in the face of the barb wire. The flowers, representing the forces for peace and hope, find themselves enveloped in between the words of prayer. The colour has seemingly turned to blue, which could be a reference to the signs of peace in heaven, which would signal the coming of life on earth. The familiar black background can be glimpsed in the bottom right of the painting. Here it refers to the endless passage of night and day in detention, of lost time and wasted lives.

Figure 14. Luay Falah Jeawan, Allah has the Last Word, Water Colours, !mx1.3m, Liverpool, NSW, 2003.

Honor your Mother and your Father. This style, called *Naskh*, which means "copying," was developed in the tenth century, and refined into a fine art form in Turkey in the sixteenth century. Since then, it has become the generally accepted script for writing in the Qur'an. *Naskh* is legible and clear and was adapted as the preferred style for typesetting and printing. It is a small script whose lines are thin and letter shapes are round. For Hameed Aqbaly, these words in Arabic had special meaning. His widowed mother, whom he contacted regularly by phone, was still living in Iraq, this being a source of constant concern. As much as he would have liked to bring her out to Australia, he knew it would be impossible for her to obtain a visa to come here. Equally, he was worried that he would never be granted a permanent visa to remain and to work in Australia. Even though in his own country he was a qualified mathematician, his temporary visa in Australia prevented him from obtaining permanent employment. He was obliged to take on whatever job, usually low paid, menial work, that was available.

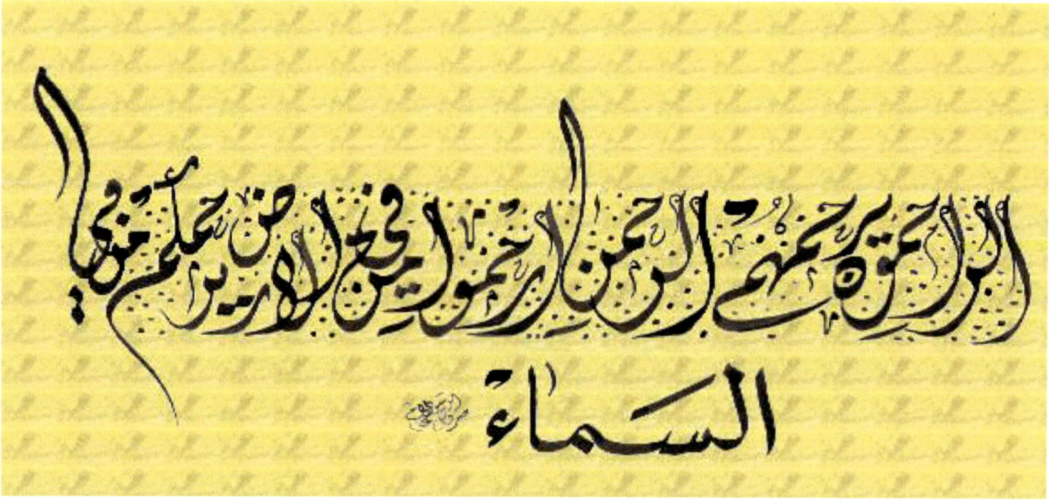

Figure 15. Luay Falah Jeawan, , *Blessed are the Merciful,* Water Colours on Paper,1m x 1.5m, Liverpool, NSW, 2003.

Figure 16. Luay Falah Jeawan, A Refugee's Dream, Ink on paper, Woomera Detention Centre, South Australia, 2002.

Figure 17. Art therapy Program for the children from Woomera Detention Centre, Liverpool, Sydney.2003, Photograph by Ibtihal Samarayi.

Figure 18. Art therapy Program for the children from Woomera Detention Centre, Liverpool, Sydney.2003, Photograph by Ibtihal Samarayi.

It has been through the telling of my story that I have found the greatest release of negative emotions. This strategy has so far proved to be the most expedient in allowing me to focus on the positive aspects of the experience, that is, the insight and understanding I have gained concerning the plight and needs of other war refugees attempting to find safety in Western countries like Australia. In creating series after series of sketches relating to war memories in preparation for my paintings, I feel I have finally "opened the box" on all my hitherto repressed memories. Finally, it has been the direct confrontation of traumatic memories that has helped immensely in creating for me a psychological distance from the troublesome events of war. Thus, by means of this strategy, I have derived a triple advantage: first, as a means of exorcising the most pernicious of my intrusive memories; second, as a solid piece of psychological armory for my own protection; and, third, I have gained through the experience an effective means of assisting fellow refugees through a sympathetic presentation of the similar difficulties they face as traumatized migrants escaping from their own countries' horrors.

CONCLUSION

This chapter has attempted to offer new directions in thought about Islam in the hope of restoring justice to a religious ideology currently under siege, a siege brought on partly by deliberate acts of hijacking this ideology but largely through lack of sound education about it, both within Muslim and non-Muslim regimes, and the misunderstanding and bigotry that necessarily follows from this lack of education. The chapter has attempted to do this restoration utilizing a range of disciplinary strategies from historical and theological appraisal through to artistic expression and analysis. Throughout, its consistent theme has been that better understanding of Islam will serve to enhance the West's self-understanding, to draw us closer to the plight of countless millions who suffer one way or another through the displacement that characterizes so many contemporary Muslims' experiences, and to inch just a little closer to solving what is arguably the world's current most threatening conflict between peoples.

REFERENCES

Adang, C (1996) *Muslim writers on Judaism and the Hebrew bible: From Ibn Rabban to Ibn Hazm.* Leiden: E. J. Brill.

Ahmed, L. (1992). *Women and gender in Islam: Historical roots of a modern debate.* New haven: Yale University Press.

Al-Ghazzali, A. (1991). *The book of religious learnings.* New Delhi: Islamic Book Services.

Amin., O., (2007). Influence of Muslim Philosophy on the West. (accessed 10 Jul 2007) *http://www.renaissance.com.pk/JunRefl2y3.html.*

Aquinas, T. (1936). *Summa theologica.(tr. L. Shapcote)* London: Burns and Oates.

Aristotle (1985). *Nicomachean ethics. (tr. T. Irwin)* Indianapolis: Hackett.

Aristotle (1992). *The Politics. (tr. T. Sinclair)* Harmondsworth: Penguin.

Armstrong, K. (1999). *A history of God.* London: Vintage.

Armstrong, K. (2001). *The battle for God: Fundamentalism in Judaism, Christianity and Islam.* London: Harper Collins.

Augustine (1972). *City of God.* Harmondsworth, UK: Penguin.

Bat Ye'or (2002). *Islam and dhimmitude: Where civilizations collide.* Madison, NJ: Associated Universities Presses.

Butterworth, E. and Blake, A. (1993). *The introduction of Arabic philosophy into Europe.* Toronto: Brill Academic Publishers.

Habermas, J. (1972). *Knowledge and human interests, (tr. J. Shapiro)* London: Heinemann.

Habermas, J. (1974). *Theory and practice. (tr. J. Viertal)* London: Heinemann.

Haddad, Y. and Esposito, J. (1998). *Islam, gender and social change.* Oxford: Oxford University Press.

Hawi, S. (1973). Ibn Tufayl's Hayy Ibn Yaqzan: Its structure, literary aspects and methods. *Islamic Culture*, 47: 191-211.

Hoyland, R (2001). *Arabia and the Arabs: From the Bronze Age to the coming of Islam.* London: Routledge.

Kasher, H. (1995). Maimonides' view of circumcision as a factor uniting the Jewish and Muslim communities. In R. Nettler (ed.) (1995). *Medieval and modern perspectives on Muslim-Jewish relations.* (pp. 103-108) Oxford: Harwood Academic Publishers.

Khalidi. T. (2O0l). *The Muslim Jesus: Sayings and stories in Islamic literature.* Cambndge, MASS: Harvard University Press.

Kogan, B. (1985). *Averroes and the metaphysics of causation.* New York: SUNY Press.

Kramer, M. (ed.) (1999). *The Jewish discovery of Islam.* Tel Aviv: The Moshe Dayan Center for Middle eastern and African Studies, Tel Aviv University.

Landau, R. (1962). *The Arab heritage of western civilization.* New York: Arab Information Centre.

Lewis, B. (1987). *Islam: From the Prophet Muhammad to the capture of Constantinople.* (Volumes I and II) Oxford: Oxford University Press.

Lewis, B. (2002). *The Arabs in history.* Oxford: Oxford University Press.

Lovat, T. (2005). Educating about Islam and learning about self: An approach for our times. *Religious Education*, 100: 38-51.
http://www.findarticles.com/p/articles/mi_qa3783/is_200501/ai_n13487147

Lovat, T. (2006). Interpreting the scriptures of Islam and implications for the West. *International Journal of the Humanities*, 4: 63-69.
http://www.cgpublisher.com/works/6073/actions/1/4/details/history/num=6/CGDocument/fid =158656/H06_6073_TheScripturalEvidenceofIslam_final.pdf

Nasr, S. (2002) *The heart of Islam.* San Francisco: Harper.

Nettler, R. (ed.) (1995). *Medieval and modern perspectives on Muslim-Jewish relations.* Oxford: Harwood Academic Publishers.

Nettler, R. and Taji-Farouki, S (eds.) (1998). *Muslim-Jewish encounters, intellectual traditions and modern politics.* Reading: Harwood Academic Publishers.

Netton, I.R. (1989). *Allah transcendent: Studies in the structure and semiotics of Islamic philosophy, theology and cosmology*, London and New York: Routledge.

Nevo, J. (1995). 'Zionism' versus 'Judaism' in Palestinian historiography. In R. Nettler (ed.) (1995). *Medieval and modern perspectives on Muslim-Jewish relations.* (pp. 159-173) Oxford: Harwood Academic Publishers.

Nusse, A. (1993). The ideology of HAMAS: Palestinian Islamic fundamentalist thought on the Jews, Israel and Islam. In R. Nettler (ed.) *Studies in Muslim-Jewish Relations.* (pp. 97-125). Leiden: Harwood Academic Publishers.

Peters, F. (2003). *Islam.* New Jersey: Princeton University Press.

Plato (1987). *The republic. (transl. D. Lee)* Harmondsworth: Penguin.

Plato (1989). *Protagoras. (transl. C. Taylor)* Oxford: Clarendon Press.

Randel, D. (1976). Al-Farabi and the role of Arabic music theory in the Latin Middle Ages. *Journal of the American Musicological Society,* 29, 173-188.

Rogerson, B. (2003). *The prophet Muhammad.* London: Little, Brown.

The Qu'ran (1978 publication) (tr. N. Dawood) Harmondsworth: Penguin.

Salam.A., (1980), *Miramare Truste,* International Centre for Theoretical Physics, Trieste, Italy, Imperial college, London.

Samarayi, I., 2002. *Iraqi Artists as Refugees: Reading the Narratives of War;* Masters of fine Art thesis, University of Newcastle, Ourimbah Campus.

Samarayi, I., 2007. *The Impact of Detention on Iraqi Artists in Australia and the Use of Art Practice as a Method of Healing*; PhD thesis, University of Newcastle, Ourimbah Campus.

Shatzmiller, M. (1993). *Crusaders and Muslims in twelfth-century Syria.* Leiden: E.J. Brill.

Urvoy, D., (1991). *Ibn Rushed (Averroes).* Routledge, New York.

Van Den Bergh, S., (1954). *Averroes' Tahafut Al-Tahafut: The Incoherence of the Incoherence.,*Volume 1. London: Luzac and Co.

In: Human Rights Issues in the 21st Century
Editors: M.S. Becker and J.N. Schneider, pp. 73-101
ISBN 978-1-60456-119-7

Chapter 4

A HUMAN RIGHTS PERSPECTIVE ON DETENTION FOR RE-EDUCATION: IS LABOUR A RIGHT OR AN OBLIGATION TO PERFORM?

Na Jiang
CCLCJ at University of Durham

ABSTRACT

During detention for re-education, the nature of labour seems to be compulsory. The prohibition of such labour has been recognised and codified into international human rights law, whereas there are some exceptions to this prohibition in some major human rights instruments. There remains the question of whether labour is a right or an obligation to perform. This study examines the nature of labour looking at the relevant provisions among international human rights standards and use of detention for re-education from the perspective of human rights. The right to work is fundamentally incompatible with a regime of forced labour. If compulsory work or service is permitted, it must be an implied exception to the right to work. China has the obligation to prohibit forced labour and protect the right to labour as one of basic human rights as a party to the International Covenant on Economic, Social and Cultural Rights (ICESCR), Equal Remuneration Convention (ILO100), Remuneration Policy Convention (ILO122) and Convention concerning the Prohibition and Immediate Action for the Elimination of the Worst Forms of Child Labour (ILO182). Any Chinese system in detention for re-education should be compatible with the nature of labour enshrined by these treaties.

I. INTRODUCTION

During detention for re-education, forced or compulsory labour continues to exist in this modern age. It has the effect of violating both civil and socio-economic rights, even amounting to slavery and servitude. The prohibition of such labour has been recognised and codified into international human rights law. The Universal Declaration of Human Rights (UDHR), ICESCR[1], the European Social Charter (ESC), American Declaration on the

Rights and Duties of Man (ADRDM), African Charter of Human and People's Rights (ACHPR) and ILO122 provide for the right to work, to free choice of employment, or to protection against unemployment. Various international and regional instruments have been adopted to protect the freedom of labour and also to reform its systems by the introduction of compulsory provisions to which State parties should adhere. Yet there are some exceptions to the prohibition of forced labour in some major human rights instruments. Both ADRDM XXXVII and ACHPR Article 29(6) even treat work as a duty of individuals. There remains the question of whether labour is a right or an obligation to perform.

China is a party to the ICESCR having concerns with socio-economic rights relating to work, but has not yet become a party to the International Covenant on Civil and Political Rights (ICCPR)[2] which expressly prohibits forced labour. China is still exploring what effect acceptance of the ICCPR would have on its domestic practice, including detention for re-education. The present situation concerned is that China consistently executes the policy of prohibiting forced labour in practice on the basis of pertinent laws.[3] It also allows for two kinds of 'lawful' systems, namely, Reform through Labour (RTL) and Re-education through Labour (RETL), to exist in detention for re-education. Both systems contain the same compulsory element in labour as a legal obligation of criminals under RTL or offenders undergoing RETL during their detention for re-education. This study examines the nature of labour looking at the relevant provisions in international human rights law and use of detention for re-education from the perspective of human rights.

II. Labour Provisions in International Human Rights Law

A. General

International human rights law deals with, *inter alia*, a series of socio-economic rights relating to labour or prohibition of forced labour. Some labour provisions may help explain the nature of labour in the development of international law.

The Covenant of the League of Nations (CLN)[4] expressly prohibits the slave trade[5] and requires 'fair and humane conditions of labour'[6]. Without reference to forced labour, the requirement of 'fair and humane conditions of labour' implicitly precludes any labour lacking such conditions, including forced labour. The Slavery, Servitude, Forced Labour and Similar Institutions and Practices Convention of 1926 (SSFL),[7] adopted by the League of Nations (LN) in 1926, came into effect in 1927 and is mandated to both suppress slave trade[8] and prohibit forced labour.[9] It has been described as 'the first true international human rights law treaty'.[10]

The United Nations (UN), European Commission, Organisation of American States (OAS) and Organization of African Unity (OAU) have over a long period actively engaged in the process of standard setting in the prevention of forced labour. The UDHR in 1948, ADRDM adopted by the OAS in 1948[11], and ACHPR adopted by the OAU in 1981 and brought into force in 1986,[12] all prohibit forced labour. The ICESCR adopted by the General Assembly (GA) in 1966 and in force from 1976,[13] and the European Social Charter[14] adopted by the Council of Europe in 1961, entered into force in 1965 and revised in 1996, guarantee the right to work, and rights concerning pay and conditions of work, rest and leisure of workers. This equally applies to forced labourers and seems to contribute to prohibition of forced labour. The Supplementary Convention on the Abolition of Slavery, the Slave Trade, and Institutions and Practices Similar to Slavery (SCA),[15] in force from 1957, adopted the approach of simply referring to the SSFL and other instruments on forced or compulsory labour in the Preamble. Differently, the ICCPR adopted in 1966, European Convention for the Protection of Human Rights and Fundamental Freedoms (ECHR) in 1953 and American Convention on Human Rights (ACHR) in 1978 expressly prohibit forced labour and list the relevant exceptions in their provisions. The International Convention on the Protection of the Rights of All Migrant Workers and Members of Their Families[16] adopted in 1990 and entered into force in 2003 also explicitly prohibits such labour with certain exceptions, but this treaty only applies to migrant workers and members of their families.

Since the establishment of the International Labour Organization (ILO) in 1919, a series of special instruments has contributed to the development of international human rights instruments in the field of forced labour. The Convention concerning Forced or Compulsory Labour (ILO29),[17] which came into force in 1932, defined the forced labour that should be prohibited, whilst also including the permissible forms of compulsory work or service as exceptions and detailing both the conditions for and restrictions on the imposition and performance of such labour. The Abolition of Forced Labour Convention (ILO105),[18] in force from 1959, also listed the limits on its imposition. Such details 'have served as a model for most general human rights treaties'[19] on forced labour. Furthermore, the ILO100,[20] entering into force in 1953, and ILO122,[21] coming into force in 1965, specify a range of socio-economic rights concerning work. These rights in work are equally applicable to those performing forced labour.

These general considerations appear to suffice to review the overall development of the major instruments on the prohibition of forced labour. These labour provisions appear to indicate that the right to labour is not compatible with forced labour and forced labour should be prohibited. This will be further explored from the treaties of significance to China and potential customary international law concerned as follows.

B. The ICCPR

With the signing of the ICCPR in 1998, China appears not to defeat its object or purpose, whereas it has not yet imposed on China treaty obligations. Only after ratifying the ICCPR, China will have to undertake more international human rights obligations, involving those concerning prohibition of forced labour. The labour provisions will influence China's practice after its ratification in the near future.

B.1. The Scope of Prohibition of Forced Labour

Derived from ILO29 Article 2, ICCPR Article 8(3) stipulates the prohibition of forced or compulsory labour and imposes the absolute and immediate obligation on State parties to prevent it. This also allows for a few exceptions to the general prohibition. The specific scope of prohibition entails the following elements.

B.1.1. General Scope

ICCPR Article 8(3)(a) states that '[N]o one shall be required to perform forced or compulsory labour'. Generally, it obliges States to prohibit all forms of forced or compulsory labour beyond slavery and servitude respectively in Article 8(1) and (2). While 'the borders between slavery and servitude and other forms of forced or compulsory labour are not hard and fast'[22], it is still essential to distinguish them from one another in order to precisely interpret relevant obligations on forced labour.

'Slavery is the status or condition of a person over whom any or all of the powers attaching to the right of ownership are exercised', as stipulated in SSFL Article 1(1). This means the exploitation of human beings by human beings with immunity on the basis of ownership.[23] 'Servitude' occurs where one human being actually has legal powers over another to effectively exercise other forms of economic exploitation or dominance over another, without the protection of ownership.[24] This appears to include all forms of slavery-like practices beyond slavery. Both slavery and servitude are prohibited in any event, regardless of voluntariness or involuntariness.[25]

Different from the above two, 'forced or compulsory labour' is 'all work or service which is extracted from any person under the menace of any penalty and for which the said person has not offered himself voluntarily' pursuant to ILO29 Article 2(1). The generally accepted definition intimates the essential requirements that the States or private parties extract any work or service from any persons and punishments are threatened if they fail to offer it voluntarily. Among them, compulsion is the fundamental character of forced labour, distinguished from slavery and servitude with ownership or effective dominance of one person over another. This appears to indicate that forced labour is compulsory and the forced labourer must be unhappy with compulsion. On the contrary, slavery and servitude does not necessarily contain the compulsory element, and slaves would not be unhappy with compulsion; but with the pain or work.

Without limitation to Article 8(3)(a), the words 'No one' appear to broadly include States and private persons that are likely to practise forced labour, while the prohibition of forced labour is mainly directed at State parties[26]. Article 8(3)(a) guarantees freedom from forced labour and prohibits both States and private persons from compelling anyone to perform any work against their will. It also obligates State parties to prevent private persons from engaging in such practices by including various positive measures. This is universally applicable to any circumstances concerning forced labour, even where States 'extensively regulate the labour market or themselves control it within the scope of a planned economy.'[27]

While some States, such as China, provide for the nature of work as both a right and duty of citizens, the right to work should not in theory or in practice contain the provision of the duty to work[28]. 'Every general duty to work imposed by State parties that carries a penal sanction'[29] is likely to meet both requirements of forced labour and thus breach its prohibition under Article 8(3)(a).[30] Yet there is no such violation in 'the mere lapsing of unemployment assistance when a person refuses to accept work not corresponding to his qualifications'.[31] Without satisfying any conditions required for forced labour, such vagrancy should not be prohibited and any forms of its prohibitions appear to breach Article 8(3)(a).

Additionally, these requirements of forced labour are also important elements for the Human Rights Committee (HRCom) to consider whether facts amount to forced labour or not in a particular case for the purpose of its admissibility. For example, the HRCom dismissed the case of *Silva et al v. Zambia* because the authors had not sufficiently substantiated 'how the taxation of their inducement allowance could be seen as constituting forced labour' under Article 8(3)(a).[32]

B.1.2. Exceptions

Different from Article 8(1) and (2), Article 8(3)(a) permits derogations in certain circumstances as part of the definition of forced labour, under five primary types of cases.

B.1.2.1. Hard Labour as Punishment for a Crime

The prohibition of forced labour, by Article 8(3)(b), 'shall not be held to preclude, in countries where imprisonment with hard labour may be imposed as a punishment for a crime, the performance of hard labour in pursuance of a sentence to such punishment by a competent court.' Literally, this appears to expressly regulate that hard labour, as a punishment for a crime is a legally permissible form of compulsory work or service and not an exception to forced labour. This formulation seems to be reasonable considering the practice of some States where competent courts impose sentences of imprisonment with hard labour by law.[33] Yet it is actually not different from the exception to the general prohibition of forced labour from a legal perspective.

Article 8(3)(b) allows for imprisonment with hard labour, rendered by judgement of a competent court, to be imposed as punishment for a statutorily defined crime. Several primary requirements and procedural guarantees should be noted. Firstly, it tends to apply only to imprisonment with hard labour and not light labour. The 'classical forms of forced labour in work colonies or camps'[34] are good examples of hard labour. Accordingly, the punishment relating to forced labour appears to be imposed for serious offences only, which is another requirement. Under ICCPR Article 10(3), however, penitentiary systems shall 'comprise treatment of prisoners the essential aim of which shall be their reformation and social rehabilitation', which appears to leave no space for hard labour to simply punish criminals. Secondly, the punishment is imposed only for a statutorily defined crime. Considering that crimes are serious offences, this appears to exclude the light offences, which are punishable by administrative punishment such as a fine. Thirdly, it also entails the imposition of the punishment only through a criminal sentence rendered by a competent court according to a law explicitly stipulating such punishment. The criminal sentence must have an explicit statement of the punishment for its performance in pursuance of a sentence'.[35] This sentence should be rendered by the competent court rather than administrative authorities. This court should supply with all of judicial guarantees, e.g., those contained in ICCPR Articles 9 and 14.[1] Hence, the only way to impose hard labour as punishment for a crime is the criminal conviction by a competent court on the basis of a law expressly providing for it and the sentence of the court must explicitly state it.

[1] See B.2 Other Relevant Provisions.

B.1.2.2. Work In Detention

Article 8(3)(c) precludes four categories of compulsory work or service from the term of forced or compulsory labour'. The first is any 'work or service... normally required of a person who is under detention in consequence of a lawful order of a court, or of a person during conditional release from such detention' without being precluded by Article 8(3)(b). Article 8(3)(c)(i) deals with routine work that persons under detention have to do, diverse from the above hard labour. Here work is limited to such routine work or service as 'normally required of a person' during detention or 'conditional release from such detention', e.g., cleaning cells, preparing food.

This detention broadly includes pre-trial detention on the grounds 'contained in the court decision' and 'other forms of judicially imposed custody' pursuant to Article 9.[36] Pre-trial detainees seem not to be compelled to work without the grounds for detention in the court decision, whereas it is possible 'in consequence of lawful order of a court'. The words mean that the lawful order of a court must expressly state the work or service as punishment, similar to 'in pursuance of a sentence' in Article 8(3)(b). This leaves no room for an administrative authority to make specific directives on such work without explicit lawful order of a court as a legal basis.

Article 9 ICCPR prohibits all forms of arbitrary arrest or detention, except for ones 'on such grounds and in accordance with such procedure as are established by law'. This appears to allow any forms of 'judicially imposed custody' rendered by a competent court pursuant to law in the above-mentioned detention. It also requires the lawful administrative detention must be directly reviewed by a competent court in the way of proceedings.

In view of the penitentiary system in Article 10(3), prison labour has the essential aim of the 'reformation and social rehabilitation' of prisoners. The work by prisoners during conditional release also appears to follow the same approach. Hence, the routine work in Article 8(3)(c)(i) tends to have the character of the social rehabilitation of persons undergoing detention or those on conditional release from it.

B.1.2.3. Military and National Service

The second category of exception is any 'service of a military character and, in countries where conscientious objection' is recognised, 'any national service required by law of conscientious objectors'. Article 8(3)(c)(ii) addresses military and national service as another exception. This involves all forms of military service and any national one that is required by law of conscientious objectors in countries which recognise conscientious objection.

The military and national service is qualified with conscientious objection or objectors. This formulation results from the practice of a few States to recognise this right, whereas the right of conscientious objection appears not to be inferred from such qualifications.

B.1.2.4. Duties in Cases of Emergency

Exceptions will also apply in circumstances where any service is 'exacted in cases of emergency or calamity threatening the life or well-being of the community'[37]. Article 8(3)(c)(iii) deals with duties in the event of all emergencies or calamities, regardless of public or local, which threaten 'the life or well-being of the community'. Without an explicit list of such emergencies or calamities in this provision or significant discussions in the working groups of the HRCom, ILO29 Article 2(2)(d) appears to be helpful in elaborating on this exception. It specifies situations such as war, fire, flood, famine, earthquake, violent epidemic or epizootic diseases, invasion by animals, insect or vegetable pests.

B.1.2.5. Normal Civic Obligations

The fourth is any 'work or service which forms part of normal civil obligations'. Article 8(3)(c)(iv) provides for another exception, that is, any forms of work or service that amount to normal civil obligations, without a specification of such obligations. This provision derives from, albeit differs from, ILO29 Article 2(2)(b) and (e).

Considering this relationship between the two provisions, these normal civil obligations appear to refer to such forced labour that recognise that it is absolutely necessary to fulfil State functions and unable to be accomplished in non-forcible manners. This seems to primarily include both professional duties and most traditional civic obligations. However, traditional obligations are likely to be related to emergencies or calamities and thus have been overlapped by Article 8(3)(c)(iii). Hence, they appear to be professional duties and traditional civic obligations without falling into the category of the duties in emergency.

B.2. Other Relevant Provisions

Apart from ICCPR Article 8(3), some of other provisions in the ICCPR appear to relate to the prohibition of forced labour. These are mainly Articles 9, 10 and 14.

Specifically, ICCPR Article 9 details 'the right to liberty and security of person'. This contains a series of human rights procedural guarantees to restrict the deprivation of personal liberty and security. Article 9(1) requires the principles of legality and prohibition of arbitrariness; Article 9(2) deals with the right to information; Article 9(3) addresses special rights for those in detention. Article 9(4) requires anyone 'who is deprived of his liberty by arrest or detention' to be entitled with the right to have the detention decided in court without delay. This allows for courts only to decide whether the detention is lawful or not. Article 9(4) stipulates the right of the victims of unlawful arrest or detention to compensation.

Moreover, Article 10 addresses the right of detainees to be treated with humanity and dignity. Humane treatment and respect for human dignity is essential to the reformation and social rehabilitation of prisoners in penitentiary systems. Article 14 details the procedural guarantees in civil and criminal trials, which equally applies to both RTL and RETL.

Additionally, there are more relevant provisions in international human rights law. These will be examined in the following sections:

C. International Treaties Concerned

C.1. The Icescr

Since the 27th June 2001, China has been a party to the ICESCR and this treaty has had a legally binding force on China. There are now a range of obligations imposed upon China and some of these are worthy of further discussion.

Similar to the UDHR, the ICESCR does not have a provision expressly dealing with forced labour, but has a number of concerns with a range of socio-economic rights relating to work to imply its prohibition. They mainly contain Articles 2(2) and 3 respectively dealing with non-discrimination and equality, Article 6 on the right to freely chosen work, Article 7 concerning the right to just and favourable conditions of work, Article 8 on the rights relating to trade unions and Article 11 on the right to an adequate standard of living and the right to food and living. Among them, the relevant rights contained in Articles 2(2), 3, 6 and 7 basically conflict with forced labour with the compulsory element and might be breached in the implementation of compulsory work. Accordingly, the prohibition of forced labour appears to contribute to protecting these rights and protection of the right to work implies this prohibition.

Article 2(2) generally stipulates the obligation of State parties to guarantee the principle of non-discrimination in protecting human rights enunciated in the ICESCR. Specifically, by Article 3, these parties are obliged to 'ensure the equal right of men and women to the enjoyment of all economic, social and cultural rights' required in this treaty. This equality principle appears to be the application of non-discrimination in the protection of such rights between men and women.

Article 6(1) 'includes the right of everyone to the opportunity to gain his living by work which he freely chooses or accepts'. This essentially includes the right to free choice of employment as found under UDHR Article 23(1), but under the ICESCR the right has been expanded to include the opportunity to gain a living. Accordingly, the qualified and progressive obligation that State parties should undertake is to safeguard these rights and aim at its full realization[38] through 'appropriate steps'[39]. These measures are 'technical and vocational guidance and training programmes, policies and techniques to achieve steady economic, social and cultural development and full and productive employment under conditions safeguarding fundamental political and economic freedoms to the individual' under Article 6(2).

State parties, by Article 7, also undertake the obligation to recognise the right of everyone to the enjoyment of just and favourable conditions of work'. Matters concerning forced labour are not addressed here, while the performance of this labour appears to run counter to the requirements of the above rights on work. Article 7(a) ensures fair wage and a decent living for protection of the right to fair pay. It also emphasises 'work of equal value' 'without distinction of any kind', particularly between women and men, as a requirement for 'equal pay for equal work'. Article 7(b) requires the safeguard of 'safe and healthy working conditions' to protect the right to proper working conditions. Article 7(c) is the only provision to provide for the right of equal opportunity to be promoted, subject to considerations of seniority and competence only. Article 7(d) provides for the right to 'rest, leisure and reasonable limitation of working hours and periodic holidays with pay, as well as remuneration for public holidays'. This appears to regard five distinct rights, differing from UDHR Article 24.

Additionally, the above rights are non-derogable in any circumstances under the ICESCR. By Article 5(2), no 'derogation from any of the fundamental human rights recognised or existing in any country in virtue of law, conventions, regulations or custom shall be admitted'. This is equally applicable to the right to work as an economic right.

C.2. The ILO100

Upon its ratification on 2nd November 1990, China became a party to this treaty. It should assume the following treaty obligations on the rights in work.

ILO100 Article 2(1) obliges its State parties, 'by means appropriate to the methods in operation for determining rates of remuneration', to 'promote and, insofar as is consistent with such methods, ensure the application to all workers of the principle of equal remuneration for men and women workers for work of equal value'.[40] This obligation is qualified and progressive in form, which requires China to take appropriate measures to promote and ensure the application of equal remuneration principle.

'Remuneration' 'includes the ordinary, basic or minimum wage or salary and any additional emoluments whatsoever payable directly or indirectly, whether in cash or in kind, by the employer to the worker and arising out of the worker's employment'.[41] The principle of 'equal remuneration for men and women workers for work of equal value' refers to rates of remuneration established without discrimination based on sex'.[42] However, differential rates between workers are not necessarily contrary to the principle. This depends on whether this divergence corresponds, 'without regard to sex, to differences, as determined by such objective appraisal, in the work to be performed'.[43]

C.3 The ILO122

ILO122 began to have legal effect on China following its date of ratification on 17th December 1997. There are several primary obligations on labour.

By Article 1(1), China 'shall declare and pursue, as a major goal, an active policy designed to promote full, productive and freely chosen employment'. This permits its progressive realisation of the main goal by implementing an active policy and its obligation is qualified and progressive in form.

China has to ensure several aims to be gradually realised by the above means. Under Article 1(2), these aims are to ensure that there is 'work for all who are available for and seeking work'; that such 'work is as productive as possible'; and that there is 'freedom of choice of employment and the fullest possible opportunity for each worker to qualify for, and to use his skills and endowments in, a job for which he is well suited' without any discrimination.

Article 1(3) stressed that 'the stage and level of economic development and the mutual relationships between employment objectives and other economic and social objectives' should be considered in policy-making. It also noted that methods should be 'appropriate to national conditions and practices'. Accordingly, China has the obligation to recognise these issues to make a reasonable policy and take proper methods to implement the policy in the light of such conditions and practices.

C.4 The ILO182[44]

China ratified the ILO182 on 8th August 2002 and has been a party to this treaty since that time. Among the 16 Articles, Articles 1, 2, 3 and 6 relate to forced labour and set out China's obligations.

Article 1 requires China to 'take immediate and effective measures to secure the prohibition and elimination of the worst forms of child labour as a matter of urgency'. This obligation is qualified and progressive in form. In the ILO182, 'the term *child* shall apply to all persons under the age of 18'.[45]

Article 3 defined the phrase of 'the worst forms of child labour' in detail. By it, 'all forms of slavery or practices similar to slavery, such as the sale and trafficking of children, debt bondage and serfdom and forced or compulsory labour, including forced or compulsory recruitment of children for use in armed conflict' fall into the category of such child labour.[46]

Hence, China is obliged to take immediate and effective measures to prohibit children from being subject to the worst forms of child labour, including forced labour, in order to strengthen the implementing of the ILO182.

D. Possible Customary International Law Concerned

With the development of international human rights law, some norms mentioned above are likely to demonstrate a customary feature.[47] Such a feature would be helpful to delineate the nature of the labour. The first problem is whether the prohibition of forced labour is a customary rule.

Among the above instruments that explicitly mention forced labour, the location of its prohibition is alongside the prohibition of slavery as 'one of the first human rights...in public international law'[48] within the anti-slavery norms. This appears to show the relationship between forced or compulsory labour and slavery or slavery-like practices. This is also evidenced by the SSFL, which emphasises measures taken to prevent forced labour 'from developing into conditions analogous to slavery'. Similarly, the inclusion of the ILO29 in Supplementary Convention on the Abolition of Slavery, the Slave Trade, and Institutions and Practices Similar to Slavery Preamble also considered the potentially grave consequences of forced labour and its position in international law.

Nonetheless, the above reasoning seems not to show that forced labour is a form of slavery or servitude. These three inter-related concepts are essentially diverse in both nature and degree. Moreover, anti-slavery norms are non-derogable in any circumstances, while it is not the case for the prohibition of forced labour as has already been outlined. Such divergence is worthy of note given the close relationship that appears to exist between forced labour and slavery or servitude. The prohibition on forced labour as a potential rule of customary international law should be justified by the nature of the prohibition itself rather than because of its relation with slavery.

The key difference between the two is the fact that despite the recognition given to the forced labour in major international human rights instruments, exceptions often exist whereby the legal coverage of the prohibition is greatly reduced. One of these exceptions is hard labour as punishment for a crime, which is included in ILO29 Article 2(2), ICCPR Article 8(3)(c), ECHR Article 4(3), ACHR Article 6(2) and CMW Article 11(3). The exception of work in detention is detailed in ILO29 Article 2(2), ICCPR Article 8(3)(c)(i), ECHR Article 4(3)(a), ACHR Article 6(3)(a) and CMW Article 11(4)(a). Another is military and national service in ADRDM XXXIV, ILO29 Article 2(2), ICCPR Article 8(3)(c)(ii), ECHR Article 4(3)(b) and ACHR Article 6(3)(b). The exception of duties in emergency is regulated in ADRDM

XXXIV, ILO29 Article 2(2), ICCPR Article 8(3)(c)(iii), ECHR Article 4(3)(c), ACHR Article 6(3)(c) and International Convention on the Protection of the Rights of All Migrant Workers and Members of Their Families (CMW) Article 11(4)(b). Normal civic obligations are contained in ADRDM XXXIV, ILO29 Article 2(2), ICCPR Article 8(3)(c)(iv), ECHR Article 4(3)(d), ACHR Article 6(3)(d) and CMW Article 11(4)(c).

This seems to indicate the broad recognition of the prohibition of forced labour, whereas it is difficult to justify that such labour has been generally recognized by States as law. Moreover, reports of the UN, the ILO and other intergovernmental organizations appear to 'show an unacceptable extent to which forced labour practices are still used, and their apparent link with undemocratic structures and other structural causes of gross violations of human dignity.'[49] There is no sufficient evidence to suggest that States engage in a general practice of prohibiting forced labour, thereby greatly weakening any arguments that the prohibition is a rule of customary international law.

The other issue is to explore whether above socio-economic rights relating to work are customary. Firstly, the right to work, to free choice of employment, or to protection against unemployment have not been universally recognised in all of the major international instruments. At least one of the three rights is found in many instruments, e.g., the UDHR, ICESCR, ESC, ADRDM, ACHPR and ILO122, and even non-derogable in cases under the ICESCR and ACHPR. Yet both ADRDM XXXVII and ACHPR Article 29(6) treat labour as a duty of individuals. This appears to go against the right to work and thus defeat the customary feature of the right to work in international law.

Secondly, not all major instruments concerned recognise the rights concerning pay and conditions of work. For instance, UDHR Article 23(3), ICESCR Article 7(a)(i), ESC I, (4) provide for the right to fair pay, while others, such as the ACHPR remain silent. Unlike the UDHR, ACHPR, ICESCR and ESC, the ADRDM fails to mention the right to equal pay for equal work. Different from the ADRDM, the UDHR, ICESCR, ACHPR and ESC seems to stipulate the right to proper working conditions. The right to promotion is only prescribed in ICESCR Article 7(c). Such rights are even derogable in exceptional circumstances under the ESC.[50] Such examples illustrate some of the reasons behind the non-customary character of these rights.

Thirdly, the right to rest and leisure appears to indicate the absence of general recognition in international law. While the UDHR, ICESCR, ESC and many ILO instruments contain provisions on such rights, the ACHPR makes no comparable reference. This is also derogable in certain cases pursuant to the ESC.[51]

III LABOUR PROVISIONS IN CHINA'S PRACTICE

The situation in China concerning forced labour is that China seems to consistently implement a policy of prohibition in practice on the basis of pertinent laws[52]. This contributes to prohibition of forced labour and protection of the right to labour. But permissible forms of compulsory work or service potentially exist in detention for re-education. It relates to two kinds of 'lawful' systems, namely, Reform through Labour and Re-education through Labour. It is desirable to examine whether China's practice recognizes labour as a right or an obligation to perform.

Article 46 of the Criminal Law of the PRC, adopted in 1997 (1997CL) stipulates RTL, such that any criminal 'who is sentenced to fixed-term imprisonment or life imprisonment' shall serve his term either in the prison or another place stipulated 'for the execution'. 'Anyone who is able to work shall do it to accept education and reform through labour.'[53] Article 69 of the Law on Prisons of the PRC, adopted in 1994 (1994PL) also provides that any criminal 'who is able to work shall do labour'. RTL is a means by which to enforce criminal detention, fixed-term imprisonment, life imprisonment and the death penalty with a suspension of execution to educate and reform criminals serving sentences involving the above sanctions.[54] Since RTL results from criminal sanctions imposed or passed by competent courts and according to the 1997CL, this compulsory work seems to be the permissible form required by ICCPR Article 8(3)(b) and not forced labour prohibited by ICCPR Article 8(3)(a).

Nonetheless, it is RETL that might conflict with the provisions of the ICCPR and other human rights instruments concerned. This unique system has undergone approximately 50 years' development in the Chinese judicial systems. Without a clear official definition, Chinese scholars usually describe it in a variety of ways and have presented some generally accepted views[55] according to the current legislation of China. At present, offenders subject to RETL are usually those who are above the age of 16 and whose illegal acts or petty crimes are 'not serious enough for criminal punishments'[56]. After RETL Administrative Committees examine and approve RETL decisions, control offices of RETL take offenders in to educate them through labour for one to three years, with an additional year if necessary.[57] As a special punishment decided by the administrative departments for justice, it entails depriving persons undergoing RETL of personal liberty for not less than one year,[58] similar to RTL.

A. The Common Constitutional Basis in Legal Practice

Since both RTL and RETL concern work and labour, their common constitutional basis is Article 42 of the Constitution of the PRC, adopted in 1982 (1982Constitution), which stipulates that work is the right and 'glorious duty of every able-bodied citizen.' This means that work is a constitutional right and duty of Chinese citizens so that every able-bodied citizen has the obligation on the work, regardless of whether citizens are willing or not. This is diverse from the provisions on the right to work in the ICCPR and ICESCR.

Pursuant to ICCPR Article 8(3)(a), the State parties are obliged not to compel them to work with all positive measures, including legal ones. The right to work is optional and does not necessarily imply the duty to work, which is compulsory in nature. Meanwhile, ICESCR Article 6(1) also provides for the right to work, comprising the individual's claim or opportunity 'to gain his living by work which he freely chooses or accepts'. Hence, the general duty to work that could be imposed with a penal sanction by States tends to constitute forced or compulsory labour against ICCPR Article 8(3)(a) and ICESCR Article 6(1).

Despite that, the above constitutional clause was reasonable under the circumstances of the planned economy in history. From the establishment of a market economy in the 1980s, it has had an increasing tendency to demonstrate a series of shortcomings inconsistent with contemporary China.

Early in 1952, the Decision on the Issue of Work Employment (DIWE) provided for the policy on the general assignment and work employment, which appears to deem the right to work as the right to require the State to offer each citizen employment. Further, the Constitution of the PRC in 1954 (1954Constitution) tends to take the means of planned management to ensure the right of citizens to obtain employment in Article 91. With the socialistic alteration finished in 1956, a labour system under the planned management was gradually established to pertain to planned economic system. The highly concentrated management system guaranteed every able-bodied citizen an occupation without the menace of unemployment and prohibited a random floating work force. Hence, the right to work became a right to be guaranteed work but this also involved a duty to work without the freedom to choose. This was evidenced by both the principle of distribution according to work in Constitution of the PRC in 1975 (1975Constitution) Article 9 and 'glorious duty of every able-bodied citizen" to work in Constitution of the PRC in 1978 (1978Constitution) Article 10 and 1982Constitution Article 42.

On the one hand, these provisions on the duty to work contributed to the good social order, the income equality of everyone in the sense of equalitarian ideas, and the stable living standard of citizens under the planned economy. As a historical result, the labour system was able to successfully avoid the disordered state happened under the market economy and resulted in the good order of society. Since the State undertook the obligation to assign to every citizen some form of employment, citizens really enjoyed the equal right of obtaining it and even income equality. Without risk of unemployment or bankruptcy, every citizen had stable work and income for a peaceful life. A belief that 'an advantage of socialistic society is that everyone has food and work' had been generally accepted by the public in China.

On the other hand, these provisions about the obligation to work tend to lead to theoretical disorder, practical difficulty, and inconsistency among legal systems. Such negative influence may be addressed in detail as follows.

Firstly, the legal duty is compulsory and the legal right is optional in theory. If work is a right, citizens can choose it or give it up at will. If work is a duty, citizens must fulfil their own legal obligations; otherwise they have to be punished. Both difference and contradiction appear not to give rise to work as both a right and duty. Moreover, neither the Constitutions of China nor other laws provided for any sanctions against those able-bodied citizens who failed to participate in labour market. As 1999 Amendment of 1982Constitution Article 6 states, the State adheres to 'the distribution system with the distribution according to work remaining dominant and the coexistence of a variety of distribution', during the stage of socialism. In practice, with the system of market economy gradually established and improved, the means of distributing income to every citizen are diverse. Chinese citizens can gain personal economic income through saving interests, bonus stock, bonus, premiums, rent and even inheritance. These means are beneficial complements of the way of distribution according to work.

Secondly, the present situation tends to leave no room for work as a legal duty of citizens for two primary reasons. At present, the size of the work force in China is of such a scale that it is impossible to find work for every citizen at the same time. Under the circumstances of a market economy, a certain unemployment rate is retained to promote labour competition and improve work efficiency. It is also the case in, and there is no exception to, China. Thus, it is impossible or impractical to ensure the employment of every citizen in contemporary China.

Thirdly, two points are worthy of note concerning legal conflicts among legal systems. One point is that the duty to work by every citizen is inconsistent with the retirement system enshrined in 1982Constitution Article 44. This system applies to retired 'workers and staff in enterprises and undertakings' and 'functionaries of organs of state', whose livelihood 'is ensured by the state and society'. Since they retire due to age rather than work capacity, lots of able-bodied citizens must leave work positions according to the retirement system and do not continue fulfiling their duties. The system is designed to allow them to have a rest and to peacefully spend their later years, whereas the 1982Constitution requires all able-bodied citizens to continue participating in work and this tends to deprive them of the right to retire. The other is easily to confuse the duty to work with that of criminals to labour. As indicated in 1994PL Articles 7(2) and 69, to participate in labour is the legal obligation of every able-bodied criminal and a compulsory means of the State to compel criminals to reform themselves through labour. This special duty of criminals is similar to, and blurred its difference with, provisions on the universal duty of citizens to work. In fact, the duty to work is at the civil level, universally applicable to all able-bodied citizens in China. Conversely, the duty of persons undergoing RTL or RETL is at the criminal level, which only applies to able-bodied ones subject to RTL or RETL.

Furthermore, it is very unlikely that nobody will participate in work, even if the 1982Constitution cancels the legal duty of work, for several primary reasons. Firstly, in most States, Constitutions emphasize the right of citizens to work without explicit regulations on the duty to work. It is unheard of for there to be no citizen in work, but better protection of the right to work, in these States. This advantageous experience could be fully considered in China's further legal reforms on labour provisions.

Secondly, in history, there are neither express provisions on the duty to work in the 1954Constitution, or 1975Constitution, nor the above phenomenon to appear. In fact, work has become a practical necessity and even lifestyle for most Chinese citizens. Specifically, work is the essential and primary means for the majority to live, develop, and to seek social welfare. Since the abolition of the exploitation system in China, most Chinese have had the negative attitude towards all forms of unearned income. This means that most Chinese citizens are willing to do some work as the primary means to maintain their own subsistence, development, and welfare. Moreover, quite a lot of citizens regard work as the lifestyle and interests of their lives and are unwilling to give up work because the course of work contributes to realizing the value of life and acquiring happiness.

Thirdly, it is a moral idea that citizens should work for both social development and States' richness in China. Chinese citizens also take cognizance of the important correlation between public interests of States and personal interests of citizens. This moral idea and strong awareness render Chinese citizens to do work, even if the 1982Constitution abolished citizens' duty to work.

Fourthly, some unearned income of citizens tends not to cause any direct harm to the State, society and others in practice. Thus, it is not necessary to resort to legal means to prohibit these income, but desirable to protect it to a certain degree.

In brief, it is not necessary, reasonable, or feasible to stipulate work as a legal obligation of Chinese citizens, and thus labour should not be determined as a legal duty of such citizens. Together with legal conflicts with both the ICCPR and ICESCR, the common constitutional basis of RTL and RETL should be revised as the right to labour in uniformity with the above international human rights instruments.

B. Practices of RTL

B.1. General

Before 1994, the main legal basis of RTL was the Regulations on Reform through Labour of the PRC in 1954, which entitled RTL to emphasize the importance of RTL in reforming prisoners as a measure. With the promulgation of the 1994PL, however, RTL was literally replaced with Reform through Education (RTE), including RTL and three other means, which are designed to correctly 'punish and reform prisoners, and prevent and reduce crimes'.[59] Together with 1997CL Article 46, the above constitutes the primary legal bases of RTL, which mainly covers a series of regulations as follows.

As the State organs for executing criminal punishments, prisons and other RTL institutions apply the principle of combining punishment with reform and education through labour in implementation,[60] so as to transform criminals into law abiding citizens.[61] Specifically, prisons execute the death penalty with a two-year suspension of execution, life imprisonment, or fixed-term imprisonment; detention houses instead execute fixed-term imprisonment, 'if the remaining term of sentence is not more than one year' before being handed over for execution; criminal detention is mainly executed by public security organs in its detention houses, pursuant to Article 213 in the Criminal Procedure Law of the PRC, adopted in 1996 (1996CPL). Juvenile delinquents execute their criminal punishments and perform labour for education and reform in remand homes.

According to the 1994PL, education and reform of prisoners involve the principles of 'suiting education to different persons'[2], 'suiting education to different types'[3], and 'persuading prisoners through reasoning'[4]. Meanwhile, the present reform contains ideological education,[62] cultural education[63], occupational and technical education[64] in its content, with such methods as combination of collective and individual education and of education inside prison and social education.[65] Similarly, detention houses compel convicted criminals into performing productive labour and impose political education on them.[66] Additionally, unconvicted persons may be organized to perform appropriate labour under the circumstance of no impediment for investigation or trial,[67] where such labour is not forced or compulsory.

Several points are worthy of mention on the difference between RTL and RETL. The first is the nature of punishments. RTL is related to criminal punishment imposed for criminal offences, but RETL is administrative punishment imposed for petty crimes and illegal acts, the degree of which has not reached the level of criminal punishment. The second is executive bodies. Prisons, detention houses and remand homes are responsible for implementing RTL, whereas the control offices of RETL are RETL intuitions. The third is executive bases. RTL is implemented on the ground of sentences rendered by competent courts, while RETL is carried out in pursuance of decisions made by police in the name of RETL Administrative Committees (RETLACs).

2 The principle of 'suiting education to different persons' refers to take different measures to educate and reform offenders in the light of their different characteristics and conditions.

3 It means to take different measures to educate and reform offenders according to the type of criminal punishment imposed on each offender.

4 It means to focus on educating offenders and prohibit administrating or controlling them in a simple and crude way.

B.2. Violations of International Human Rights Instruments

B.2.1. Forced Labour

As stated above, RTL seems to conform with the permissible form of compulsory work or service indicated in ICCPR Article 8(3)(b), and so does not fall within the category of forced labour. But this is not the case for two reasons.

First, in all cases, there will be no express statement on performance of any labour or service in the sentence rendered by a competent court. This creates uncertainty and therefore does not satisfy the permission given in Article 8(3)(b). There is no sentence by a competent court to express such punishment as labour in the practice of RTL. Even standard samples in judicial documents are short of a clear statement on RTL as punishment.[68] Meanwhile, neither legal provisions nor academic papers require the court sentence to explicitly affirm this labour as punishment.

Second, RTL institutions tend to assign productive tasks according to criminals' practical conditions, in order to meet the requirements of reform in enforcement or employment after their release. According to the 1994PL, prisons rationally organize prisoners to participate in labour in the light of their individual conditions.[69] The reform on juvenile delinquents shall conform to their characteristics and favour improving an elementary education and work skills.[70] Meanwhile, a prison shall make reference to the State's relevant regulations on working hours to decide them for prisoners and ensure the right to rest on statutory festivals and holidays, despite some possible adjustments under special circumstances.[71] Hence, such labour appears not so 'hard' as 'the classical forms of forced labour in work colonies or camps'[72].

Moreover, RTL tends not to belong to any exceptions of forced labour in ICCPR Article 8(3)(c). Despite the fact that RTL is a kind of work or service required of detainees during the detention, this punishment appears not to be explicitly stated in a 'lawful order of a court' as the exception enshrined in Article 8(3)(c)(i), not to mention others in Article 8(3)(c).

Therefore, RTL tends not to fall within the legal exceptions protected but to be forced labour prohibited by ICCPR Article 8(3).

B..2.2. Other Violations

In China, the prison system has both functions, namely, supervision and reform of criminals, and production of economic efficiency for historical reasons.[73] Despite that the State safeguards funds pursuant to the 1994PL and financial provisions from the State are annually on the increase, they seem not to meet all practical needs for prison work. Thus, many RTL institutions have contracts with their enterprises in order to further develop economy to complement deficit with productive interests.[74]

It seems that criminals undergoing RTL are placed at the disposal of private parties, rather than 'under the supervision and control of a public authority'[75]. This is against the obligation to prevent them from such practices in ICCPR Article 8(3)(b). However, it is not true in fact. As 1994PL Article 2(1) stated, prisons are the State organs to execute criminal punishments. Together with other RTL institutions, prisons are responsible for implementation of criminal sanctions, including supervision and control of criminals who take part in labour. Pursuant to Regulations on Reform through Labour of the PRC in 1954 (1954R-RTL) Article 30, productive profits from RTL should serve for State economic construction, and thus appear to be mainly used to complement the deficit with poor State provisions.

The situation of criminals in China appears not be consistent with the nature of prisons as a body to execute criminal punishments enshrined in the 1994PL. This also tends to result in a series of disadvantages in the present management of prisons as follows.

First, some RTL institutions force criminals to do overtime or highly intensive labour under financial pressure.[76] Since 1994PL Article 71 permits to adjust labour time under special circumstances, leaving a room for its arbitrary expansion, prisons are likely to expand labour time when encountering financial difficulties. In practice, the labour intensity and expansion of time are increasing without maximum limits because productive labour quotas are quite high and some prison labour is comparatively hard. This tends to occupy necessary time for education and reform activities and influence the right to rest and entertainment.[77] Hence, the above provisions run contrary to ICESCR Article 7.

Second, prisoners are merely able to acquire limited labour remuneration. 1994PL Article 72 stipulates that prisons should pay labour remuneration to prisoners that participate in productive labour according to relevant provisions, while this fails to be implemented in practice as it should be by law. Some prison officials still remain the traditional ideas that RTL is punitive and prisoners should not obtain any remuneration from their punitive labour. In addition to insufficient funds, most prisons fail to pay labour remuneration in the form of wage,[78] and thus prisoners generally acquire material objects, money awards and pocket money.[79] It appears not to be real wage,[80] but slight economic compensation, which is much less than the remuneration that prisons should pay and is probably different among diverse prisoners who do the same labour. This tends to be contrary to ICESCR Article 7(1).

Third, labour conditions cannot satisfy the requirements of due standards and prisoners' productive safety lacks necessary protection in some prisons. 1994PL Article 72 requires certain protection relating to prison labour, whereas not all prisons in fact effectively implemented the systems on labour safety. Some prisons even organize prisoners to perform labour outside, which increases the possible number of unexpected accidents in the performance of labour.[81] This also tends to go contrary to ICESCR Article 7.

Fourth, both labour insurance and compensation appear inadequate. 1994PL Article 73 provides for the compensation for injuries or death in labour of prisoners in reference to relevant regulations on national labour insurance. This tends to be mistakenly regarded as an optional provision so that some prisons failed to fully carry it out according to judicial practice. The amount of damages should be quite high by the relevant provisions, while lots of prisons claimed no sufficient funds and had to pay less in implementation, without referring to them.[82]

Fifth, some officials of RTL institutions cannot properly apply the principle of equality and justice to criminal punishments in implementation.[83] Apart from the 1996CPL, 1997CL Article 4 regulates the equal application of laws to citizens. However, prisons tend to welcome convicts with some professional skills, and refuse to accept the elder, the weak, the ill and the disabled,[84] considering improvement of economic efficiency. This tends to deviate from requirements in ICESCR Article 2(2).

C. Practices of RETL

Among the various legal forms of current legislations on RETL, the Decision of the State Council Regarding the Question of Rehabilitation Through Labour, approved on 1st August 1957 (1957D-RETL), Supplementary Provisions of the State Council for Rehabilitation Through Labour, approved on 29th November 1979 (1979SP-RETL), Trial Method on RETL issued in 1982 (1982TM-RETL), and Regulations on Public Security Bodies Handling RETL Cases (2002R-RETL) are the primary legal bases of RETL. Since the applicable scope of RETL appears wider and wider in order to meet so-called objective requirements, the 2002R-RETL tends to expand to all intentional illegal acts not falling within the scope of current criminal punishments. At present, offenders on the programme of RETL are usually those who are above the age of 16 and whose illegal acts or petty crimes are 'not serious enough for criminal punishments'.[85] With the difference between petty crimes and illegal acts, it might as well be addressed in a two-pronged approach.

C.1. Petty crimes

Among those that form the basis of a RETL order, petty crimes are criminal conducts, despite not being serious enough for criminal punishments. They tend to have several primary features as follows.

(1) Decisions Made by Administrative Departments for Justice

Once RETLACs have examined and approved RETL decisions[86], control offices of RETL will take in the offenders concerned to educate them through labour for one to three years, with possibility of an additional year if necessary. Thus, it is a special punishment decided by administrative departments for justice, rather than a sentence made by a competent court.

(2) No determination of a Criminal Charge

Moreover, this imposition of RETL tends to, but fails to, constitute the determination of a criminal charge. It could be analyzed from two perspectives, namely:

On the one hand, RETL appears to be a criminal sanction, because of its severity and so, in this respect, imposing it on persons involved seems to constitute the determination of a criminal charge.

Since this system infringes on the right to personal liberty, the length of its term and the treatment during this term appear to be primary factors in weighing its degree of severity. According to the 1997CL, the term of 'criminal detention shall be not less than one month but not more than 6 months' and that of 'public surveillance shall be not less than three months but not more than two years'. Compared with two kinds of criminal punishments, the legal minimum term of RETL is twelve times the minimum term of criminal detention and four times that of public surveillance. Its legal maximum term is four times that of criminal detention and twice that of public surveillance. Hence, from the length of the term, this system is much severer than both criminal detention and public surveillance.

Furthermore, for several reasons the treatment of persons undergoing RETL is more restrictive than those under public surveillance and detention as criminal punishments for several reasons. As an open penalty, public surveillance only partially restricts personal freedom and is carried out locally, nearby the neighborhood of convicted persons. People sentenced to criminal detention are detained in a place in the neighborhood and allowed to return home once or twice every month. Yet people under RETL are tightly guarded in special institutions and can be conditionally permitted by the institutions to go home on festivals or holidays. In addition, "one day in administrative detention" or "custody shall be considered one day of the term decided", similar to provisions on criminal detention in 1997CL Article 44. But it is different from those on public surveillance, which is the lightest criminal punishment in 1997CL Article 41, about which it states that "one day in custody shall be considered two days of the term sentenced."

Additionally, both RETL and RTL may bring similar legal consequences in sentencing subsequent criminal punishments. The Decision on Handling Convicts undergoing RTL and Persons undergoing RETL with Escape or Repeat Offenses in 1981 (1981DHC), specified RETL as legal circumstances in sentencing heavier punishments. This is actually to treat repeat offenders equally with recidivism in criminal laws in respect of sentencing.

Meanwhile, on the practical level, some abnormal phenomena also indicate the imbalance of severity between RETL and criminal punishments. In cases of complicity, principal or adult offenders may be sentenced to light criminal punishments for periods shorter than several years of RETL subject to accessory or juvenile offenders. This appears not to protect or educate but to punish minors more severely, as the term of RETL is much longer than that of criminal punishments. It is no wonder that offenders prefer criminal punishments of short terms for crimes to RETL for illegal acts and this severe punishment of RETL thus works against the aims of education and reform. Therefore, the severity of RETL far exceeds that of criminal detention, not to mention public surveillance.

On the other hand, the procedure of RETL lacks a proper trial and leaves no room for a criminal charge. According to the Law on Administrative Punishments adopted in 1996 (1996APL), administrative organs should inform both parties of relevant facts, reasons, legal bases and rights in examination, involving the right to request a hearing for decisions. It seems that the offender has the chance of defending himself or herself before the decision-making stage.

However, there is no such provision in regulatory documents on RETL until the 2002R-RETL. According to its Article 25, the public hearing mainly applies to RETL cases with the possible term of RETL decisions for no less than two years, or with juvenile suspects. It also precludes offenders who organize or use superstitious cults to commit illegal or unlawful acts, and those who inject or ingest drugs. It seems that the long period of RETL is applicable to only petty crimes punishable by RETL, while not all these crimes have the possibility to apply RETL for two years or more and thus are held in a public hearing, without detailed guidelines to determine terms.

Even if individuals attend a hearing, it is police that hear RETL cases to make decisions in the name of the RETLACs. This is far from the requirements of 'a sentence.....by a competent court' or 'a lawful order of a court' in ICCPR Article 8(3). Hence, there is no such proper criminal trial that satisfies ICCPR Article 14 to really constitute the determination of a criminal charge.

(3) Potential Violation of the ICCPR

Regardless of whether RETL has proper criminal trial or not, it always tends to violate the prohibition of forced or compulsory labour in ICCPR Article 8 for several reasons.

First, this system requires the combination of political education and productive labour under strict disciplines during a certain period[87]. If persons undergoing RETL refuse to obey disciplinary measures on forced labour, further punishment may be imposed, which may include deduction of relevant payment, warning, demerit, or expanding its period. Thus, it conforms to the general definition of forced or compulsory labour.

Second, RETL tends not to be hard labour as punishment for petty crimes. It is not hard labour because persons undergoing RETL mainly do labour on labour-intensive, simply-operated agriculture, handicraft, working and building materials industries, of which the kind or quota is assigned in the light of their sex, age, physical powers and technical conditions[88]. Although such labour is the punishment for petty crimes, the way to impose it is not criminal conviction by a competent court on the basis of a law expressly providing for it, but simply are administrative decisions without explicit punishment.

Third, RETL is really not 'work in detention', as its basis is not 'a lawful order of a court' 'in accordance with such procedure as are established by law'. Here 'law' means national laws formulated by the State legislature, but administrative decisions are made by RETLACs according to non-national laws by other bodies. Under the 1982Constitution, Legislation Law of the PRC (2000LL) Article 8 stipulates that 'only national laws may be enacted' by the National People Congress (NPC) 'and the Standing Committee thereof' 'in respect of matters relating to' 'compulsory measures' 'involving restriction of personal freedom'. Since no regulatory documents on RETL relating to 'personal freedom' were formulated 'by the NPC and the Standing Committee thereof', all legal bases of RETL tend to go against the 1982Constitution and 2000LL. Hence, the legal bases involved appear to be actually ineffective.

Since the punitive feature of RETL precludes it from military and national service, duties in cases of emergency, and normal civic obligations, RETL tends not to fall under exceptions in the Article 8(3)(c), but to be really forced labour.

Furthermore, RETL constitutes forced or compulsory labour because of its constitutional basis, apart from the improper procedure and insufficient legal bases. As the above indicated, 1982Constitution Article 42 violates the prohibition of forced labour under ICCPR Article 8(3)(a) and the right to work in ICESCR Article 6(1).

C.2. Illegal acts

C.2.1. Administrative Feature

Another kinds of conduct for which RETL can be imposed are illegal acts not punishable by criminal punishments. They are not criminal or serious enough to incur criminal punishments, and RETL is an administrative sanction for several reasons.

First, whether in legislation or practice, procedures for the examination and approval of RETL cases for illegal acts basically tend to be an administrative decision, far from being judicial trial by a competent court.

According to the 1996APL, administrative organs should inform both parties of relevant facts, reasons, legal bases and rights in examination, involving the right to request a hearing for decisions. It seems that the offender has the chance of defending himself or herself before the decision-making stage. However, there is no such provision in regulatory documents on RETL until the 2002R-RETL. According to its Article 25, the public hearing mainly applies to all RETL cases with the possible term of RETL decisions for no less than two years, or with juvenile suspects. It also precludes offenders who organize or use superstitious cults to commit illegal or unlawful acts and those who inject or ingest drugs. With such a limited scope of RETL cases, there is no chance of hearing or defence for most of them in examination and approval.

In practice, the hearing system has been gradually established underway and undue deprivation of this hearing has been corrected in some areas.[89]

For example, the Beijing Municipal Public Security Bureau (BMPSB) established a new system, the hearing, for examination and approval of RETL cases in August 2003 according to the 2002R-RETL. On 4th September 2003, it heard the first RETL case involving theft and repeated drug injection by the suspect, Wang, in public, with participation of a lawyer and 3 officials from Beijing Municipal RETLAC at the BMPSB.[90] Police insisted on applying RETL for 2 years and 9 months to Wang because of his illegal acts, while the lawyer argued for the reduction or exemption of the 1 year and 3 months of RETL due to the mitigating factor of his confession. After this debate in hearing, the hearing group submitted views of both sides to the RETLAC for final decisions.[91]

More important, regardless of hearing or not, it is an examination and approval Committee composed of department directors in the police that handle RETL cases and make relevant decisions under the 2002R-RETL. In fact, the police are exclusively responsible for examining and approving decisions of RETL in the name of the RETLAC, and even take the box-ticking approach to decide it in writing. This oversimplified and outdated form appears to deviate from requirements of the open, transparent, multi-sided participation necessary for judicial procedures, not to mention a proper trial. As reported in 2003, police in Wuhan City imposed RETL on a taxi driver found guilty of charging excessive fees twice.[92] Even if ostensibly this committee decided RETL, the police in effect control the RETL decision-making[93] and operate in camera.

Second, administrative reconsideration is one of the remedial means designed to correct improper decisions of RETL. Persons undergoing RETL may apply for it to the RETLAC at a higher level or to the municipal government of the people, if disagreeing with such decisions.[94] Where the RETLAC is chosen, police at the same level should accept applications for reconsideration of RETL cases and make decisions of administrative reconsideration in their name.[95] This is an internal enquiry only by the police, lacking any external scrutiny.

Meanwhile, such reconsiderations lack hearings available for a comprehensive and rational examination of original RETL decisions and fail to stop wrong ones in enforcement[96]. In *Gao's Case*, for instance, the police reported his case to the RETLAC of Sanmenxia City for a decision of two-year RETL because Gao had complained to the police of his county about the police sub-station many times.[97] Hence, this reconsideration is totally an administrative procedure under the disposal of the police or municipal governments.

Third, most persons undergoing RETL fail to resort to administrative litigation as the other means to remedy possible wrongs in RETL decisions, despite availability of provisions for such remedy.

Following establishment of administrative litigation in the 1990APL, the 2002R-RETL also specified that those who refuse to obey RETL decisions in RETL institutions may directly bring them to the PC.[98] This procedure required judicial examination and trials for RETL cases in courts with the police to attend in the name of the RETLAC at the same level.[99]

However, the rare application of administrative litigation was reported just to be around 25% of RETL cases in 2003[100] and has not apparently increased since. The potential reasons may result from several failings of this procedure.

First, current relevant provisions of laws and regulations provide the necessary procedures for reconsideration before administrative litigation of RETL. It appears to actually hamper the right to choose between them as an obstacle to the final realisation of the right of appeal, and even deprives the party of the right to choose the reconsideration or the lawsuit.

Second, RETL decisions had begun to have legal effect and were being executed before the administrative litigation came into effect in execution. This appears too late or insufficient to rectify improper decisions and remedy legal rights and interests of persons undergoing RETL.

C.2.2. Violation of Prohibition of Forced Labour

C.2.2.1. Retl at the Initial Stage

At the beginning, RETL was not only a measure for arranging employment to reduce social unemployment and give a reasonable salary under the salary assessment system, but also a measure for compulsory education and reform in nature. It aimed to assign employment and transform 'those who had the ability to work but idled about' without 'decent work' and those who 'violated law and discipline' into new self-sufficient and self-reliant people.[101] This tends to violate some Articles in the ICCPR and ICESCR as follows.

First, basic characteristics of RETL consist of the general definition of forced labour and thus it runs contrary to the prohibition in ICCPR Article 8(3)(a). On the basis of the constitutional right and duty to work, citizens had to work, otherwise they could be taken into RETL institutions to do labour as punishment. This indicates that RETL has the obvious feature of involuntary labour that violates Article 8(3)(a), apart from both ICCPR Article 8(3)(a) and ICESCR Article 6(1).

Second, persons undergoing RETL do work to promote social rehabilitation, which is not based on court decisions. This does not conform to the requirements of 'work in detention' as an exception of forced labour, or protection of the right to liberty of person by national laws, and so is contrary to ICCPR Articles 8(3)(c)(ii) and 9.

Third, both the duty to work and forcible employment assignment appear to influence the labouror's free choice of work and go against protection of the right to work under ICESCR Article 6(1).

C.2.2.2. The Present RETL

In the period of re-establishment of RETL, RETL evolved as 'an administrative measure' to impose compulsory education and reform, a method of 'dealing with internal contradictions among people', and then became an administrative penalty.[102] The purpose was changed to one of turning those subject to RETL into law-abiding persons who had sufficient "cultural knowledge and productive skills, were useful to society, respected public ethics, and loved the country and labour".[103] This tends to go contrary to the same articles as stated above.

First, this universal duty to work in the 1982Constitution tends to run contrary to the obligation of States not to compel citizens to work in ICCPR Article 8(3)(a), and the opportunity to freely choose work against protection of the right to work under ICESCR Article 6(1).

Second, persons undergoing RETL are taken into RETL institutions to do labour as punishment against their will, which is consistent with the general definition of forced labour. But their work is not grounded on court decisions as legal bases and does not fall into the exceptions to forced labour, and of such grounds and procedures 'as are established by law' not to ensure the right to liberty of person by law.

Hence, RETL appears to be forced labour defined in ICCPR Article 8(3) and lead to restriction of personal liberty against ICCPR Article 9.

C.2.2.3. Other Violations of Human Rights Instruments

Despite the humanitarian care in certain aspects, [104] the protection of the legal rights of persons under RETL remains a problem. Apart from the above-mentioned system of RETL itself, other relevant concerns also violate international human rights instruments.

Specifically, some offenders undergoing RETL do overtime labour in enterprises of RETL institutions.[105] The practice of overtime labour tends to go contrary to the protection from it in 1982TM-RETL Article 32 and ICESCR Article 7.

Moreover, only some prisons pay labour remuneration to persons undergoing RETL who do labour in China, though 1957D-RETL No.2, 1982TM-RETL Article 45 and Labour Law of the PRC adopted in 1994 Article 3 require labour remuneration for them. The No.2 RETL institutions of Gansu Province began to first practice the system of moderate wages for persons undergoing RETL in China from 2002,[106] followed by Guangdong province and Beijing City from 2003.[107]

IV. CONCLUSION

This study has shown that labour is a right and not an obligation to perform in detention for re-education from the perspective of human rights. On the one hand, it is the case under international human rights standards. International human rights law prohibits slavery or servitude without derogations, but permits several exceptions to the prohibition of forced labour. These exceptions contribute to part of the definition of forced labour, which appears to clarify when compulsory work or service is not forced labour, rather than when forced labour is permissible. Even the permissible forms of compulsory work might violate the relevant States' human rights obligations, for example, where compulsory work or service amounts to forced labour or is appointed in a discriminatory way. Since forced labour is strictly prohibited, the exceptions tend not to leave any room for such labour that may be forced or compulsory as an obligation in international human rights law. Hence, the nature of labour could be a right only and not an obligation.

Moreover, the idea of the right to work as an economic right is fundamentally incompatible with a regime of forced labour. If compulsory work or service is permitted, it must be an implied exception to the right to work, which would not change the nature of labour from a right to an obligation. States must provide just and favorable conditions of work in private sectors to prevent exploitation.

On the other hand, China has the obligation to prohibit forced labour and protect the right to labour as one of basic human rights as a party to the ICESCR, ILO100, LO122 and ILO182. These human rights standards attach special significance to the right to labour, treaty obligations concerning which may be contravened by certain forms of domestic legal systems. Any system that involves the obligation to labour in China's practice might be incompatible with the nature of labour in principle.

Specifically, China should undertake the obligation to prohibit forced labour from being subject to those under the age of 18, by the ILO182. Meanwhile, its obligations contain the protection of such rights of labourer in work as the rights to non-discrimination and equality, to free choice of work, to just and favourable conditions of work pursuant to the ICESCR, ILO100 and ILO122. These treaty obligations involve the prohibition of forced labour and do not allow for any forms of human rights breaches concerned. In the performance of compulsory work or service, any individual instances may constitute violations of the relevant right.

After the ratification of the ICCPR, China will undertake more treaty obligations concerned with labour, ICCPR Article 8(3) entails for China the obligation to prohibit forced labour in principle, with certain permissible forms of compulsory work or service. These are hard labour as punishment for a crime; work in detention; military and national service; duties in emergency; and normal civic obligations.

Although RTL and RETL are lawful sanctions in China as permissible compulsory work, both systems appear to take labour as an obligation and breach the relevant human rights standards. Apparently, neither RTL nor RETL would meet the procedural requirements provided in Article 8(3)(b) or (3)(c)(i). Without the due process, any of them appears to be forced labour prohibited by ICCPR Article 8(3)(a). Essentially, both systems recognize the obligation to labour, which conflicts with the nature of labour in international human rights law.

Furthermore, the two systems have the same legal basis in the 1982Constitution—the duty to work. This reflects the national value on work with Chinese characteristics and constitutes the basic reason for the difference from the relevant Western value. The duty appears inconsistent with the prohibition of forced labour in ICCPR Articles 8(3)(a) and the right to work required by both ICESCR Article 6(1) and ILO122 Article 1(2)(c). As a party to the ICESCR and ILO122, China has the treaty obligation to protect the right to work from being violated by particular or systematic instances. The obligation to labour should be revised as the right to labour, together with its obvious conflicts with the practical situation of China.

REFERENCES

[1] UN Doc. A/RES/2200A (XXI), 993/UNTS/3.
[2] UN Doc. A/RES/2200A (XXI), 999/UNTS/171.
[3] Labour Law of the PRC, adopted in 1994 (1994LL) Articles 3, 96, Criminal Law of the PRC, adopted in 1997 (1997CL) Article 244.
[4] Malcolm D. Evans (Ed.)(2003). *Blackstone's International Law Documents* (6th edition, pp.1-7). Oxford: Oxford University Press.
[5] CLN Article 22.
[6] CLN Article 23(a).
[7] 60/LNTS/253.
[8] SSFL Article 4.
[9] SSFL Article 5; Nina Lassen (1988). Slavery and Slavery-Like Practices: United Nations Standards and Implementation. *Nordic Journal of International Law, 57,* 197-227.
[10] Paul Sieghart (1983). *The International Law of Human Rights* (233). Oxford: Clarendon Press.
[11] OAS/RES/XXX.
[12] 21/ILM/58/1982.
[13] 993/UNT/S3.
[14] ETS/163.
[15] 226/UNTS/3.
[16] UN Doc.A/RES/45/158, annex.
[17] 39/UNTS/55.
[18] 320/UNTS/291.
[19] Krzysztof Drzewicki (2001). The Right to Work and Rights in Work. In A. Eide, and C. Krause, and A. Rosas (Eds.), *Economic, Social and Cultural Rights: A Textbook* (pp.223-243). Dordrecht: Nijhoff. Paul Sieghart (1983). *The International Law of Human Rights* (pp.230-233). Oxford: Clarendon Press.
[20] 165/UNTS/303 .
[21] 569/UNTS/65.
[22] Manfred Nowak (1993). *U.N. Covenant on Civil and Political Rights: CCPR Commentary* (146). Kehl am Rhein; Strasbourg; Arlington: Engel.
[23] Yoram Dinstein (1981). The Right to Life, Physical Integrity, and Liberty. In Louis Henkin (Ed.), *The International Bill of Rights: the Covenant on Civil and Political Rights* (pp.114-137). New York: Columbia. Sarah Joseph *et al.* (Eds.) (2004). *The International Covenant on Civil and Political Rights, Cases, Materials, and Commentary* (2nd edition, 295). Oxford: Oxford University Press.
[24] Sarah Joseph *et al.* (Eds.) (2004). *The International Covenant on Civil and Political Rights, Cases, Materials, and Commentary* (2nd edition, 295). Oxford: Oxford University Press. SCA Section III. Manfred Nowak (1993). *U.N. Covenant on Civil and Political Rights: CCPR Commentary* (148). Kehl am Rhein; Strasbourg; Arlington: Engel.

[25] Yoram Dinstein (1981). The Right to Life, Physical Integrity, and Liberty. In Louis Henkin (Ed.), *The International Bill of Rights: the Covenant on Civil and Political Rights* (pp.114-137). New York: Columbia.
[26] Manfred Nowak (1993). *U.N. Covenant on Civil and Political Rights: CCPR Commentary* (150). Kehl am Rhein; Strasbourg; Arlington: Engel.
[27] Ibid.
[28] Ibid. ICESCR Article 6(1).
[29] Manfred Nowak (1993). *U.N. Covenant on Civil and Political Rights: CCPR Commentary* (151). Kehl am Rhein; Strasbourg; Arlington: Engel.
[30] Yoram Dinstein (1981). The Right to Life, Physical Integrity, and Liberty. In Louis Henkin (Ed.), *The International Bill of Rights: the Covenant on Civil and Political Rights* (pp.114-137). New York: Columbia.
[31] Manfred Nowak (1993). *U.N. Covenant on Civil and Political Rights: CCPR Commentary* (151). Kehl am Rhein; Strasbourg; Arlington: Engel.
[32] Silva *et al* v. Zambia (Communication No.825-828/1999).
[33] Manfred Nowak (1993). *U.N. Covenant on Civil and Political Rights: CCPR Commentary* (152). Kehl am Rhein; Strasbourg; Arlington: Engel.
[34] Ibid.
[35] ICCPR Article 8(3)(b).
[36] Manfred Nowak (1993). *U.N. Covenant on Civil and Political Rights: CCPR Commentary* (153). Kehl am Rhein; Strasbourg; Arlington: Engel.
[37] ICCPR Article 8(3)(c)(iii).
[38] ICESCR Article 6(2).
[39] ICESCR Article 6(1).
[40] ILO100 Article 1(1).
[41] ILO100 Article 1(a).
[42] ILO100 Article 1(b).
[43] ILO100 Article 3(3).
[44] 38/ILM/1207(1999).
[45] ILO182 Article 2.
[46] ILO182 Article 3.
[47] Generally, customary international norms consist of two factors, namely, State practice consistent with the norm, and the acceptance by these States. See Theodor Meron (1989). *Human Rights and Humanitarian Norms as Customary Law* (pp.3-4). Oxford: Clarendon Press. Mark E. Villiger (1985). *Customary International Law and Treaties: A Study of Their Interactions and Interrelations with Special Consideration of the 1969 Vienna Convention on the Law of Treaties* (37). Dordrecht; Lancaster: Nijhoff.
[48] Nina Lassen (1988). Slavery and Slavery-Like Practices: United Nations Standards and Implementation. *Nordic Journal of International Law, 57,* 197.
[49] Krzysztof Drzewicki (2001). The Right to Work and Rights in Work. In A. Eide, C. Krause, and A. Rosas (Eds.), *Economic, Social and Cultural Rights: A Textbook* (pp.223-243). Dordrecht: Nijhoff.
[50] Paul Sieghart (1983). *The International Law of Human Rights* (220). Oxford: Clarendon Press.
[51] Ibid. (224).
[52] 1994LL Articles 3, 96, 1997CL Article 244.

[53] 1997CL Article 46.
[54] Ma Jihong (2003). Some Cognitions about Reform Through Labour. *Journal of Guizhou Police Officer Vocational College, 4*, 52-55. China Comments (2004). Is RETL RTL? [Laodong Jiaoyang Shi Laodong Gaizao Ma] [webpage]. http://news.xinhuanet.com/banyt/2004-05/12/content_1464763.htm.
[55] Wang Hengqin (2003). *New Considerations of Reform to RETL in China'a Prisons [Zhongguo Jianyu Laodong Jiaoyang Gaige Xinlun]*. Beijing: Publishing House of Qunzhong [Qunzhong Chubanshe].
[56] Chen Zexian (1999). The System of Rehabilitation Through Labor and Reform of Criminals Through Education in China. In Liu Hainian *et al.* (Eds.), *Human Rights and Administration of Justice* (172-188). Beijing: China Legal Publishing House. Zou Keyuan (2001). The 'Re-education Through Labour' System in China's Legal Reform. *Criminal Law Forum, 12,* 459-485.
[57] Zhao Bingzhi, Chen Zhijun, Wan Yunfeng, and Liao Wanli (2003). Plans of Legal Reform on the Chinese RETL System. In Zhao Bingzhi *et al* (Eds.), *Research Report on the Development of Criminal Law* (514-540). Beijing: Publishing House of the Chinese People's Pubic Security University.
[58] Jiang Jinfang (2002). The Legal Course and Realistic Questions on the RETL System [Laodong Jiaoyang Zhidu De Fazhi Licheng Ji Xianshi Wenti]. In Chu Huaizhi, Chen Xingliang, and Zhang Shaoyan (Eds.), *Sense and Order----Research on the System of RETL in China* (33-48). Beijing: Law Press.
[59] 1994PL Article 1.
[60] 1994PL Article 3.
[61] 1994PL Article 2.
[62] 1994PL Article 62.
[63] Ibid.
[64] 1994PL Articles 64 and 65.
[65] 1994PL Article 63.
[66] Regulations on Detention Houses of the PRC, adopted in 1990 (1990R-DH) Article 9
[67] Ibid.
[68] China Court (2007). First-Instance Judgments [Yishen Panjueshu] [webpage]. http://www.chinacourt.org/ajdq/cpws.php?location=0409010000.
[69] 1994PL Article 70.
[70] 1994PL Article 75.
[71] 1994PL Article 71.
[72] Manfred Nowak (1993). *U.N. Covenant on Civil and Political Rights: CCPR Commentary* (152). Kehl am Rhein; Strasbourg; Arlington: Engel.
[73] Feng Jiancang (2004). Studies on International Human Rights Conventions and the Human Rights Guarantee inside Chinese Prisons (Part Two). *Justice of China, 6,* 37-39.
[74] Ibid.
[75] ILO29 Article 2(2)(c).
[76] Jiang Weiren (2004). Prison System and Reform Quality [Jianyu Tizhi Yu Gaige Zhiliang]. *Politics and Law [Zhengzhi Yu Falv], 2,* 150-152..
[77] Feng Jiancang (2004). Studies on International Human Rights Conventions and the Human Rights Guarantee inside Chinese Prisons (Part Two). *Justice of China, 6,* 37-39.
[78] Ibid.

[79] Ibid.
[80] Liu Jian and Cai Gaoqiang (2004). On the Prisoners' Right of Properly Living Standard Under Our State's System of the Prison--Regard International Human Rights Convention as the Visual Angle. *Journal of Henan Judicial Police Vocational College, 1,* 10-14.
[81] Feng Jiancang (2004). Studies on International Human Rights Conventions and the Human Rights Guarantee inside Chinese Prisons (Part Two). *Justice of China, 6,* 37-39.
[82] Ibid.
[83] Ibid.
[84] Ibid.
[85] 1957D-RETL No.1; 1982TM-RETL Article 10; 2002R-RETL Article 9.
[86] 2002R-RETL Article 2.
[87] 1982TM-RETL Article 28.
[88] 1982TM-RETL Articles 39-40.
[89] hao Xin (2003). The Suspect Strives for Rights for Voluntary Confession [Fanzui Xianyiren Weizhudong Tanbao Zhengquanyi] [webpage]. <http://www.people. com. cn/GB/paper1787/10091/924866.html>.
[90] Li Jinghua, and Niu Aimin (2003). Beijing First Held A Public Hearing of the RETL Case in the Whole Nation of China [Beijing Zai Quanguo Shuaixian Dui Laodong Jiaoyang Anjian Gongkai Lingxun] [webpage]. <http://news.xinhuanet.com/ zhengfu/2003-09/05/content_1064313.htm>.
[91] Zhao Xin (2003). The Suspect Strives for Rights for Voluntary Confession [Fanzui Xianyiren Weizhudong Tanbao Zhengquanyi] [webpage]. http://www.people.com.cn/GB/paper1787/10091/924866.html.
[92] Zhongguo Fazhi Wang (2004). Where is the RETL System Way Out? [Laodong Jiaoyang Zhidu De Chulu Zai Nali] [webpage], <http://www.law.cn /news/ztbd/ hjzdbg/ 20043102134447>.
[93] Chen Ruihua (2001). Historical Examination and Reflections on Re-education through Labour [Laodong Jiaoyang De Lishi KaoCha Yu Fansi]. *Peking University Law Journal, 6.*
[94] 2002R-RETL Article 72(1).
[95] 2002R-RETL Article 72(2).
[96] 2002R-RETL Article 74.
[97] Zhang Yibang, and Tang Jinggang (2004). A Court Sentenced to Cancel the Decision of RETL [Fayuan Panjue Cexiao Laojiao Jueding] [webpage]. <http:// txy. hnby.com.cn/henan/smxs/smxs/zyb/t20041215_7448.htm>.
[98] 2002R-RETL Article 73(1).
[99] 2002R-RETL Article 73(2).
[100] Tian Yu, and Chen Fei (2006). Xiao Yang Emphasizes to Remove Irresponsible Judges [Xiao Yang Qiangdiao Jianjue Chanchu Faguan Duiwu Zhong De Haichun Zhima] [webpage]. http://china.rednet.cn/c/2006/06/30/926847.htm.
[101] The 1957D-RETL.
[102] 1982TM-RETL Article 2.
[103] Ibid.
[104] Xinhua Net (2003). Beijing Reeducation Center First to Have Flowers in Every Room [webpage]. <http://news.xinhuanet.com/english/2003-02/09/content_ 721038. htm>.

Xinhua Net (2002). Falun Gong Practitioner Lin Shenli Released After Receiving Humanitarian Care [webpage]. <http://news.xinhuanet.com /english/2002-02/24/content_288165.htm>. Xinhua Net (2001). Family Reunion in Reeducation-through-labour Center [webpage]. <http:// english.people.com. cn/200301 /31/eng20030131_111004.shtml>.

[105] Wang Jue (2004). Reflections on the Implementation of the Community Service. *Justice of China, 1,* 52-54.

[106] Yang Xiaobo (2003). Gansu Province First Practices the System of Moderate Wages for Persons undergoing RETL [Gansu Sheng Shouxian Shijian Gei Laojiao Renyuan Fa Shidang Gongzi] [webpage]. <http://www.chinacourt. org/public/ detail.php?id= 81258>.

[107] Guangzhou Ribao (2004). Guangdong Province Plans to Extend the System of Labour Remuneration for Persons undergoing RETL This Year [Guangdong Sheng Jinnian Ni Tuiguang Laojiao Renyuan Laodong Baochou Zhidu]. <http:// law. anhuinews. com/system/2004/02/06/000556631.shtml>.

In: Human Rights Issues in the 21st Century
Editors: M.S. Becker and J.N. Schneider, pp. 103-132
ISBN 978-1-60456-119-7

Chapter 5

"GIRL SOLDIERS" AND ARMED CONFLICT IN AFRICA

Noëlle Quénivet and Shilan Shah-Davis
University of the West of England, Bristol, United Kingdom

ABSTRACT

Africa is at the epicentre of the child soldier phenomenon. Armed groups and forces using children cover the continent. In fact, children have been drawn into (whether through forced measures or 'voluntarily') nearly every one of its myriad wars. However, whilst the endemic link between children (and boys in particular) and armed conflict in Africa is generally becoming increasingly well documented, the specific correlation between girls and warfare in Africa remains under-researched and less well documented. Consequently this chapter focuses on "girl soldiers" and armed conflict in Africa. It is contended that girls, in their status firstly as females, and secondly as children, are markedly disadvantaged and discriminated against from a social and cultural point of view even in peacetime. Therefore arguably, they are in an even more vulnerable and susceptible position during conflict.

The first part of this chapter explores how girls in Africa become part of an armed conflict. Research denotes that whilst the majority are either abducted or forcibly recruited, some girls 'willingly' join armed groups to obtain things–*inter alia* protection, education and training, a sense of belonging/purpose, money, power–denied to them in civilian life. This in turn depicts that such girls are not passive victims but active agents with a strong sense of agency and ability to exercise choice.

The second part of this chapter examines the experiences of the girls once they are part (whether forcibly or 'voluntarily') of the armed group/force. Within the group, girls suffer from grave violations and abuses that have lasting mental, emotional, and physical repercussions. One such violation is sexual violence, (which also forms the focus of this section) as although not universal, it is a daily fare inside most armed groups in Africa and is even experienced by girls who joined without obvious coercion.

In the second part, the roles girls perform within armed groups are also analysed as they too have an important bearing on the experiences encountered. Research indicates that within an armed group, girls perform a wide variety of roles–roles that do not necessarily conform to simplistic gender stereotypes. Therefore some "girl soldiers" are fighters and take a direct part in hostilities, whereas others serve in a more supportive role such as cooks, porters, domestic labourers, spies, etc. However, it is important to note that the majority of the girls' roles are fluid, multiple, and overlapping.

Finally, in both parts of this chapter, the relevant international law (human rights law, international humanitarian law, and international criminal law in particular) pertaining to the issues is also considered. Fundamentally, international law makes it clear that the rights and dignity of girls must be protected at all times. However, such protection may recede when girls, exercising their agency, willingly participate in hostilities.

INTRODUCTION

Africa is considered to be at the epicentre of armed conflicts in the world today. Most of the armed conflicts on this continent occur within State borders. In such localised conflicts (grounded in nationalistic, ethnic, and religious dissensions), "opposing sides do not distinguish between children and adults" (Madubuike-Ekwe, 2005: 30). In actual fact due to the nature and pattern of the warfare (Klaus 1999: 12), more and more children have become the primary targets of armed forces and opposition groups, and consequently, tens of thousands of children are either killed directly or die through other injury, disease, (Klaus 1999: 15) and malnutrition every year in these conflicts in Africa. Moreover, girls are particularly targeted because of their age and gender. In fact it is contended that even in peacetime girls in Africa are "significantly disadvantaged from a social and cultural point of view" (Holst-Roness, 2006: 7) owing to their status in society first as females, and secondly as children. Discriminatory behaviour, attitudes, and practices that negatively affect their fundamental rights such as right to life, health, dignity, education and physical integrity are commonplace and merely continue (if not exasperated) during times of war. It is also argued that during wartime the vulnerability of girls further increases because the traditional protection afforded to them by their families and communities is disrupted or unavailable as a result of displacement or separation (Holst-Roness, 2006: 6).

When talking about "girls and armed conflict" it is important to note that this can be viewed from two perspectives: civilian girls who are affected by war and girl soldiers (Jesseman, 2001: 144). As civilians, girls suffer physically and psychologically from the impact of the armed conflict. Being female, they are often subjected to sexual offences as a means of control and humiliation of the community to which they belong. Under such circumstances rape is used as a weapon of war and girls become easy targets.[1] The consequences of such gender-based violence are devastating as girls suffer from forced or unwanted pregnancies, sexually transmitted diseases including HIV/AIDS, and rejection from their own families and communities due to the shame of having been raped or having given birth to a child out of wedlock. Furthermore, many of these girls are then caught in a vicious cycle, whereby, unable to support themselves through any other means, they enter the sex trade. Girls are also targeted because as children they represent the next generation, the future generation of the enemy that must be wiped out. For example, during the genocide in Rwanda, the extremist Hutu radio station, Radio Libre Mille Collines, repeatedly encouraged the Interahamwe[2] militia to kill Tutsi children with the slogan "To destroy the big rats, you

1 For example, during the storm of Freetown in Sierra Leone, over a thousand of girls were raped (Klaus 1999: 15).
2 Militia group that was backed by the Hutu-led government up to and during the Rwandan genocide.

must kill the little rats" (Hilsum, 1994). Indeed, over 300,000 children were killed during the Rwandan genocide (Klaus 1999: 9-10).

During armed conflicts families flee their homes to find a safe place. In the process, children get separated from their parents (Klaus 1999: 14) and it is often in these situations that children are abducted or coerced into joining armed groups. In some instances, families and communities find refuge in camps. For example, in 2006 there were 935,000 children living in camps in Uganda alone (UNICEF, 2006). The living conditions and security levels in the camps are appalling. Hunger, disease, insecurity, and malnutrition are rampant, resulting in very high child mortality rates.[3] Moreover, "the loss of homes, land, cattle and other livestock has also meant the loss of a way of life" (Redress, 2006: 10). In this context, children are often the least protected. Furthermore, due to the increased pressure put on children to support themselves or their families, girls, and particularly adolescents, fall prey to sexual exploitation. In 2002 a report published by Save the Children and the United Nations High Commissioner for Refugees, which later became known as the "food for sex" scandal, exposed widespread sexual exploitation and abuse by United Nations and NGO personnel working in camps in Liberia, Sierra Leone, and Guinea (UNHCR and Save the Children, 2002).

Inevitably, armed conflicts have an emotional and psychological impact on children. In addition to the trauma created by what they have witnessed and/or endured, children are also affected by the loss of their parents and close relatives. Consequently many children are diagnosed with various types of post-traumatic stress disorder syndromes (Adam, 1999). Indeed, as children are best protected from the effects of armed conflict by the community and the family (Save the Children, 2005: 4), much of their well-being hinges upon the strength and resistance of these elements (Mazurana and Carlson, 2006: 2). However it is also at this moment that families and communities as well as educational, health, and social care services are put under stress. Furthermore, some members may wish to take sides in the conflict, thereby leaving the family and the community and making the family a possible target for reprisals. The loss of parents and, more generally close relatives, has a considerable impact on the development of children. It also makes them more vulnerable to abuses perpetrated by relatives or other individuals. In other instances they are left to head households alone (Mazurana and Carlson, 2006: 2).

Not only do girls suffer from the effects of armed conflict upon their families, communities, and themselves, they are also sometimes drawn into the conflict, in that they take actively part in the conflict. By being forced to become part of the conflict or by voluntarily joining sides, girls experience a range of violations to their human dignity. Notwithstanding, some of them fully participate in the conflict and become perpetrators of crimes under international law.

This chapter focuses on such girls in armed conflict, i.e. those who are not only passive victims of the conflict but become (whether willingly or not) part of the conflict itself. Once integrated in the armed forces or armed opposition groups these "girl soldiers" suffer from victimisation and/or become active participants in the perpetration of war crimes. Thus these girls are cast in the contradictory roles of both victim and perpetrator of human rights violations. The first section of this chapter explains and analyses how girls become part of the

---

3 Beginning of 1997, at the height of the crisis in the Democratic Republic of Congo, between 20 and 40 children died every day in the camp Tingi-Tingi (Klaus, 1999: 14).

conflict, while the second part describes their experiences in armed conflicts. Both issues are examined in light of the relevant international law, and in particular, human rights law, international humanitarian law, and international criminal law.

1. Becoming Part of the Conflict

There is no doubt that more and more children, and girls in particular, are frequently being used in armed conflicts in Africa. In fact, it is estimated that in recent African conflicts, girls comprise 30 – 40% of all child combatants (Park, 2006: 321).

The reasons why children are recruited are manifold. In military terms, the rapid changes in weapons technology have allowed for the creation of light weapons, such as the AK47 which can be easily stripped, reassembled, loaded, and fired by any child. Moreover, it is contended that children are often used to terrorise the population, for they are known to be unaware of concepts such as mercy and sympathy which only develop with age (Boyden, 1994: 260). They are also regarded as "expendable, less demanding and easier to manipulate than adult soldiers" (Fonseka, 2001: 69). Due to their young age, "children can [...] act relatively inconspicuously in war zones, observing troop deployments, dispositions of weapons and noting logistical arrangements without attracting undue attention" (Faulkner, 2001: 494). In addition, children are cheaper to maintain than adults.

Whilst girls are recruited for the aforementioned reasons, it is important to ask what additional qualities do girls possess that render them appealing to armed groups. Girls are recruited because in addition to fighting, they are also able to do the 'domestic' chores around the camp and provide sexual services for the male soldiers.

Generally children become part of the conflict in two different ways. First, they may be used or abducted and subsequently forced to participate in the hostilities; second, they may be recruited either forcefully or voluntarily. Furthermore, research shows that most girls fight alongside armed opposition groups rather than in governmental forces, an exception being the recruitment of girls by the government in Sierra Leone (Twum-Danso, 2003).

1.1. Abduction

"Most armed groups recruit children by force" (Madubuike-Ekwe, 2005: 33). In the last few decades, abduction and kidnapping have become the main ways to forcefully include girls in armed groups. Sadly, abductions are reported in almost every African conflict (Mischkowski, 2005). In some countries, abduction of children, including girls, has reached a level of automaticity. For example, during the second part of the 1980s, RENAMO systematically abducted children to participate in activities against the government of Mozambique (Legrand and Weissman, 1995). This is due to the fact that "[t]he abduction of women and girls to serve as porters, farmers, cooks, cleaners, launderers, tailors and sex workers is perhaps the crudest form of asset transfer in civil war, in this case, women's productive labour" (Turshen, 2001: 61). Often girls are "taken by force while working in fields or when a village was under attack" (Save the Children, 2005: 11). In other instances, girls are abducted while on their way to and from school (Redress, 2006: 12) or from school buses raided by armed groups.

While recent reports relating to the way girls get involved in armed conflicts underline the tactics of abduction, one must bear in mind that international law does not prohibit abduction of children for use in armed conflict *per se*. Article 29 of the 1990 African Charter on the Rights and Welfare of the Child (African Child Charter) prohibits abduction as such, but this prohibition does not specifically relate to the context of armed conflict.[4] What international law does condemn however, is the use of children in armed conflict.

The 1977 Additional Protocols (AP) were the first international legal instruments to regulate the participation of children below 15 years of age in hostilities, barring children from "tak[ing] a direct part in hostilities." This terminology is encapsulated in article 77(2) AP I relating to international armed conflict.[5] In contrast, article 4(3)(c) AP II does not use the adjective "direct", thus encompassing functions such as "gathering information, transmitting orders, transporting munitions or foodstuffs or committing acts of sabotage" (Dutli, 1990). This distinction in terminology prompted the International Committee of the Red Cross (ICRC) to comment that since "[t]he intention of the drafters of the article was clearly to keep children under fifteen outside armed conflict", indirect participation in *international* armed conflict should also be ruled out.[6] A resolution adopted at the 26th International Conference of the Red Cross and Red Crescent in 1995 reinforces this position inasmuch as it declares that "parties to conflict take every feasible step to ensure that children under the age of 18 years do not take part in hostilities," thereby refraining from using any adjective. The Abo Turku declaration, which is considered to encapsulate minimum standards of humanity, also stresses that children should not take part in acts of violence, thereby setting a higher standard than the "direct participation" expression enshrined in AP I.[7] Consequently it appears that under customary international humanitarian law, the expression "participation in hostilities" encompasses both direct and indirect acts that affect the enemy forces. Rule 137 of the study of customary international humanitarian law confirms this by stating that "[c]hildren must not be allowed to take part in hostilities" neither in international nor in non-international armed conflict (Henckaerts, 2005: 210).

Children's participation in armed conflict is also prohibited under human rights law. Article 38 of the Convention on the Rights of the Child (CRC), which is applicable in peacetime as well as in times of armed conflict, prohibits the *direct* participation of children (below 15 years of age) in hostilities. The Optional Protocol to the Convention on the Rights of the Child on the Involvement of Children in Armed Conflict (OP) uses similar wording, but stipulates the age of 18. Notwithstanding, one may argue that due to the nature of the wording used ('do not take *direct* part in hostilities') in the aforementioned instruments, they seemingly allow for the indirect participation in hostilities. There is however concurrence between the CRC, the OP and international humanitarian law instruments in that they all

4 Undoubtedly abduction violates the right to liberty and security as enshrined in article 9 of the International Covenant on Civil and Political Rights and article 6 of the African Charter on Human and Peoples' Rights.

5 According to the Rutaganda case, "[t]o take a 'direct' part in the hostilities means acts of war which by their nature or purpose are likely to cause actual harm to the personnel and equipment of the enemy armed forces." (Rutaganda, 1999: §100).

6 "The intention of the drafters of the article was clearly to keep children under fifteen outside armed conflict, and consequently they should not be required to perform such services." (Sandoz, Swinarski & Zimmermann (APII), 1987, §3187).

7 The Abo Turku declaration reads "Children who have not yet attained the age of fifteen years shall not be recruited in or allowed to join armed forces or armed groups or allowed to take part in acts of violence. All efforts shall be made not to allow persons below the age of 18 to take part in acts of violence." See also Meron &. Rosas, 1991: 375-381.

forbid the direct participation in hostilities. Yet, as stipulated above, AP I that governs international armed conflict should be interpreted so as to also ban indirect participation, a proposition supported by customary international law. In the case of *DRC* v. *Uganda* (2005: §219) the International Court of Justice (ICJ) found that Uganda had breached article 38(2) and (3) of the CRC and articles 1, 2, 3(3), 4, 5 and 6 of the OP. Regrettably however, the ICJ did not make any reference to article 77 of AP I, thereby leaving it open as to how the various rules interact.

In cases of non-international armed conflict (governed by AP II), by virtue of the *lex specialis* character of international humanitarian law, AP II supersedes the CRC and its OP. Nevertheless, inasmuch as AP II is rarely applicable either because a conflict does not reach the threshold set in article 1(1) or because a State does not concede its applicability, article 38 of the CRC and article 1 of the OP are the only legal instruments applicable in non-international armed conflicts falling within the scope of Common Article 3 of the Geneva Conventions (although it does not mention the participation of children in hostilities). Consequently, one must refer to the norms established in customary international law that prohibit the participation, both direct and indirect, of children in non-international armed conflict. In "situations of internal disturbances and tensions, such as riots, isolated and sporadic acts of violence and other acts of a similar nature" the only applicable instruments are the CRC and OP. In a nutshell, the protection afforded to children in such situations is not very satisfactory. Moreover, in contrast to international humanitarian law, the CRC does not bind non-State entities such as armed opposition groups.[8] As a result "children may still be exposed to considerable dangers on the battlefield [despite the adoption of the Protocol]" (Helle, 2000; Fontana, 1997). In terms of non-binding human rights documents, the Paris Commitments adopted in February 2007 generally refer to the use of children below 18 in armed conflicts. However, paragraph 6 of the document specifically uses the expression "used them to participate actively in hostilities," again indicating that participation must take an active or direct form.

A growing body of international criminal law deals with the use of children under the age of 15 in armed conflicts. According to the Statute of the International Criminal Court, it is a crime to make children participate in armed conflicts. During the negotiation process it was argued that the expression "participate actively," as enounced in article 8(2)(b)(xxvi) in the context of international armed conflict and 8(2)(e)(vii) in the context of non-international armed conflict,[9] covers not only direct participation in combat activities but also military-related activities such as scouting, spying, sabotage, and the use of children as couriers (Draft Statute and Draft Final Act of ICC, 1998: 25, footnote 12). This also includes activities at the front line (even though they may not have a military component *stricto sensu*) such as taking supplies to the front line. The deployment of the word "using" is additional proof of the wish of the drafters of the ICC Statute to prohibit the participation of children in hostilities generally rather than in combat only. Yet, activities "unrelated to the hostilities such as food deliveries to an airbase [or] the use of domestic staff in an officer's married accommodation" (Draft Statute and Draft Final Act of ICC, 1998: 25, footnote 12) would not qualify as

8 A notable exception is the Sudan People's Liberation Movement and the South Sudan Independence Movement which in July 1995 committed themselves to the CRC (Save the Children Sweden, 1996).

9 Here, it must be noted that the threshold of applicability for non-international armed conflicts is lower since it does not require that the conflict falls within the purview of Additional Protocol II. The crime of using children in armed conflict may also be committed in Common Article 3 conflicts.

participation in the hostilities. Consequently, when applied in the context of armed opposition groups, this infers that domestic labour, cooking and similar activities do not qualify as participation in the hostilities and are therefore not prohibited by international law.

The only piece of jurisprudence relating to the participation of children in hostilities is the decision of the Appeals Chamber of the Special Court for Sierra Leone in the *Norman* case in 2004. Article 4(c) of the Statute of the Special Court for Sierra Leone provides that "[t]he Special Court shall have the power to prosecute persons who committed the following serious violations of international humanitarian law: [...] c) Conscripting or enlisting children under the age of 15 years into armed forces or groups or using them to participate actively in hostilities." On the basis of this provision and by analysing other relevant instruments, the Court came to the conclusion that the recruitment and the use of children under the age of 15 to participate actively in hostilities was unlawful as a matter of customary international law. Interestingly, neither the Court nor the *amicus curiae* submissions discuss the issue of "active" or "direct" participation in the hostilities. For example, UNICEF speaks of the various aforementioned international humanitarian law and human rights law documents without even employing a qualifying adjective (*Norman*, 2004: §7). Again, this conveys the impression that both direct and indirect participation in the hostilities are unlawful.

Consequently, it seems that on the international level there is a consensus that both direct and indirect participation are banned.

On the regional level, the current state of the law is rather unclear. Indeed treaty law employs language similar to the aforementioned instruments while soft law espouses a broader definition of participation and even ventures into defining the notion of "child soldiers."

Article 22(2) of the African Child Charter requires States to ensure that "no child shall take a direct part in hostilities and refrain in particular from recruiting a child," thereby echoing article 77(2) AP I. The Protocol to the African Charter on Human and Peoples' Rights on the Rights of Women in Africa mirrors this position inasmuch as it imparts in article 11(4) that "no child, especially girls under 18 years of age, take a direct part in hostilities and that no child is recruited as a soldier." Like the aforementioned international instruments, regional documents speak of *direct* participation. Unfortunately, it is uncertain whether an all-embracing interpretation, similar to that adopted for the universal instruments, can be applied to them. For this, an examination of the soft law documents is necessary.

First, the Maputo Declaration adopted in 1999 does not refer to the notion of direct participation. Point 2 of the declaration encourages States "to take all necessary measures to ensure [...] no child under 18 years of age takes part in armed conflict." Furthermore, the Declaration tends to prefer employing the word "use:" The first point bans "the use of any child under 18 years of age by any armed force or armed group" while the third point "condemn[s] the use of children as soldiers by armed opposition groups."

Second, the 1997 Cape Town Principles go beyond the interpretation provided in the Maputo Declaration, using an even more encompassing definition. Notably, instead of defining participation in armed conflict, it focuses on "child soldiers," describing them as "[a]ny person under 18 years of age who is part of any kind of regular or irregular armed force or armed group in any capacity, including but not limited to cooks, porters, messengers and anyone accompanying such groups, other than family members. It includes girls recruited for sexual purposes and forced marriage. It does not, therefore, only refer to a child who is carrying or has carried arms." Such a definition is also espoused by Graça Machel in her follow-up book where she states that “a child soldier is any child – boy or girl – under the age of 18, who is [...] recruited or used in hostilities by armed forces. [...] Child soldiers are used for forced sexual services, as combatants, messengers, porters and cooks[...]. The majority are boys, but a significant proportion overall are girls” (Machel, 2001: 7). This definition embraces a broader interpretation than the provisions of the International Criminal Court Statute as it covers many tasks that are unrelated to the hostilities.

It appears that the rationale behind the adoption of the Cape Town Principles and the Maputo Declaration is the protection of children, while the Additional Protocols to the Geneva Conventions aim to define a combatant in the context of the general military operations. As an interpretative tool of international humanitarian and international criminal law provisions, the definition contained in the Cape Town principles is therefore inappropriate. It is however imperative to retain this definition when assisting girls after an armed conflict and helping them through the disarmament, demobilisation, and reintegration process.[10]

Thus, in light of the soft law documents adopted in Africa and bearing in mind the previous discussion on the interpretation of universal instruments, one may surmise that the treaties using the word “direct” must be interpreted as covering both direct and indirect participation.

Both universal and regional documents ban direct and indirect participation of children in armed conflict. Unfortunately, in reality the majority of girls do not directly *participate* in the hostilities.

With regard to indirect participation, two broad categories can be identified. Some girls are indirectly participating in the hostilities by spying, scouting, taking part in sabotage and working as couriers. Bearing in mind the definition of “participation” discussed above, such activities are covered and “is therefore not limited to taking a direct part in combat or deployment to the frontlines” (Smith, 2004: 1146). On the other hand, the definition does not cover the second broad category which includes ‘domestic’ activities such as cooking, fetching water and firewood, cleaning, caring for the sick and wounded, i.e. activities in which girls are regularly involved. Although these activities are “vital for group survival in terms of logistics” (Holst-Roness, 2006: 14) and “fundamental to the continuation of fighting as it sustain[s] the armed group” (Park, 2006: 324) they do not appear to fall within the scope of any of the aforementioned examples.

Inopportunely, these three categories, exemplified by the fighter, the spy, and the cook, do often overlap. It is quite common for girls to be involved in all these activities. Strictly speaking, one must then examine on a case-by-case basis what was the focus of their activities in order to determine their participation in the conflict. This is a strenuous task as it would involve interviewing a substantial number of girls, obtaining enough factual evidence of their activities and then assessing the time spent on each task. Furthermore, an objective test in terms of time management for example may fail to take into consideration the feelings of the girls who perhaps viewed the situation from a different perspective. Some may indeed be proud to state that they were part of the fighting forces even when their main duties consisted of cooking and running the camp of the armed opposition group. This will be a difficult balance that a court will need to strike.

10 This also explains why international organisations as well as non-governmental organisations have widely adopted the definition in the Cape Town Principles (Holst-Roness, 2006: 12).

The language used both in international humanitarian law as well as in human rights law "perpetuates an understanding of the child soldier as combatant, excluding many girls because of perceptions that they hold only non-combatant roles" (Kays, 2004: 7). In other words, whereas the actual participation of boys in armed conflict concurs with the legal definition of participation, this does not always hold true for girls since they are involved in an array of activities that are related to military operations but whose purpose is not necessarily "to cause harm to the personnel or equipment of the enemy forces" (Sandoz, Swinarski and Zimmermann (API), 1987, §1942).

1.2. Recruitment

Another method of integrating girls into armed forces and armed opposition groups is through recruitment. The word "recruitment" literally means joining the armed forces. Hence, the concept covers two types of actions. First, compulsory or obligatory conscription in the armed forces once a child has reached a certain age (often called military service); second, enlistment which denotes the activity of entering in the armed forces, either on a voluntary or forced basis.[11] Since girls are unlikely to be conscripted, the focus of this chapter is on the second type of recruitment.

1.2.1. Forced Recruitment/Enlistment

Forced recruitment of girls in government and armed opposition forces occurred in *inter alia* Angola (IRIN News, 2003) and Sierra Leone (Mitchell, 2003-2004: 86-87). A method commonly used to forcefully recruit children is press-ganging, "where armed militia groups…roam the streets and public gathering places, including school gates, to round up individuals they come across" (Madubuike-Ekwe, 2005: 33). Such groups also raid schools and orphanages. A notorious example is the LRA capture in 1996 of 136 girls from St. Mary's College, an Aboke school in Northern Uganda (De Termmerman, 2001). Similarly, in 2001 armed groups in Burundi abducted 300 children (including girls) from schools and forced them to carry military equipment or help wounded soldiers (Wessells, 2006: 41). In some instances children are intimidated so that they "voluntarily" join up. In other cases the school curriculum contains military elements, thereby, contributing to the indoctrination of the children who may then wish to join "willingly", yet are not fully able to understand the different competing ideologies and realise the implications of their decisions and actions.

Reports highlight that despite legal safeguards set by States to combat forced recruitment, inefficiency, corruption, and structural inadequacies mar the system. "As a result, forced recruitment occurs even in states where legislation is in place to prohibit compulsory military service before the age of eighteen" (Bald, 2002: 548). One of the reasons for this is that in many States the age of a person is not properly documented, thereby facilitating the recruitment of minors. Furthermore, because of the lack of punishment for armed groups recruiting children, forced recruitment became endemic in some conflicts such as the one in Sierra Leone (Mitchell, 2003-2004: 85-86).

11 See in particular UNICEF amicus brief in the Norman Judgment, footnote 1 on page 2.

1.2.2. "Voluntary"[12] Recruitment

Not all children and girls in particular are forced into soldiering. Many choose to join an armed group of their own volition. In Africa, a main contrast between government armed forces and other armed opposition groups is that the former tends to be overwhelmingly male, and the latter tends to involve both males and females. To a certain extent this may be because everyone in a guerrilla camp is self-identified as a member of the group, whereas the same does not apply to the civilian population within which government armed forces live (Happold, 2005: 14). Notwithstanding, girls' motives for joining or "volunteering" are distinct and basically seem to lie in the personal circumstances surrounding their lives and the local environment.

Poverty is often cited as one of the key determinants influencing girls' decisions to join armed groups (Happold, 2005: 14). Poor girls have the strongest economic and social incentives to join as providing for their basic survival needs and those of their families is a constant source of anxiety and uncertainty for them. They therefore join armed groups as a means to sustain themselves and often their families.

Furthermore, during war, many schools are destroyed, teachers flee, and public resources flow increasingly on the war effort rather than to services such as education. Children's lack of access to education weighs heavily upon them, because most children, especially girls, view education as their hope for the future and a better life. Denied this, many begin searching for other venues where they develop skills and competencies that can enable them to build their future. Military life often provides one such venue. As averred by a 16 year old girl who had been a commander with the RUF in Sierra Leone, "I'm proud of what I learned – how to speak to groups, organise people, command, use weapons. I never got this from the government. How else am I supposed to have a future? If I had it to do again, I'd join again." (Wessells, 2006: 50) In addition, lack of education also restricts children's choice of employment, making enlistment into an armed force or group an attractive option. For example, the Alliance of Democratic Forces for the Liberation of Congo-Zaire easily recruited by claiming that it would offer a $100 monthly pay (Redress, 2006: 19).

It is also well documented that the loss or absence of family frequently leads to children joining armed groups (Happold, 2005: 13). Moreover, in relation to girls there seems to be a high correlation between domestic exploitation, physical and/or sexual abuse at home and their decision to volunteer (Keairns, 2002: 3). Girls living in abusive situations see an armed group as providing a better "family" environment than the one they are living with.

Children are heavily influenced by social, community and family values, and by peer pressure. In fact, societal attitudes advanced by community leaders, teachers, parents, and their peers can "direct children to the conclusion that that they best way of...displaying maturity and becoming a full member of the collective is to join the struggle" (Happold, 2005: 14). Moreover, girls often join armed groups because their "significant others" (boyfriends, husbands, brothers, etc.) have already joined the movement (Keairns, 2002: 3).

Children also join armed groups out of a desire for revenge. Victimisation, whether it occurs inside a family or at the hands of a government force or an armed opposition group, compels many children, especially girls, to become soldiers (Wessells, 2006: 49). As Marjory, a young Liberian fighter explains, "The rape ...made me feel very angry. I couldn't sit still and do nothing about it. I wanted to take revenge" (Taylor, 2006).

---

12 Voluntary in this context is sometimes referred to as unforced recruitment.

Structural conditions in the midst of conflict also encourage children to join armed groups. Surrounded by violence and chaos, children, and girls in particular, often decide that they are safer as members of an armed group, rather than going about by themselves (Singer, 2005: 64). In addition to protection, being a member of an armed group gives a girl a sense of equality and respect. Furthermore, a sense of physical power is also achieved if she is given a gun to use or carry.

"Generally speaking, girls who [volunteer have] some notion that their life would be improved by joining" (Keairns, 2002: 3).

1.2.3. Prohibition of Recruitment under International Law

The recruitment of children, whether forced or voluntary, is regulated by both international humanitarian law and human rights law. "The prohibition against recruitment is separate and independent from the prohibition against the use" (Smith, 2004: 1147). Irrespective of whether a child is indeed taking part in the hostilities, his/her recruitment is itself sufficient to violate international law norms set out in international humanitarian law, human rights law, and international criminal law.

According to international humanitarian law and, more particularly, the Additional Protocol I, States must refrain from recruiting children under 15. Yet, under article 77(2) AP I, if such children voluntarily enlist in the armed forces, there is no obligation upon the State to refuse the new recruit. The Commentary to the Additional Protocol explains that the Committee that designed this provision "noted that sometimes, especially in occupied territories and in wars of national liberation, it would not be realistic to totally prohibit voluntary participation of children under fifteen" (Sandoz, Swinarski and Zimmermann (API), 1987, §3184). In contrast, according to article 4(3)(c) AP II that covers non-international armed conflicts, States as well as armed opposition groups are barred from recruiting children under 15 even if they voluntarily join. The ICRC commentary defends this viewpoint inasmuch as it states that "[n]ot only can a child not be recruited, or enlist himself, but furthermore he will not be 'allowed to take part in hostilities'" (Sandoz, Swinarski and Zimmermann (APII), 1987, §4557). This general prohibition of recruitment in non-international armed conflicts is very welcome because the great majority of cases of recruitment of girls, be they voluntary or compulsory, nowadays take place in the context of civil wars. The study of customary international humanitarian law also confirms in rule 136 that children cannot be recruited in armed forces or armed opposition groups both in international and non-international armed conflicts (Henckaerts, 2005: 210).

Human rights law instruments also impose upon States restrictions regarding recruitment. First, the issue of the distinction between voluntary and forced recruitment must be considered. Article 38 of the CRC affirms that "State Parties shall refrain from recruiting any person who was not attained the age of fifteen years into their armed forces." This is a laudable provision inasmuch as it is applicable both in peacetime and in times of armed conflict, thereby leaving aside the difficult question of qualification of the conflict. Moreover, it does not distinguish between voluntary and forced recruitment. In contrast, the OP prohibits, under article 2, the compulsory recruitment of persons under the age of 18. Furthermore, according to the OP, States are required to ensure that voluntary recruitment is genuine and not coerced, i.e. the informed consent of the recruits' parents or legal guardians has been obtained and the recruits are well informed about the duties involved in the military service. A similar approach was adopted by the European Commission of Human Rights in that it held that voluntary enlistment of children under the age of 18 did not amount to forced or compulsory labour (*W, X, Y, and Z v. United Kingdom*, 1968). The Commission stressed the fact that parental consent had been given and that the applicants were fully aware of the consequences of their decision. Second, the issue of age is highly disputed in human rights documents. The OP requires States under article 3(1) to raise the legal age for military voluntary recruitment. The latter provision has been met with criticism because it only raises the age of recruitment to 16. Upon ratification, States must deposit a binding declaration setting out the standards in place to meet their legal obligations in pursuance of the Optional Protocol. In contrast, the age of recruitment according to the Convention 182 of the International Labour Organization is 18 years. In other words, there are, depending on which human rights instruments States have ratified, three age thresholds: 15, 16, and 18. Undoubtedly, this leads to great legal uncertainty. Third, human rights law instruments adopt different standards depending on the parties to the conflict. The CRC provision only focuses on the traditional armed forces and does not refer to non-State actors. As many contemporary conflicts are of non-international nature and pit armed opposition groups against each other, it is imperative that there are provisions relating to non-State actors. Hence, the OP adopts a more stringent position, asserting that "armed groups that are distinct from the armed forces of a State should not, under any circumstances, recruit or use in hostilities persons under the age of 18 years." One of the main flaws of this provision however is that the OP, and more generally, any human rights instruments, cannot bind non-State actors as they cannot sign up to the agreement/s in the first place. In addition, "the beneficiaries of the rules –children– have no enforceable rights" (Madubuike-Ekwe, 2005: 35). As a result, the legal value of this provision is severely weakened. On the other hand, States are, in accordance with the OP, required to criminalise forced recruitment carried out by armed opposition groups. As one author notes, "[p]redictably, states have bound potential opponents with stronger obligations than they are prepared to accept for themselves" (Harvey, 2000). Nevertheless, one must note that those States which ratified ILO Convention 182 have been urged via Recommendation 190 to make forced or compulsory recruitment of children under 18 a criminal offence.

Moreover, international law has criminalised the recruitment of children under 15 despite the fact that Additional Protocol I does not mention recruitment as a grave breach. In the aforementioned case of *Prosecutor v. Norman* which was heard by the Special Court for Sierra Leone, it was held that recruitment of children under the age of 15 was prohibited under customary international law (*Norman*, 2004). Furthermore, the Court asserted, though on dubious grounds, that the prohibition of recruitment entailed individual liability since at least 1996 (Meisenberg, 2004). The ICC Statute clearly spells out that recruitment is considered as a war crime under article 8(2)(e)(vii) in non-international armed conflict and article 8(2)(b)(xxvi) in international armed conflict. Interestingly, the general notion of "recruitment" used in international humanitarian law has been split into two different concepts, conscription and enlistment. Thus, the ICC Statute provides that "conscripting or enlisting children under the age of fifteen years" is a crime.[13] This delineation was agreed upon after the United States expressed its concerns that the word "recruitment" could encompass the mere administrative act of putting the name of an individual on a list. A

13 In the context of non-international armed conflict, this prohibition concerns recruitment "into armed forces or groups" (article 8(2)(e)(vii)) while in the context of international armed conflict, it refers to recruitment "into the national armed forces" (article 8(2)(b)(xxvi)).

further distinction embedded in international humanitarian law, i.e. that between voluntary and forced recruitment, does not seem to be reflected in international criminal law. Indeed, the ICC Statute does not refer to the degree of voluntariness in joining the armed groups. Thus, Smith argues that "the forcible or voluntary nature of the recruitment is not an element of the crime" (Smith, 2004: 1148). In the *Norman* judgment (that pertains to a non-international armed conflict), neither the Special Court for Sierra Leone nor the *amicus* brief submitted by UNICEF distinguish between the different forms of recruitment. Yet, this may be due to the fact that according to international humanitarian law pertaining to non-international armed conflict, both voluntary and forced recruitment are prohibited.

On the regional level, the African Child Charter prohibits under article 22(2) the recruitment, both voluntary and compulsory, of children under 18 in armed conflict. Nevertheless, as it does not provide for compulsory registration of birth for the purpose of stating the chronological age but only in relation to name and nationality (under article 6(2) and 6(4)),[14] its efficacy is seriously limited in the context of recruitment.

As a result it is generally agreed that as a matter of customary international law, the recruitment of children, whether voluntary or forced, whether in international or in non-international armed conflict, under the age of 15 into armed forces is prohibited. This is confirmed by the abovementioned *Norman* jurisprudence. There might be an emerging norm barring the compulsory recruitment of children under 18, but this does not seem to be universally accepted at the moment.

The discussion above clearly demonstrates the various ways in which girls become part of a conflict. It further highlights that the discriminatory behaviour experienced by girls in peacetime merely continues during armed conflict. To a certain extent such discrimination can also be seen in the legal provisions relating to the use of child soldiers, i.e. in their direct or indirect participation in hostilities. Due to the nature of the activities carried out by girls (based on gendered expectations) their role in the armed conflict is viewed as *indirect* and, hence, falls outside the ambit of the general protection offered to children by international law. Such discrimination however is not evident in the legal framework pertaining to the recruitment of children.

It can also be concluded from the above analysis that girls are not always forcibly recruited in armed groups but sometimes make a conscious decision (usually due to personal circumstances surrounding their lives) to join. This, in turn, challenges the presumption that girls can only be forcefully drawn into armed conflict, and, therefore, can only be regarded as victims of the conflict. In fact, by opting to join an armed group through their own volition girls are demonstrating that they have the ability to exercise their agency in this context.

However when considering the victimcy or agency of such girls one must bear in mind the complexity of the issue, i.e. it is not easy to simply label girls as either victims or agents, as often they are both. Similarly, once girls are integrated in the armed groups (whether forcibly or voluntarily) they can still be both victims and agents, as examined in the next section relating to the experiences of "girl soldiers."

---

14 For a discussion on this issue, see Lloyd, 2002: 26.

2. Experiences of "Girl Soldiers" in Armed Groups

The readily available image of children with guns must be reconsidered in that children, and especially girls, play manifold roles in times of armed conflict. While some describe their primary role as fighters, others list duties such as portering, cleaning, providing medical assistance, gathering information, cooking (Save the Children, 2005: 11), taking care of younger children and running errands for breastfeeding mothers (McKay, 2004: 23), helping to loot villages (Utas, 2005: 59), taking part in abducting and training other children (Holst-Roness, 2006: 13). Generally speaking, girls "are forced to provide the majority of domestic and agricultural labor that sustains the fighting forces" (Mazurana and Carlson, 2006: 14). Whilst girls feel empowered as members of such groups this empowerment is only limited to the civilian population and is not recognised within the armed group. In fact, girls (usually deemed to be the least powerful members) are likely to be victimised unless they are considered as useful fighters (Utas, 2005: 74). Therefore, girl soldiers' experiences in armed conflict are a combination of passively suffering violations, often of a sexual nature, and actively and willingly engaging in hostilities.

2.1. Violations Suffered by Girl Soldiers

Within the armed groups girls suffer from various violations to their personal dignity. One such form of violence that deserves particular attention is sexual violence as at some point most "girl soldiers" have been and are likely to be subjected to it.

2.1.1. Sexual Violence

Their lives are steeped in hardship, danger, and exposure to different forms of violence, including gender-based violence. Girls are subjected to various kinds of sexual violence, including gang rapes, sexual torture, and serial rapes by different individual male members of the group (Park, 2006: 327). For example, in Liberia 75% of women and girls associated with fighting forces who came forward to be disarmed and demobilised stated that they had been sexually assaulted (Holst-Roness, 2006: 13). In fact, sexual violence, and rape in particular, is often used not only as a source of punishment, but also as a means of subjugation since it profoundly "violates girls' sense of safety and bodily integrity and can lead girls to see themselves as impure and damaged" (Wessells, 2006: 94). As described by a girl from the Democratic Republic of Congo who had joined an armed group at the age of 12, "One day rebels attacked the village where I lived. I hid and watched as they killed my relatives and raped my mother and sisters. I thought if I joined their army, I would be safe. In the army...I was often beaten and raped by the other soldiers. One day, a commander wanted me to become his wife, so I tried to escape. They caught me, whipped me, and raped me every night for many days" (U.S. State Department, 2004: 5).

Girls are also given as "wives" to men or boys in "bush marriages" (also referred to as "AK-47 marriages") as a reward for good fighting (Park, 2006: 327). In certain conflicts such as in Sierra Leone, 60% of girls involved with fighting forces were bush wives (McKay and Mazurana, 2004: 92). This phenomenon is also prevalent in Liberia, Angola (IRIN News,

2003), the Democratic Republic of Congo (Mazurana and Carlson, 2006: 10), and Uganda.[15] "Girls are typically 'taken' or 'allocated' as the sexual partner of a particular member of the armed group." (Save the Children, 2005: 15; Mazurana and Carlson, 2006: 5) Nevertheless, although the choice of attribution was not made by the girls, they often declared that this situation provided them with safety as other men in the group would not abuse them (Save the Children, 2005: 15). Furthermore, many conflicts show that girls, in order to avoid repeated rapes by several men who may use excessive force, preferred to "choose" a particular man. Additionally being the wife of a commander enhances the status of girls within the group (Park, 2006: 327).

It is also contended that providing sexual services is inevitably part of a girl's "duty" within the armed group.[16] For example, in the conflicts in Uganda and Sierra Leone girls, whether or not they took part in hostilities, were required to provide sexual services as their combat role was considered secondary (Alfredson, 2001: 5) (despite the fact that they "went through training and took part in combat" (Honwana, 2000b). In other cases, girls were not required to fight but to perform activities of a sexual nature. For instance, in the Democratic Republic of Congo, it is reported that some "girls were sent to be prostitutes and get information from the enemy" (Twum-Danso, 2003) while the great majority were used as sexual slaves (Verhey, 2004). Similar activities were also reported during the conflict in Angola (IRIN News, 2003). In fact, girls are often abducted with the objective of turning them into sexual slaves (Mischkowski, 2005).

It is worth noting that whilst the use of girls as sex slaves is contemptible, the issue is more complex then it may appear initially. In some circumstances, girls in armed groups decide to be the "wife" of a soldier because they need protection. Girls may also become emotionally attached to their "husbands" and see themselves in a *de facto* marital relationship (Wessells, 2006: 95), which outsiders would regard as exploitative and grounded in the abuse of power. Often the birth of a baby also adds to the girls' perceptions that the relationship is more like that of a husband and wife rather than of a captor and victim. As expressed by a girl who had lived in the bush with her RUF captor in Liberia, "I was afraid of him first...But he protected me – kept others away and got us food. He's the father of my baby and we should be properly married" (Wessels, 2006: 95). Notwithstanding, the strategy of having a "husband" can backfire if the man turns out to be cruel, transmits a sexual infection, or dies leaving the girl unprotected.

2.1.2. The Prohibition of Sexual Violence in International Law

Sexual violence is generally banned by international law, via a set of norms stipulated in human rights law, international humanitarian law, and international criminal law. Each *corpus juris* will be examined in turn.

2.1.2.1. Prohibition of Sexual Offences under Human Rights Law and International Humanitarian Law

Under human rights law, sexual offences are not prohibited *per se*. Rather, they fall within two categories: violation of one's personal dignity and sexual exploitation and abuse.

---

15 This is not a new practice as the attribution of girls to particular men also occurred in Mozambique under the name of the "wives of captor-husbands" during the decolonisation process (McKay, 2004: 21).

16 However, boys can also be used as sex slaves (Twum-Danso, 2003).

The protection of one's personal dignity is encapsulated in *inter alia* article 5 of the Universal Declaration of Human Rights and article 7 of the International Covenant on Civil and Political Rights. On the regional level, article 5 of the African Charter on Human and Peoples' Rights and article 3 of its Protocol on the Rights of Women in Africa also specifically protect the right to dignity. Undoubtedly, sexual offences encroach upon one's personal dignity and are therefore prohibited under human rights law. A solid body of jurisprudence (see e.g. *de Mejia v. Peru*, 1996) and various United Nations reports (see e.g. Special Rapporteur on Violence against Women, 1999: §18) also confirm that rape and other forms of sexual violence violate the fundamental right to dignity. Moreover, this right is also recognised within the context of the prohibition of ill-treatment, degrading treatment, and torture. It is acknowledged that rape and other sexual offences can be considered as a form of torture (Blatt, 1997: 821).

Sexual exploitation is any abuse of a position of vulnerability, differential power, or trust for sexual purposes and includes profiting monetarily, socially or politically from the sexual exploitation of another (United Nations Inter-Agency Standing Committee, 2002). Sexual abuse denotes the actual or threatened physical intrusion of a sexual nature either by force or under unequal or coercive conditions (United Nations Inter-Agency Standing Committee, 2002). Article 34 of the CRC prohibits all forms of sexual abuse and exploitation against children (during peacetime and war). This is also echoed in article 27 of the African Child Charter. Although both provisions provide girl soldiers with some level of protection, only States that have ratified the Convention and the Charter are bound by their provisions. Consequently, armed groups (whose male members are the main perpetrators of sexual violence against girl soldiers) are not legally bound by the provisions of either instrument. Furthermore, article 11 of the Protocol to the African Charter on Human and Peoples' Rights on the Rights of Women stipulates that "States Parties undertake to protect asylum seeking women, refugees, returnees and internally displaced persons, against all forms of violence, rape and other forms of sexual exploitation, and to ensure that such acts are considered war crimes, genocide and/or crimes against humanity and that their perpetrators are brought to justice before a competent criminal jurisdiction." Interestingly however, no specific reference is made to girl soldiers. What emerges in international and regional human rights law is a blanket prohibition on the sexual exploitation and abuse. Therefore in order to ensure that girl soldiers are given the appropriate protection, specific provisions, prohibiting the sexual violence of girls abducted or recruited by armed groups and forces, need to be incorporated as human rights violations (Leibig, 2005).

In international humanitarian law, rape and other forms of sexual offences are prohibited both under conventional instruments such as the Geneva Conventions and the Additional Protocols, and under customary law. As the ICTY summarised "[r]ape in time of war is specifically prohibited by treaty law: The Geneva Conventions of 1949, Additional Protocol I of 1977 and Additional Protocol II of 1977. Other serious sexual assaults are expressly or implicitly prohibited in various provisions of the same treaties" (*Furundzija*, 1998: §165). Article 27 of the Geneva Convention IV spells out that "[w]omen shall be especially protected against any attack on their honour, in particular against rape, enforced prostitution, or any form of indecent assault," a prohibition reiterated in article 76(1) AP I. In non-international armed conflict sexual offences are proscribed under article 4(1) AP II. Furthermore, it is well established that rape in times of conflict is prohibited under customary rules (Meron, 1993: 424; Bassiouni and Manikas, 1996: 578). Rule 93 of the study on customary international humanitarian law confirms that "[r]ape and other forms of sexual violence are prohibited" in international and non-international armed conflict (Henckaerts, 2005: 206).

2.1.2.2. Prohibition of Sexual Offences under International Criminal Law

Whilst various legal instruments pertaining to international humanitarian law and human rights law prohibit sexual offences, none of them seem to provide a definition of a sexual offence. Consequently, international criminal tribunals have created their own definition of sexual violence and rape by recourse to definitions enshrined in various national legislation (*Furundzija*, 1998). Traditionally, sexual offences comprised of two elements: an act of a sexual nature and the absence of consent. While the international criminal tribunals seem to have reached a consensus on what constitutes an act of a sexual nature, the jurisprudence on the issue of consent is not as homogeneous. In the context of the sexual violence experienced by girl soldiers, three types of incidents deserve particular attention: isolated cases of rape and sexual violence, repetitive incidents of rape and sexual violence (falling within the category of enforced prostitution or sexual slavery), and, finally, forced marriage. The ensuing discussion focuses primarily on the issue of consent (or the absence thereof) as the experiences of girl soldiers demonstrate that their perception of the incident often differs from the legal requirements.

2.1.2.2.1. Rape and Sexual Violence

The International Criminal Tribunal for Rwanda defined sexual violence as "any act of a sexual nature which is committed on a person under circumstances which are coercive" (*Akayesu*, 1998: §598). Subsequently, when interpreting the term coercive the International Criminal Tribunal for the Former Yugoslavia broadened its meaning to include a sexual act that was "non-consensual or non-voluntary" (*Kunarac*, 2001, §437-438). In the Elements of Crimes document[17] of the International Criminal Court a similar stance is taken: "The invasion was committed by force, or by threat of force or coercion, such as that caused by fear of violence, duress, detention, psychological oppression or abuse of power, against such person or another person, or by taking advantage of a coercive environment, or the invasion was committed against a person incapable of giving genuine consent" (Elements of Crimes, 2000). Therefore it is evident that besides the physical sexual act, two additional yardsticks used to decide upon the legality of the act are consent and the presence of elements of coercion. Yet, the ICTY in the case of *Kvocka* went a step further and embraced the informed-consent doctrine. It explained that consent is connected to "a variety of other specified circumstances which made the victim particularly vulnerable or negated her ability to make an informed refusal" (*Kvocka*, 2001, §177). As the ICTY judgment was delivered after the adoption of the ICC Statute, this new definition of consent was not incorporated in the Statute by the drafters. Rather, the ICC definition implies that some force or coercion must be present and the doctrine of *informed* choice is not applicable.[18]

---

17 The Elements of Crime document was drafted at the same time as the Statute of the International Criminal Court. It aims to define the elements of the crimes upon which the Court has jurisdiction.

18 Several authors militate in favour of the informed consent theory, see Boon, 2001: 625 and Hansen-Young, 2005-2006: 490.

The issue of consent as an affirmative defense is also governed by Rule 70(a)-(c) of the Principles of Evidence in Cases of Sexual Assault in the Rules of Procedure and Evidence which stipulates a two-prong test (ICC Rules of Procedure and Evidence, 2002). First, the Court must establish whether the victim had the legal capacity to give consent and, second, the Court must assess the circumstances and determine whether they can be characterized as coercive so as to undermine the victim's ability to exercise his/her agency. The ICC rules of procedure link consent to the "victim's ability to give voluntary and genuine consent" (ICC Rules of Procedure and Evidence, 2002: Rule 70 (a), (b) and (c)). In most cases relating to rape and sexual violence the prosecution focuses on establishing that the circumstances were such that the woman could not consent to the sexual encounter. In relation to girl soldiers one would expect the prosecution to centre upon the first part of the test, i.e. the legal capacity. Amazingly, in cases brought before the ICTY, the issue of age was never raised (even in one of the most notorious incidents relating to the selling of two girls (*Kunarac*, 2001, §775)). It is also of paramount importance to show that the girl did not consent to the sexual offence, which as mentioned above, can be difficult to ascertain in certain cases. For example, girls sometimes exercise their agency when "consenting" to be sexually abused in exchange for protection. Yet, due to the coercive environment in which these girls are living, the law may not take account of their agency.

2.1.2.2.2. Enforced Prostitution and Sexual Slavery

Many girls are also subjected to repetitive and often systematic incidents of rape and sexual violence. Such incidents fall within the legal categorisation (in international law) of enforced prostitution and sexual slavery.

When joining the fighting forces it is doubtful that they did so with the aim of working as prostitutes and, therefore, obviously did not consent to such encounters. Similarly, girls who were abducted/recruited for the purpose of providing sexual services to the armed groups did not consent to such abuses either. Hence, prostitution can be ruled out and the concept of forced/enforced prostitution examined.

Forced prostitution is a crime under international law[19] and is generally described as the "conditions of control over a person who is coerced by another to engage in sexual activities" (Report of the Special Rapporteur on Contemporary Forms of Slavery, 1998: §10). Furthermore, the Elements of Crime for article 7(1)(g)(3) of the ICC Statute aver that the use of force or threat thereof is not necessary; Fear of violence, duress, detention, psychological oppression or abuse of power as well as taking advantage of a coercive environment can also vitiate consent. However, paragraph 3 of the Elements of Crime for article 7(1)(g)(3) explains that the perpetrator must obtain or expect to obtain monetary or material benefit. Outwardly, this provision cannot be used against individual members of the armed opposition groups since they are not gaining anything from making the girls available to fellow fighters. However, it may be contended that the victim may as well expect a certain gain or advantage, thereby allowing for the prosecution of those who abuse "enforced prostitutes" (Oosterveld, 2004: 645). In some conflicts in Africa "[w]hile money is not a part of [the] transaction, the children are expected to perform sexual and other services in return for protection and staying alive" (Alfredson, 2001: 6). In such cases (as presented in the *Kunarac* case before the ICTY

19 In the famous Batavia case, enforced prostitution was considered a war crime (Batavia, 1946: 122).

(*Kunarac*, 2001; and *Kunarac*, 2002)), it must be demonstrated that the fellow fighter had knowledge of the circumstances surrounding the girls' activities.

Unlike for (en)forced prostitution, consent is not a possible defense for sexual slavery because slavery is a *jus cogens* crime, and therefore "a person cannot under any circumstances, consent to be enslaved or subject to slavery. Thus it follows that a person accused of slavery cannot raise consent of the victim as a defence" (Special Rapporteur on Contemporary Forms of Slavery , 2000: §51). This position was reinforced by the ICTY jurisprudence and clearly stresses that "lack of consent does not have to be proved by the Prosecution as an element of the crime" (*Kunarac*, 2002: §120).

Sexual slavery denotes a situation where a person lacks control over his/her body and personality, and his/her physical environment is controlled by another person, usually in the form of captivity or detention. As many "girl soldiers" end up trapped, unable to leave the group or resist the pressure, their situation can be compared to that of captivity. Both those who detain girls and those who have sex with girls whom they know are detained for *inter alia* sexual purposes, can be indicted for sexual slavery (*Kunarac*, 2001; and *Kunarac*, 2002).

To date sexual slavery has not been prosecuted as such by an *ad hoc* international criminal tribunal. Rather, it has been prosecuted under the heading of enslavement which is described in the ICTY jurisprudence as "the exercise of any or all of the powers attaching to the right of ownership over a person" (*Kunarac*, 2001, §540). However, such a definition is not reflected in the ICC Statute which defines the term sexual slavery in the following manner: "The perpetrator exercised any or all of the powers attaching to the right of ownership over one or more persons, such as by purchasing, selling, lending or bartering such a person or persons, or by imposing on them a similar deprivation of liberty" (Elements of Crimes, 2000). This definition creates the impression that some exchange must take place. Notwithstanding, the use of the word "such as" and the second part of the sentence "imposing on [victims] a similar deprivation of liberty" seem to lend more room for interpretation. Consequently, members of armed opposition groups who repeatedly sexually abuse girls could be prosecuted for sexual slavery.

2.1.2.2.3. Forced Marriage

Forced marriage is the legal terminology used to describe the concept of "bush-wives." In a landmark decision the Trial Chamber of the Special Court for Sierra Leone allowed the Prosecution to amend indictments so as to include a new count of "crimes against humanity – other inhumane acts (forced marriage)" (*Prosecutor v. Issa Hassan Sesay, Morris Kallon, and Augustine Gbao*, 2004). As Park notes, this "is a significant precedent [because] it addresses the prevalent 'bush-wife phenomenon' in many conflicts around the world, [...] it is the first prosecution of a gender-specific crime against humanity that is perpetrated within an armed group [and because] forced marriage is overwhelmingly perpetrated against girls, the prosecution of this crime addresses the specific experience of girls in war" (Park, 2006: 328). This case started on May 3, 2007 and it is expected that the Court will provide a legal definition of "forced marriage" and treat it as a crime *per se*. When considering forced marriage in the context of girl soldiers' experiences, the issue of agency re-emerges and must be borne in mind by the Court.

2.2. Participation

When considering the experiences of girl soldiers it is also very important to examine their participation in the armed groups. Indeed "[i]n all conflicts, children can take, and some choose to take, an active role in supporting violence. Children make calculated decisions during armed conflict about how to access shelter, food, medicine, and best ways to keep themselves and their family members safe" (Mazurana and Carlson, 2006: 2).

Girls, "[o]nce recruited, either voluntarily or forcibly, into a military regime, [...] are forced to fight, kill, steal food [...]" (Hackenberg, 2000: 422). After being forced to perform ritualistic killings such as killing their family or their relatives, girls are then provided with training on how to operate weapons. Children gradually enter a process of military socialisation aimed at transforming them into killing machines, a practice witnessed in *inter alia* Mozambique (Legrand and Weissman, 1995; Thompson, 1999: 193), Liberia (Dallaire, 2007: 13), and Uganda (Mischkowski, 2005: 4). Generally, girls who are living in such an environment tend to lose their personality and identity (Honwana, 2000a: 67) as well as any connection to the real world (Faulkner, 2001: 495). Furthermore, by living in such a violent world (where disorder and arbitrariness are common place), they lose touch with any concepts of morality which may have been inculcated to them before they joined to join the groups (Alfredson, 2001: 7; Maslen, 1999: 25). Therefore, one questions whether girls trapped in such a situation are still able to genuinely consent to their participation in the conflict, or are simply the means to an end for the armed group. Indeed "[c]hildren participating in hostilities are a deadly threat, not only to themselves, but also to the persons whom their impassioned and immature nature may lead them to shoot at" (Dutli, 1990: 421). African conflicts show that many children, trapped in a world of sustained and orchestrated violence, turn into merciless killers (Faulkner, 2001: 499; Maslen, 1999: 24; Honwana, 2000: 65). As expressed by Faulkner, they become "a horde of insensate killers" (Faulkner, 2001: 495).

Nevertheless, it is reported that girl soldiers often felt empowered through their experiences of fighting, bearing arms,[20] and killing (Twum-Danso, 2003). For some, being in the armed group meant enhanced opportunities, autonomy, and respect (West, 2000: 187). Additionally, "[c]hanges in the gender roles ascribed to women and girls can sometimes be seen as positive developments; girls do mature more quickly when faced with armed conflict and acquire new levels of responsibility and independence" (Holst-Roness, 2006: 8). Paradoxically, the conflict offers girls the opportunity to positively change their behaviour, lives, and relationships to men, family, elders, community, and society (Meintjes, Pillay and Turshen, 2001: 7). Thus, when girls subsequently try to reintegrate the civil society at the end of the armed conflict, they often have to conceal their role as combatants and adopt a subservient attitude in line with gendered customs and traditions (IRIN News, 2003). Furthermore, whilst the girls may mature rapidly in such an environment, they do so without moral and ethical guidance (Chitalia and Odeh, 2004).

Many girls are full participants in the armed conflict. Their participation ranges from committing atrocities to helping out with cooking or managing the camp. Generally, those who attained positions of command and became leaders are those who committed the worst atrocities. These girls gained their equal status to male fighters by demonstrating that they fully engaged in combat activities and were able and willing to kill (Holst-Roness, 2006: 15).

20 Possession of a weapon often conferred a certain status within the group (Dallaire, 2007: 13).

In fact, in Liberia, Uganda, and Sierra Leone, girls who wished to attain a certain status within the armed group knew that they had to commit murders, punish and execute fellow child soldiers as well as press-gang other children into armed groups (Twum-Danso, 2003). Therefore, girls should not only be seen as reluctant participants in armed conflicts but also as active agents.

Girls sometimes carry out tasks that fall within the legal definition of participation in armed conflict (as examined above). They are therefore considered, under international humanitarian law as combatants in international armed conflicts or participants to the hostilities in non-international armed conflict, and as a result lose the protection normally afforded to them as civilians. Indeed, from the moment they join the armed forces or the armed opposition group they fall within the category of combatant, whether or not they are truly engaged in frontline combat activities or not (Maslen, 1999: 25). Children "lose their inviolability as non-combatants; indeed, they become 'legitimate' military targets, individuals whose death or disablement result in that weakening of the armed forces of the enemy which is the only legitimate aim in war" (Cohn and Goodwin-Gill, 1993: 45).

"[I]nasmuch as girls are entitled to the full *protection* of IHL, they also incur the relevant *obligations* set forth in that law" (Holst-Roness, 2006: 5). The obligations relate to respecting international humanitarian law and the failure to do so entails criminal liability for grave breaches and war crimes under customary international law.

When many girls actively participate in hostilities, it may be contended that they commit war crimes. As a result, one needs to ask whether they should be prosecuted. Simply arguing that children, and girls in particular, should not be prosecuted fails to recognise the reality that girls are inevitably "thoughtful, insightful and active agents who shape their own lives" (Mazurana and Carlson, 2006: 2). Indeed, the Special Court for Sierra Leone expressly allows for the prosecution of children between the ages of 15 and 18 at the time of the commission of the crimes.

In general, any discussion on the prosecution of girl soldiers should ensure that the culpability of these individuals, the coercive environment in the armed group, the desire to rehabilitate such children as well as the call for retribution among the victims are factors taken into account (Custer, 2005: 449). Undoubtedly, as the United Nations Secretary-General noted in his report on the Statute of the Special Court for Sierra Leone, a tension exists between the need to ensure that the judicial system in place is credible in the eyes of the local population i.e. that children are prosecuted, and the desire to ensure that the rehabilitation of child soldiers is not endangered (Report on Establishment of a Special Court for Sierra Leone, 2000: §35).

Conclusion

There is undoubtedly an endemic link between girls and armed conflict in Africa. Research indicates that initially girl soldiers were mostly invisible; basically the prevailing view was that girl soldiers were only present in literally a handful of conflicts. Nevertheless, emerging literature depicted otherwise and showed that girls were part of many armed groups. Subsequently it was recognised that girls were definitely involved in armed conflicts on the African continent. Notwithstanding, they were usually described as "camp followers" who provided labour and support but were not child soldiers *per se* (Wessells, 2006: 85). As a result, the term child soldiers represented boy soldiers, hence marginalising girl soldiers.

Recently however, a new generation of research has sketched a more comprehensive portrait of girl soldiers and revealed the complexities and variations of this phenomenon. What has emerged is a pattern of widespread use of girl soldiers and of girls' participation in various roles in armed conflicts.

This chapter has highlighted that girls enter armed groups through both forced and unforced recruitment. Whilst many girls are either abducted or forcibly coerced into joining, some enlist "voluntarily." Such girls decide to join armed groups for diverse reasons as discussed previously. However the issue that surfaces is whether such girls are in fact joining through an agency of their own? In fact, are they in the best position to make informed decisions on weighty matters such as whether to join an armed group? Moreover, being young and inexperienced, are they making decisions grounded in a romanticized notion that their lives will be better in the armed group than outside? Notwithstanding, it is important to note that not all girls who decide to become soldiers are unhappy with their decisions. In some circumstances, being a soldier offers girls access to competencies, options, respect, equality, and support that they had been unable to obtain in civilian life (Wessells, 2006: 92).

It has already been asserted that girls in their status, firstly as females, and secondly as children, are markedly disadvantaged and discriminated against from a social and cultural point of view even in peacetime. This inequity merely continues during armed conflict. For instance, rape, sexual slavery and forced "marriages," though not universal, are a daily fare against girls inside most armed groups. Sexual violence is also used as a means of subjugation as it profoundly violates girls' dignity and bodily integrity. Consequently, such girls emerge as passive victims of armed conflicts.

However, as stipulated in the earlier discussion, not all girls in armed groups are passive victims, some play a direct and active role in the hostilities (primarily as combatants). Moreover, many girls (whether forcibly recruited or not), once in the armed group, consciously negotiate or construct their roles and position within the group. For example they may decide to become the "wife' of a soldier to ensure their protection. Similarly, they may become willing participants in committing atrocities, or even go beyond their regular military duties in the expectation of being rewarded or positively acknowledged by their commanders and other male members of the group. In effect, many girls, having started as victims, often become perpetrators of violent and horrible deeds. This raises the question whether these girls in their actions are demonstrating a certain level of agency. Moreover, can they be considered as "real" agents or are they in fact still victims of their social setting?

Agency "concerns events of which an individual is the perpetrator, in the sense that the individual could, at any phase in a given sequence of conduct, have acted differently. Whatever happened would not have happened if that individual had not intervened" (Honwana, 2005: 48). Thus the agent must have transformative capacity – "the power to intervene or to refrain from intervention" (Honwana, 2005: 48). Do girls in armed groups have such a capacity? The simple answer is yes, albeit, limited. From the examples given above, it can be seen that some girls do in fact "manipulate" situations in order to turn them into "opportunities." As Honwana explains, "these...[girls]...exercise what I would call a 'tactical agency'. By 'tactical agency' I mean a specific type of agency that is devised to cope with the concrete, immediate conditions of their lives in order to maximise the circumstances created by their military and violent environment" (Honwana, 2005: 49). Notwithstanding, it could be argued that the girl soldiers' actions are constrained by their weak position and therefore in reality they are acting in relation to a specific event rather than looking at the long-term consequences of their actions (Honwana, 1990: 75-76). Accordingly, in the context of girl soldiers it is indeed a fine line between victimcy and agency.

Broadly speaking, international law seeks to protect child soldiers. For instance, the recruitment and use of children in armed conflict is clearly prohibited. But on the same front international law does acknowledge that children can be full participants/agents in hostilities. However, the current trend in international law is to try and remove all children from the battlefield, thereby exhibiting its unwillingness to accept that children may have the ability to make decisions based on agency, albeit tactical or strategic.

With regards to incidents involving sexual violence, international law views women and girls as victims, and perhaps rightly so. It is worth noting however, that whilst sexual violence is contemptible, the reality of the incidents may be more complex than as they may initially appear. As explained above, in some circumstances girls may make tactical/strategic decisions (be it in coercive settings) relating to their survival and overall position in the armed group.

To conclude, preventing the recruitment, usage, and exploitation of girls in armed conflict is a monumental challenge of our time. Whilst international law (through international human rights law, international humanitarian law, and international criminal law) deals with these issues, the question is to what extent do States, armed groups and individuals who carry out these activities and actions comply with the law. Furthermore, what can be done to encourage the aforementioned parties to comply with these provisions?

Thus whilst there is growing recognition that girls are endemically involved in, or are part of, armed conflicts in Africa, what needs to be tackled now is the problem itself e.g. why children are recruited and used by armed groups, why girls join such groups, why girls are exploited, and why girls are willingly participating in the conflicts. It is only when these issues have been answered that the law can be maximised to its full potential to protect the girl soldiers.

References

Literature

Adam, H. (1999). "Trauma und Versöhnung. Die Lehren aus der Praxis". *Kinder im Krieg.* Konferenz, 25 August 1999, Friedrich-Ebert-Stiftung in Zusammenarbeit mit UNICEF. Available at: http://64.233.183.104 /search?q = cache:JiacUb AOxmUJ: library. fes.de/pdf-files/iez/01374.pdf+% E2%80%9C Trauma+und+ Vers%C3% B6hnung.+ Die+Lehren+aus+ der+Praxis%E2%80%9D.+ Kinder+im+ Kriegand hl= enand ct=clnkand cd=3and gl=uk. (Last retrieved 6 August 2007.)

Alfredson, L. (2001). *Sexual Exploitation of Child Soldiers: An Exploration and Analysis of Global Dimensions and Trends.* Coalition to Stop the Use of Child Soldiers. Available at: www.reliefweb.int/rw/lib.nsf/db900SID/LGEL-5RPBPA/$FILE/csusc-exploit.pdf? Open Element. (Last retrieved 6 August 2007.)

Bald, S. H. (2002). "Searching for a Lost Childhood: Will the Special Court of Sierra Leone Find Justice for its Children". *American University International Law Review, Vol. 18*, pp 537-583.

Bassiouni, M. C., and Manikas, P. (1996). *The Law of the International Criminal Tribunal for the Former Yugoslavia.* New York: Transnational Publishers.

Blatt, D. (1997). "Recognising Rape as a Method of Torture". *New York University Review of Law and Social Change, Vol. 19*, pp 821-865.

Boyden, J. (1994). "Children's Experience of Conflict Related Emergencies: Some Implications for Relief Policy and Practice". *Disasters, Vol. 18*, pp 254-267.

Chitalia, A., and Odeh, M. (2004). "How Girl Soldiers are Punished by their Past". *Youth Advocate Program International Resource, Paper 4.* Available at: http: // www. yapi.org/rpgirlsoldiers.pdf. (Last retrieved 6 August 2007.)

Cohn, I., and Goodwin-Gill, G. S. (1993). *Child Soldiers.* Geneva: Henry Dunant Institute.

Custer, M. (2005). "Punishing Child Soldiers: The Special Court for Sierra Leone and the Lessons to Be Learned from the United States' Juvenile Justice System". *Temple International and Comparative Law, Vol. 19*, pp 449-476.

De Temmerman, E. (2001). *Aboke Girls.* Kampala: Fountain Publisher.

Dutli, M. T. (1990). "Captured Child Combatants". *International Review of the Red Cross, No. 278*, pp 421-434. Available at: http://www.icrc.org/Web/Eng/siteeng0. nsf/html/57JMEA. (Last retrieved 6 August 2007.)

Faulkner, F. (2001). "Kindergarten Killers: Morality, Murder and the Child Soldier Problem". *Third World Quarterly, Vol. 22*, pp 491-504.

Fonseka, B. (2001). "The Protection of Child Soldiers in International Law". *Asia-Pacific Journal on Human Rights and the Law, Vol. 2*, pp 69-89.

Fontana, B. (1997). "Child Soldiers and International Law". *African Security Review, Vol. 6.* Available at: www.issafrica.org/pubs/ASR/6No3/Fontana.html. (Last retrieved 6 August 2007.)

Hackenberg, M. L. (2000). "Can the Optional Protocol for the Convention on the Rights of the Child Protect the Ugandan Child Soldier?". *Indiana International and Comparative Law Review, Vol. 10*, pp 417-456.

Happold, M. (2005). *Child Soldiers in International Law.* Manchester: Manchester University Press.

Harvey, R. (2000). "Recruitment and Deployment of Child Soldiers – The Beginning of the End?". *ChildRIGHT, No. 164.* Available at http://www.essex.ac.uk/armedcon /News%20Folder/Future/2000News/Comments/DraftOPCS.htm. (Last retrieved 6 August 2007.)

Helle, D. (2000). "Optional Protocol on the Involvement of Children in Armed Conflict to the Convention on the Rights of the Child". *International Review of the Red Cross, No. 839*, pp 797-809. Available at: http://www.icrc.org/Web/Eng/siteeng0.nsf/html/57JQQE. (Last retrieved 6 August 2007.)

Henckaerts, J.-M. (2005). "Study on Customary International Humanitarian Law: A Contribution to the Understanding and Respect for the Rule of Law in Armed Conflict". *International Review of the Red Cross, No. 857*, pp 175-212. Available at: http://www.icrc.org/Web/eng/siteeng0.nsf/htmlall/review-857-p175/$File/irrc_857_ Henckaerts.pdf. (Last retrieved 6 August 2007.)

Hilsum, L. (1994). "Children flee to Burundi camps". *The Guardian*, 5 July 1994. Available at: http://www.guardian.co.uk/rwanda/story/0,,1184627,00.html. (Last retrieved 6 August 2007.)

Holst-Roness, F. T. (2006). *Violence against Girls in Africa during Armed Conflicts and Crises*. Second International Policy Conference on the African Child: Violence against Girls in Africa, International Committee of the Red Cross, Addis Ababa, 11-12 May 2006. Available at: http://www.icrc.org/Web/Eng/siteeng0.nsf/htmlall/violence-girls-conference-110506/$File/International-Policy-Conference.pdf. (Last retrieved 6 August 2007.)

Honwana, A. (2000a). "Innocents et coupables. Les enfants-soldats comme acteurs tactiques". *Politique Africaine, No. 80*, pp 58-78.

Honwana, A. (2000b). "Untold War Stories: Young Women and War in Mozambique". *African Gender Institute Newsletter, Vol. 6*, pp 7-9. Available at: web.uct.ac.za/org/agi /pubs/newsletters/vol6/war.htm. (Last retrieved 6 August 2007.)

Honwana, A. (2005). "The Pain of Agency, the Agency of Pain. Child-Soldiers as Interstitial and Tactical Agents". In A. Honwana, and F. De Boeck (Eds.), *Makers and Breakers: Children and Youth in Postcolonial Africa*, (pp 31-52). Oxford: James Currey Publishers.

IRIN (2003). "Angola: Ex-Girl Soldiers Hidden behind a Veil of Fear and Denial". *IRIN News*, 12 December 2003. Available at: http://medilinkz. org/news/news2. asp?News ID=5028. (Last retrieved 6 August 2007.)

Jesseman, C. (2001). "The Protection and Participation Rights of the Child Soldier: An African and Global Perspective". *African Human Rights Law Journal, Vol. 1*, pp 140-154.

Kays, L. (2004). *Why We Cannot Find the Hidden Girl Soldiers: A Study of Professional Attitudes towards Gender Analysis in International Conflict and Development Work*. Available at: http://64.233.183.104/search?q =cache:12P894pBU_ EJ:www. peacestudiesjournal. org.uk/docs/Child%2 520soldiers%2520final %2520version% 25203.pdf+Why+We+ Cannot+Find+ the+Hidden+ Girl+Soldiers:+ A+Study +of+ Professional+Attitudes+towards+Gender+Analysis+in+International+Conflict+and+Dev elopment+Workand hl=enand ct=clnkand cd=1and gl=uk. (Last retrieved 6 August 2007.)

Keairns, Y. E. (2002). *The Voices of Girl Child Soldiers*. New York: Quaker United Nations Office.

Klaus, M. (1999). "Kinder und Krieg – eine Bestandaufnahme". *Kinder im Krieg*. Konferenz, 25 August 1999, Friedrich-Ebert-Stiftung in Zusammenarbeit mit UNICEF. Available at: http://64.233.183.104/search?q=cache:JiacUbAOxmUJ:library.fes.de/pdf-files/iez/01374.pdf+Kinder+und+Krieg+%E2%80%93+eine+Bestandsaufnahmeand hl=enand ct=clnkand cd=1and gl=uk. (Last retrieved 6 August 2007.)

Kristen Boon, K. (2001). "Rape and Forced Pregnancy under the ICC Statute: Human Dignity, Autonomy, and Consent". *Columbia Human Rights Law Review, Vol. 32*, pp 625-676.

Lancaster, P., O'Neill, J., and Spencer, S. (2007). *Children in Conflict. Eradicating the Child Soldier Doctrine*. Research Report Prepared for the Carr Center for Human Rights and Supervised by Lieutenant-General the Honourable R.A. Dallaire. Available at: http://www.ksg.harvard.edu/cchrp/pdf/ChildSoldierReport.pdf. (Last retrieved 6 August 2007.)

Legrand, J.-C., and Weissman, F. (1995). "Les enfants soldats et usages de la violence au Mozambique". *Cultures et Conflicts, Vol. 18*, pp 165-180.

Leibig, A. (2005). "Girl Child Soldiers in Northern Uganda: Do Current Legal Frameworks Offer Sufficient Protection?". *Northwestern University Journal of International Human Rights, Vol. 3*, p 6.

Lloyd, A. (2002). "A Theoretical Analysis of the Reality of Children's Rights in Africa: An Introduction to the African Charter on the Rights and Welfare of the Child". *African Human Rights Law Journal, Vol. 2*, pp 11-32.

Machel, G. (2001). *The Impact of War on Children: A Review of Progress since the 1996 United Nations Report on the Impact of Armed Conflict on Children*. London: Hurst and Company.

Madubuike-Ekwe, J.N. (2005). "The International Legal Standards Adopted to Stop the Participation of Children in Armed Conflicts". *Annual Survey of International and Comparative Law, Vol. 11*, pp 29-48.

Maslen, S. (1999). "Kinder sind keine Soldaten – politische und rechtliche Aspekte des Phaenomens Kindersoldaten". *Kinder im Krieg*. Konferenz, 25 August 1999, Friedrich-Ebert-Stiftung in Zusammenarbeit mit UNICEF. Available at: http://64.233.183.104 search?q =cache:JiacUbAOxmUJ:library.fes.de/pdf-files/iez/01374. pdf+Kinder +und+ Krieg+%E2%80%93+eine+Bestandsaufnahmeand hl=enand ct=clnkand cd=1and gl=uk. (Last retrieved 6 August 2007.)

Mazurana, D., and and Carlson, K. (2006). *The Girl Child and Armed Conflict: Recognizing and Addressing Grave Violations of Girls' Human Rights*. United Nations Division for the Advancement of Women in Collaboration with UNICEF, EGM/DVGC/2006/EP.12. Available at: http://fic.tufts.edu/downloads /Thegirlchildan darmedconflict.pdf. (Last retrieved 6 August 2007.)

McKay S., and Mazurana, D. (2004). *Where Are the Girls? Girls in Fighting Forces in Northern Uganda, Sierra Leone and Mozambique: Their Lives during and after War*. Montreal: International Centre for Human Rights and Democratic Development. Available at: http://uwacadweb.uwyo.edu/MCKAY/Documents/girls%20ang%20v5.pdf. (Last retrieved 6 August 2007.)

McKay, S. (2004). "Reconstructing Fragile Lives: Girls' Social Reintegration in Northern Uganda and Sierra Leone". *Gender and Development, Vol. 12*, pp 19-30.

Meintjes, S., Pillay, A., and Turshen, M. (2002). *The Aftermath: Women in Post-Conflict Transformation*. London: Zed Books.

Meisenberg, S. (2004). "Customary International Law and the Recruitment of Child Soldiers". *BOFAXE No. 286E*. Available at: www.ruhr-uni-bochum.de/ifhv/publications /bofaxe/x286E.pdf. (Last retrieved 6 August 2007.)

Meron, T. (1993). "Rape as a Crime under International Humanitarian Law". *American Journal of International Law, Vol. 87*, pp 424-428.

Meron, T., and Rosas, A. (1991). "A Declaration of Minimum Humanitarian Standards". *American Journal of International Law, Vol. 85*, pp 375-381.

Mischkowski, G. (2005). *Abducted, Raped, Enslaved: The Situation of Girl Soldiers in the Case of Uganda*. Medica Mondiale. Available at: http://www.medicamondiale. org/download/doku_report/Mischkowski_GirlSoldiersUganda.pdf. (Last retrieved 6 August 2007.)

Mitchell III, A. F. (2003-04). "Sierra Leone: The Road to Childhood Ruination through Forced Recruitment of Child Soldiers and the World's Failure to Act". *Regent Journal of International Law, Vol. 2*, pp 81- 114.

Oosterveld, V. (2004). "Sexual Slavery and the International Criminal Court: Advancing International Law". *Michigan Journal of International Law, Vol. 25*, pp 605-651.

Park, A. (2006). "Other Inhumane Acts: Forced marriage, Girl Soldiers and the Special Court for Sierra Leone". *Social and Legal Studies, Vol. 15(3)*, pp 315-337.

Redress, (2006). *Victims, Perpetrators or Heroes? Child Soldiers before the International Criminal Court.* The Redress Trust, London. Available at: http://www.iccnow.org /documents/Redress_childsoldiers_report_Sep06.pdf. (Last retrieved 6 August 2007.)

Sandoz, Y., Swinarski, C., and B. Zimmermann B. (Eds.), (1987). *Commentary on the Additional Protocols of 8 June 1977 to the Geneva Conventions of 12 August 1949.* Geneva: Martinus Nijhoff and International Committee of the Red Cross.

Save the Children Sweden, (1996). "Rebel Group Pledge to Uphold Convention". *Children of War, Vol. 3.*

Save the Children, (2005). Forgotten Casualties of War: Girls in Armed Conflict. Available at: http://64.233.183.104/search?q=cache:ULzoxG0nvFAJ:www.harare.unesco.org/women/2698_GAAF%2520report.pdf+Forgotten+Casualties+of+War:+Girls+in+Armed+Conflict.and hl=enand ct=clnkand cd=1and gl=uk. (Last retrieved 6 August 2007.)

Secretary-General, Report of the Secretary-General on the Establishment of a Special Court for Sierra Leone, (2000). U.N. Doc. S/2000/915, 4 October 2000.

Singer, P. W. (2005). *Children at War.* New York: Pantheon Books.

Smith, A. (2004). "Child Recruitment and the Special Court for Sierra Leone", *Journal of International Criminal Justice, Vol. 2*, pp. 1141-1153.

Special Rapporteur on Contemporary Forms of Slavery: Systematic Rape, Sexual Slavery and Slavery-like Practices During Armed Conflict, (2000). U.N. Doc. E/CN.4/Sub.2/2000/21, 6 June 2000.

Special Rapporteur on Contemporary Forms of Slavery: Systematic Rape, Sexual Slavery and Slavery-Like Practices During Armed Conflict, (1998). U.N. Doc. E/CN.4/Sub.2/1998/13, 22 June 1998.

Special Rapporteur on Violence against Women, its Causes and Consequences: Policies and Practices that Impact Women's Reproductive Rights and Contribute to, Cause or Constitute Violence against Women, (1999). U.N. Doc. E/CN.4/1999/68/add. 4, 21 January 1999.

Taylor, D. (2006). "I wanted to take revenge". *The Guardian*, 7 July 2006. Available at: http://www.guardian.co.uk/guardianweekly/story/0,,1824246,00.html. (Last retrieved 6 August 2007.)

Thekla Hansen-Young, T. (2005-06). "Defining Rape: A Means to Achieve Justice in the Special Court of Sierra Leone". *Chicago Journal of International Law, Vol. 6*, pp 479-494.

Thompson, C. B. (1999). "Beyond Civil Society: Child Soldiers as Citizens in Mozambique". *Review of African Political Economy, No. 80*, pp 191-206.

Turshen, M. (2001). "The Political Economy of Rape". In C. O. N. Moser, and F. C. Clark (Eds.), *Victims, Perpetrators or Actors? Gender, Armed Conflict and Political Violence.* London: Zed Books.

Twum-Danso, A. (2003). *Africa's Young Soldiers. The Co-Option of Childhood.* Institute of Security Studies, Monograph No. 82. Available at: http://www.issafrica.org /Pubs /Monographs/No82/Ch3.pdf. (Last retrieved 6 August 2007.)

U.S. State Department, (2004). *Trafficking in Persons Report.* Washington DC. Available at: www.state.gov/g/tip/rls/tiprpt/2004/. (Last retrieved 6 August 2007.)

UNICEF, (2006). *Humanitarian Action: Uganda Donor Update*, 16 May 2006. Available at: http://www.reliefweb.int/rw/RWB.NSF/db900SID/LSGZ-6PUE7A?OpenDocument. (Last retrieved 6 August 2007.)

United Nations High Commissioner for Refugees (UNHCR) and Save the Children UK, (2002). *Note for Implementing and Operational Partners on Sexual Violence and Exploitation: The Experience of Refugee Children in Guinea, Liberia, and Sierra Leone: Based on Initial Findings and Recommendations from Assessment Mission 22 October - 30 November 2001*, 26 February 2002. Available at: http://www.reliefweb.int /rw/rwb.nsf /AllDocsByUNID/6010f9ed3c651c93c1256b6d00560fca. (Last retrieved 6 August 2007.)

United Nations Inter-Agency Standing Committee, (2002). *Report of the Task Force on Protection from Sexual Exploitation and Abuse in Humanitarian Crises.* Available at: http://64.233.183.104/search?q=cache:1jNv6vjNNzMJ:www.unicef.org/emerg/IASCTFR eport.pdf+Report+of+the+Task+Force+on+Protection+from+Sexual+Exploitation+and+ Abuse+in+Humanitarian+Crisesand hl=enand ct=clnkand cd=2and gl=uk. (Last retrieved 6 August 2007.)

Utas, M. (2005). "Agency of Victims. Young Women in the Liberian Civil War". In A. Honwana, and F. De Boeck (Eds.), *Makers and Breakers: Children and Youth in Postcolonial Africa*, (pp 53-80). Oxford: James Currey Publishers.

Verhey, B. (2004). *Where are the Girls? Study on Girls Associated with Armed Forces and Groups in the Democratic Republic of Congo.* Save the Children and the NGO Group.

Wessells, M. (2006). *Child Soldiers: From Violence to Protection.* Cambridge, Massachusetts: Harvard University Press.

West, H. G. (2000). "Girls with Guns: Narrating the Experience of War of FRELIMO's 'Female Detachment'". *Anthropological Quarterly, Vol. 73*, pp 180-194.

Legal Documents

African Charter on Human and Peoples' Rights, (1981). OAU Doc. CAB/LEG/67/3 rev. 5, 21 I.L.M. 58 (1982), adopted 27 June 1981, entered into force 21 October 1986.

African Charter on the Rights and Welfare of the Child, (1990). O.A.U. Doc. CAB/LEG /TSG/Rev. 1, 1 July 1990.

Agreement between the United Nations and the Government of Sierra Leone on the Establishment of a Special Court for Sierra Leone, (2002). 2178 U.N.T.S. 38342, 16 January 2002.

Cape Town Principles and Best Practice on the Prevention of Recruitment of Children into the Armed Forces and on Demobilisation and Social Reintegration of Child Soldiers in Africa, (1997). New York, UNICEF, 30 April 1997.

Convention on the Rights of the Child, (1989). 1577 U.N.T.S. 3, 20 November 1989.

Convention Relative to the Protection of Civilian Persons in Time of War, (1949). 75 U.N.T.S. 287, 12 August 1949.

European Commission of Human Rights, (1968). *W, X, Y, and Z v. United Kingdom*, 19 July 1968.

Inter-American Court of Human Rights, (1996). *Marti de Mejia v. Peru*, Case 10.970, Report No. 5/96, Inter-Am. Ct. H.R., OEA/Ser.L/V/II.91 Doc. 7, 1 March 1996.

International Court of Justice, Case Concerning Armed Activities on the Territory of the Congo (*Democratic Republic of Congo* v. *Uganda*), (2005). Judgment, 19 December 2005.

International Covenant on Civil and Political Rights, (1966). G.A. Res. 2200A (XXI), 21 U.N. GAOR (Supp. No. 16) at 52, U.N. Doc. A/6316 (16 December 1966), 999 U.N.T.S. 171, entered into force 23 March 1976.

International Labor Organization, (1999). Recommendation Concerning the Prohibition and Immediate Action for the Elimination of the Worst Forms of Child Labour, June 1999.

International Tribunal for Rwanda, *Prosecutor v. Akayesu*, (1998). Case No. ICTR-96-4-T, Judgment, 2 September 1998.

International Tribunal for Rwanda, *Prosecutor v. Rutaganda*, (1999). Case No. ICTR-96-3-T, Trial Chamber, 6 December 1999.

International Tribunal for the Former Yugoslavia, *Prosecutor v. Furundzija*, (1998). Case IT-95-17/1-T 10, Judgment, 10 December 1998.

International Tribunal for the Former Yugoslavia, *Prosecutor v. Kunarac et al.*, (2001). Case Nos. IT-96-23-T and IT-96-23/1-T, Judgment, 22 February 2001.

International Tribunal for the Former Yugoslavia, *Prosecutor v. Kunarac*, (2002). Case No. IT-96-23 and IT-96-23/1-A, Appeals Judgment, 12 June 2002.

International Tribunal for the Former Yugoslavia, *Prosecutor v. Kvocka*, (2001). Case No. IT-98-30/1, Judgment, 2 November 2001.

Maputo Declaration on the Use of Children as Soldiers, (1999). 22 April 1999.

Netherlands Temporary Court-Martial in Batavia, Trial of Washio Awochi, Judgment, 25 October 1946, in: The United Nations War Crimes Commission (ed.), Law Reports of Trials of War Criminals, Vol. XIII, Case No. 76.

Optional Protocol to the Convention on the Rights of the Child on the Involvement of Children in Armed Conflicts, (2000). General Assembly Resolution A/RES/54/263, 25 May 2000, entered into force on 12 February 2002.

Preparatory Commission for the International Criminal Court, Addendum: Part II, Finalized Draft Text of the Elements of Crimes, (2000). U.N. Doc. PCNICC/2000/1/Add.2, 2 November 2000.

Protection of the Civilian Population in Period of Armed Conflict, Resolution of the 26th International Conference of the Red Cross and Red Crescent, (1995). Available at: http://www.icrc.org/Web/Eng/siteeng0.nsf/html/57JMRV#a3 (last retrieved 15 May 2007.)

Protocol Additional to the Geneva Conventions of 12 August 1949, and Relating to the Protection of Victims of International Armed Conflicts (AP I), (1977). 1125 U.N.T.S. 609, 8 June 1977.

Protocol Additional to the Geneva Conventions of 12 August 1949, and Relating to the Protection of Victims of Non-International Armed Conflicts (AP II), (1977). 1125 U.N.T.S. 609, 8 June 1977.

Protocol to the African Charter on Human and Peoples' Rights on the Rights of Women in Africa, (2000). CAB/LEG/66.6, 13 September 2000, entered into forced 25 November 2005.

Report of the Preparatory Committee on the Establishment of an International Criminal Court, Draft Statute and Draft Final Act, (1998). UN Doc. A/Conf.183/2/Add. 1, 14 April 1998.

Rome Statute of the International Criminal Court, (1998). 2187 U.N.T.S. 3, 17 July 1998.

Rules of Procedure and Evidence of the International Criminal Court, (2002). Doc. ICC-ASP/1/3.

Special Court of Sierra Leone, Amended Consolidated Indictment, *The Prosecutor v. Issa Hassan Sesay, Morris Kallon, and Augustine Gbao*, (2004). Case No. 2004-15-PT-6181-6202, 13 May 2004.

The Paris Commitments to Protect Children from Unlawful Recruitment or Use by Armed Forces or Armed Groups, (2007). February 2007.

Universal Declaration of Human Rights, General Assembly Resolution 217 A (III), 10 December 1948.

In: Human Rights Issues in the 21st Century
Editors: M.S. Becker and J.N. Schneider, pp. 133-150
ISBN 978-1-60456-119-7

Chapter 6

REALIZING CHILDREN'S RIGHTS – PROGRESS, PROBLEMS AND PROSPECTS

Emily R. Munro
Centre For Child And Family Research, Loughborough University, United Kingdom

We have a 'collective responsibility to uphold the principles of human dignity, equality and equity at the global level...*we have a duty...to* all the worlds people...in particular, *the children of the world to whom the future belongs*'

(*Millennium Declaration*, United Nations, 2000, emphasis added)

INTRODUCTION

It is nearly twenty years since the UN General Assembly adopted the Convention on the Rights of the Child (UNCRC). Since then it has been ratified by more countries than any other international treaty – only Somalia and the United States have not yet done so. Lansdown (2002) suggests that 'during the last decade of the twentieth century the human rights of children finally became visible' (p.285). In the 21st Century the importance of children's rights and the commitments adopted by 192 countries under the UNCRC have been expanded and reaffirmed in The Millennium Declaration[1] and *A World Fit for Children* (United Nations 2000, 2002). The ongoing challenge is in realising children's rights and promoting their well-being in practice. These challenges occur at a time when countries are seeking to respond to changes brought about by globalisation[2], technological advances and changes in the world of work (Hudson and Lowe, 2004). Local, national and international engagement is required to implement policies and practice that improve children and young people's life chances and promote their rights.

1 The Millennium Declaration was adopted by 189 nations and signed by 147 heads of state
2 The impact of globalisation on human rights is subject to debate. See for discussion, Howard-Hassmann (2005).

The first part of this chapter provides a brief overview of the rights enshrined in the UNCRC and its purpose. A number of human rights violations worldwide are identified within this discussion. In the second part of the chapter, the focus changes and attention turns to the progress that one Western society has made in realising children's rights, since they ratified the UNCRC. England has been selected for in-depth exploration. In a recent review of child well-being in developed economies[3] the UK ranked the lowest country overall, closely followed by the United States (UNICEF, 2007a). A number of policy developments in England have been influenced by, or transferred from the United States (Dolowitz et al., 2000). This is of interest given that the former have ratified the UNCRC and the latter have not yet done so. The decision was also pragmatic, as the author's work aims to inform policy and practice and improve outcomes for vulnerable children and young people in England. The examination is not intended to comprehensively or systematically map the changes that have occurred in recent years, but rather to review certain developments to explore a range of factors that have contributed towards enhanced rights for children in England and those that have acted against this.

UNCRC Rights and Values

A range of commitments to the civil, political, economic, social and cultural rights of children are outlined under the umbrella of the UNCRC (Roche, 1999) and it can be viewed as an important milestone in recognising children as individuals with entitlements (Skevik, 2003). Wintersberger (1999) suggests that the UNCRC is revolutionary in its conception of children's rights because it recognises the civil and political rights of children (see also, Ben-Arieh and Boyer, 2005).

The overarching, general principles of the Convention relate to: non-discrimination (Article 2); the best interests of the child as a primary consideration (Article 3); and the right to life, survival and development (Article 6). The core rights outlined in the Convention can be clustered into groups of related articles, covering civil rights and freedoms (Articles 7, 8, 13-17, 37); family environment and alternative care (Articles 5, 9, 18, 10, 11, 19, 20, 21, 25, 29); basic health and welfare (Articles 1-3, 6, 18, 23-27); education, leisure and cultural activities (Articles 29 and 31) and special protection measures (22, 30, 32-40) (UNICEF, 1998). Within these clusters certain groups of children are identified as requiring special protection by virtue of their circumstances. These include looked after children[4], children in emergency situations, those in the youth justice system, those in situations of exploitation[5] and those belonging to minority groups.

The framework of central rights has also been described as covering the '3 Ps,' that is provisional, protective and participatory rights (Hammarberg, 1990; Wringe, 1995). Provisional rights include: the right to life; an adequate standard of living; health and education. The importance of such rights cannot be underestimated. In 2000, 10.8 million children under five years old died, over half of them from just five preventable communicable

3 Exploring material well-being, health and safety, educational well-being, family and peer relationships, behaviour and risks, subjective well-being in 21 economically advanced nations.

4 The term used in the UK to describe children in public/out-of-home care.

5 Relating to child labour, drug abuse, sexual exploitation, sale of children and other exploitation (Articles 32-36)

diseases and malnutrition. Ninety nine percent of these deaths were in developing countries (World Health Organisation, 2003).

Protective rights cover (among other things) the right not to be subject to abuse, neglect or exploitation. The recent UN study on violence against children identifies how contrary to states' human rights obligations certain forms of violence against children remain state-authorised and condoned by society (Pinheiro, 2007). Children and young people may be subjected to violence in a range of settings including the home and family, school, care and justice systems, workplaces and community. The World Health Organisation estimates that almost 53,000 child deaths in 2002 were homicides (World Health Organisation, 2006a). In sub-Saharan Africa, Egypt and Sudan, 3 million girls and women are subjected to female genital mutilation (UNICEF, 2005). It is estimated that 73 million boys and 150 million girls have experienced forced sexual intercourse or sexual violence (World Health Organisation, 2006b). While the family is generally seen as a protective environment for children, in certain cases abuse and neglectful parenting means that children's safety and well-being are promoted by separating them from their parents. In such cases, children are entitled to special assistance (Article 20).

Lansdown and Karkara (2006) note that historically children's perspectives and experiences have not been taken seriously by adults due to perceptions of children and young people's incompetence to inform decision-making. The UNCRC marks a departure from this standpoint. In relation to children's participatory rights, Article 12 is key. It states that:

> States Parties shall assure to the child who is capable of forming his or her own views the right to express those views freely in all matters affecting the child, the views of the child being given due weight in accordance with the age and maturity of the child.
>
> For this purpose, the child shall in particular be provided the opportunity to be heard in any judicial and administrative proceedings affecting the child, either directly, or through a representative or an appropriate body, in a manner consistent with the procedural rules of national law
>
> (Article 12, UN Convention on the Rights of the Child).

Recognition of children and young people's right to freedom of expression and freedom of thought, conscience and religion are also incorporated into the Convention (Article 13, 14). It has been suggested that in reality children and young people's participation is 'frequently suborned into an adult agenda, assuming that key adults are 'expert' in the needs of the child' (Leeson, 2007, p.269).

Before exploring some of the issues that arise as attempts are made to operationalise and apply the standards outlined in the UNCRC, a brief overview of the English policy context is provided for the benefit of those who are not familiar with recent developments (see for discussion, Goldthorpe, 2004; Henricson and Bainham, 2005; Parton, 2006). Following this, progress towards realising children's provisional, protective and participatory rights in England is discussed[6].

6 A survey on the UNCRC Committee's Concluding Observations on the last EU Countries' reports offers a comparative analysis of issues examined by the Committee and points of strength and weakness in the implementation of the UNCRC (Instituto degli Innocenti, 2006).

POLICY CONTEXT

Liberal welfare states such as the UK[7] have increasingly recognised the importance of investing in children to maximise their contribution to society and the economy as citizen-workers of the future (Williams, 2004, see also Dobrowolsky, 2002; Fawcett al., 2003; Lister 2003; 2006). Broadly speaking, recent reforms and policy developments in child welfare, youth policy and justice in England have drawn upon the idea that intervening early in children's lives is beneficial to prevent a range of problems in later life. The Government suggest that increased knowledge of risk factors associated with children's development and poor outcomes, including low income and parental unemployment, poor parenting, community factors, such as living in a disadvantaged neighbourhood mean that early intervention is required to improve children's life chances and forestall anti-social behaviour, crime and unemployment. Early intervention and prevention is thus presented as cost-effective and of dual benefit to individuals and society. While emphasis is placed upon investing in and safeguarding *all* children, specific groups are also targeted to receive additional support because they have been identified as being at high risk of experiencing adverse outcomes and social exclusion.

The Green Paper *Every Child Matters* (HM Government, 2003) was published alongside the formal response to the tragic death of Victoria Climbié, who although known to four different social services departments, two hospitals, two child protection teams and a family centre, suffered horrific abuse and neglect and was eventually killed by her aunt and her partner (Laming, 2003). Every Child Matters outlines universal ambitions for every child and young person, whatever their background and circumstances. The following five outcomes are emphasised:

- Be healthy
- Stay safe
- Enjoy and achieve
- Make a positive contribution
- Achieve economic well-being

The reforms were said to build on existing plans to strengthen preventative services by focusing on four key themes:

- Increasing the focus on supporting families and carers - the most critical influence on children's lives
- Ensuring necessary intervention takes place before children reach crisis point and protecting children from falling through the net
- Addressing the underlying problems identified in the report into the death of Victoria Climbié - weak accountability and poor integration
- Ensuring that the people working with children are valued, rewarded and trained (see http://www.everychildmatters.gov.uk).

7 This chapter refers to the UK government making policy specifically for England. Responsibilities for children's services in the rest of the UK are devolved to the Northern Ireland Assembly, Scottish Executive and (partially) the Welsh Assembly.

The Children Act 2004 was also introduced to provide the legal underpinning for the reforms and to support changes in the organisation and delivery of services, with emphasis placed upon multi-disciplinary working and 'joined up' services. Under this overarching framework a wide range of initiatives and changes have been implemented.

PROVISIONAL RIGHTS

Provisional rights include 'the right of every child to a standard of living adequate for the child's physical, mental, spiritual, moral and social development' (Article 27(1)). The primary responsibility for this rests with parents. However, it is recognised that states should assist parents and provide material support in cases of need (Article 27(3)). It is acknowledged that financial assistance needs to be considered in the context of a State's 'national conditions' and 'means' (Article 27(3)).

Between 1979 and 1995 child poverty in the UK tripled and over this period inequality also rose by a third (Bradbury and Jantti, 1999). Over four million children were living in households below 60 per cent of median income and one in eight children grew up in families with persistently low income (Minoff, 2006). The detrimental impact of childhood poverty is well recognised:

> Poor children are deprived of material assets, they experience higher morbidity and mortality, their activities and opportunities are constrained, they are more likely to be mentally ill and they are more likely to live in poor housing in poor neighbourhoods (Bradshaw, 2005, p.36).

In 1999 Prime Minster Tony Blair made a historic pledge to eradicate child poverty by 2020. Since then policy developments, resources and interventions have been directed at seeking to meet this commitment (Department for Work and Pensions, 2006; Minoff, 2006). The Committee on the Rights of the Child welcomed this effort in its second report (CO United Kingdom, 2002; Instituto degli Innocenti, 2006). Despite this, between 2004-05 and 2005-6 the number of children in relatively low-income families actually rose by 100,000 (UK Government, 2007). However, this should not undermine recognition of the fact that over the last decade 800,000 children have been lifted out of poverty (HM Government, 2007a). Progress has certainly been made and living standards and increased opportunities have been afforded to many families. Recently, however, the Social Exclusion Task Force have identified that there are approximately 140,000 families (2 percent) who are not benefiting from the policy initiatives that have been implemented to tackle poverty and exclusion because they are facing complex and multi-faceted problems (including poverty, not being in employment, lack of qualifications, parental mental ill health, substance misuse, poor housing and contact with the criminal justice system) (Cabinet Office, 2007). The report recognises that this can limit aspirations and reinforce cycles of deprivation and have a detrimental impact on children's standard of living and future opportunities. A strategy to respond to the these seemingly intractable problems has recently been developed (HM Government, 2007a).

Alongside an adequate standard of living, the right of the child to education is recognised in the UNCRC (Article 28). Inequalities in educational attainment, according to, among other things, socio-economic status and ethnicity are of concern. In England, a raft of policies have been implemented with the intention of addressing this issue (Department for Work and Pensions, 2006). Specialist services are being provided in universal settings in a bid to reduce the stigma of service provision. For example, the extended schools initiative seeks to support the development of one or more schools per local authority that provide a comprehensive range of services on a single site, including access to health services, adult learning and study support as well as 8am – 6pm 'wrap-around' childcare (Cummings et al., 2006). The intention is that these services will not only improve educational attainment and reduce school exclusions, but also re-engage families and community members and overcome barriers to learning.

As well as raising academic achievement, attention has been given to measures aimed at reducing the wide variations in rates of exclusion and low education attainment for certain groups. Education for children in custodial settings has not been included in this wave of targeted policy initiatives, although a wide range of other groups have benefited. In 2003, the 'Aiming Higher' initiative was introduced and targeted minority ethnic groups. Although there is still some way to go, since then there has been a rise in the proportion of minority ethnic groups achieving 5 or more A*-C grades in GCSE examinations[8]. However, in 2004-05, the exclusion rate for black pupils was around twice that for white pupils (UK Government 2007).

Attention has also been given to the low educational attainment of looked after children. Outcomes need to be considered within the wider context of children's lives and pre-care experiences, however, statistical returns reveal a striking difference in the attainment of looked after children compared to their peers. Forty three percent of the 8,100 children leaving care aged 16 or over during 2005-06 had at least one GCSE or GNVQ qualifications on leaving care. Seven percent left care with at least 5 GCSEs at grade A*-C (DfES, 2006a) compared to 59.6 percent nationally (DfES, 2006b). *Care Matters: Time for Change* (HM Government, 2007b) places the academic attainment of looked after children as a high priority on the policy agenda. Measures include giving local authorities the power to direct schools to admit children in care even when the school is fully subscribed, support for reducing absence and school exclusion and the provision of £500 a year to support the education of those children at risk of not achieving the expected standards. Local authorities are also placed under a new duty to raise the academic attainment of looked after children (Children Act 2004, sec.52). Although the commitments outlined in Care Matters were not presented as measures to promote the rights of looked after children per se, there are indications that policies are enhancing the provisional rights of this group. This is particularly significant as it indicates that longstanding legacy of the principle of less eligibility[9] may now be shifting (Ward and Munro, 2005) and that the responsibilities of the corporate parent are

---

8 In 2006, at GCSE and equivalent, 44.4 percent of Black Caribbean pupils, 46.9 percent of pupils of Mixed White and Black Caribbean heritage, 50.3 percent of Black African pupils and 46.9 percent of other black pupils achieved 5 or more A*-C grades compared to 56.9 percent nationally (DfES, 2006b).

9 For more than a century child welfare policy in England and Wales was influenced by the principle of less eligibility, that is that conditions of people in the workhouse would not be better than the conditions experienced by an independent labour of the lowest class. This was enshrined in the 1834 Poor Law and was intended to reduce reliance on the state and ensure that there was no incentive for idleness. The legacy of this principle lasted long after the act was rescinded (in the 1940s) and acted as a disincentive to offer looked after children opportunities that poor families could not afford.

increasingly recognised. Developments in terms of protective and participatory rights are also apparent.

PROTECTIVE RIGHTS

Under the Children Act 2004, children's services authorities and children's trusts as well as Local Safeguarding Children Boards, police authorities and housing authorities are all expected, 'but not legally obliged', to comply with the requirements of the UNCRC in their work with children and families' (Lyon, 2007, p.148). On a more positive note, the Act does place a duty on key agencies to discharge their functions having regard to the need to safeguard and promote the welfare of children (Sec 11(2)). Recognition that safeguarding children and promoting their welfare in service provision and delivery is important beyond the children's service arena is significant. While legislative changes provide a framework to promote and safeguard children from harm, the effectiveness of implementation is key. It is early days, but O'Brien and colleagues (2006) suggest that:

> professional communities are embracing a commitment to the education, health and care of the 'whole' rather than the 'sectoral' child, differences between professional discourses and traditions remain, particular in relation to threshold and intervention decisions (O'Brien et al., 2006, p.394).

This demonstrates how legislative reforms need to be considered alongside organisational cultures, values and beliefs, as these are also influential in terms of frontline service delivery.

In the consolidated 3rd and 4th Periodic Reports to the UN Committee on the Rights of the Child the UK Government identify these legislative changes and reforms and argue that they encompass the principles of the Convention (UK Government, 2007). However, commentators have expressed a range of alternative views. Eileen Munro (2007) notes that in parliamentary debates on the Children Bill (which preceeded the Children Act 2004), it was made clear that a rights based approach was not the basis for its policy, as requested amendments from the House of Lords that anchored the legislation in the rights framework were rejected (Munro, 2007; Hansard debates for 13 September 2004). UNICEF suggest that Every Child Matters is progress but expressed regret that the Government 'failed to take the golden opportunity to situate the five outcomes of ECM within the framework set by the UNCRC' (UNICEF, 2007b, p.2). More critically, Parton (2006) suggests that policy was driven by the desire to prevent unemployment and crime, rather than primarily to address concerns about child abuse. He also suggests that the changes increase the power of social, welfare, health and criminal justice professionals and have the potential to undermine, rather than promote civil liberties and human rights.

Every Child Matters is intended to help all children fulfil their potential and the five outcomes (be healthy, stay safe, enjoy and achieve, making a positive contribution and achieve economic well-being) are universal. However, it is recognised that certain groups, including looked after children and care leavers may need additional support and targeted services to achieve these ambitions. Research demonstrates that young people leaving public care are vulnerable to a range of adverse outcomes, including unemployment, homelessness and involvement in the criminal justice system (see Wade and Munro, 2008 for an overview). Attention was drawn to the fact that care leavers were making the transition to independence at an earlier age than their peers and that they often had to learn to manage a home and start a career or their own family shortly after leaving care (Biehal et al., 1995; Stein, 2004). Under the 'Quality Protects' initiative, central government funding was linked to specific service objectives, including targets for improvements in housing, education and training and personal support for care leavers (Department of Health, 1998). Targeted legislation (The Children (Leaving Care) Act 2000) was passed to strengthen the duties placed on local authorities to assess and meet needs, provide personal advisers and develop pathway plans for those care leavers eligible to receive services up to the age of 21 (or beyond if continuing in education). These progressive developments recognise looked after children's rights to special protection and assistance (Article 20 and 39) and include measures to promote their life chances.

Concerns have been raised that the duties placed on local authorities in relation to care leavers are being by-passed in relation to unaccompanied asylum seeking children in some local authorities (Cemlyn and Briskman, 2003; Crawley, 2007). Cemlyn and Briskman (2003) suggest that breaches of the UNCRC in the context of children seeking asylum are widespread. Issues that have been raised include: the chaotic nature of reception arrangement, variations in local authority provisions for young people, with some having no contact with social services and some 16-17 year olds receiving services under s. 17 rather than s. 20 of the Children Act 1989[10]. The transition from childhood to adulthood for young people whose claims remain unresolved when they turn 18 years of age is characterised by uncertainty and anxiety (Dennis, 2002). Some local authorities are also acting to avoid unaccompanied minors from becoming eligible for support under the Children (Leaving Care) Act 2000 (see also, Aynsley-Green, 2006). The Children's Commissioner has drawn attention to how the duties imposed under the Children Act 2004 to have regard to children's welfare in exercising their normal functions do not extend to the Immigration Service, NASS and Immigration Removal Centres, thus undermining a comprehensive safeguarding framework (Aynsley-Green, 2006). An All Party Parliamentary Group on Children and Refugees has also drawn attention to immigration detention of children and families (Bercow et al., 2006).

It should be noted that the UK government entered a reservation to Article 22 of the UNCRC arguing that effective immigration control could be compromised (see UK Government, 2007, para 5-8). This Article of the UNCRC outlines how State Parties should:

> take appropriate measures to ensure that a child who is seeking refugee status or who is considered a refugee ...receive appropriate protection and humanitarian assistance in the enjoyment of applicable rights set forth in the present Convention.

Further,

> in cases where no parents or other members of the family can be found, the child shall be accorded the same protection as any other child permanently or temporarily deprived of his or her family environment for any reason, as set forth in the present Convention.

Despite the growing body of evidence that the rights of asylum seekers are not being protected, in the UK Government's most recent report to the Committee they contend that:

10 Section 17 covers children in need. Accommodation under s.20 means children are classified as looked after children and have greater entitlements and protection.

> the interests and rights of asylum seeking children and young people are fully respected. The key human rights of children are protected under the Human Rights Act 1998, which applies, without exception, to all children in the UK (UK Government, 2007, para. 5).

While the Human Rights Act 1998 does apply to children, it was never developed as a child-centred legislative framework. McDonald (2007) also identifies how 'there has been a tendency for courts not to intervene when difficult decisions of resource provision have to be made, choosing to focus on procedural correctness rather than substantive support for Convention rights' (p.84).

Balancing the rights of individual children, or groups of children against the rights and interests of wider society also comes into focus in examining youth justice. Early intervention and prevention are prioritised in child and family policy and youth justice. However, in the former emphasis is placed on children's vulnerability and need for protection, whereas in the latter, young people are 'often granted the agency of adults and are the objects of concern and control' (Such and Walker, 2005, p.54). Critics have suggested that the emphasis placed on intervention in youth justice has resulted in a decline in the primacy afforded to 'lenient' sentences and that identification of high 'risk' groups has criminalised young people for relatively minor offences (Smith, 2003, p.137). Payne (2003) suggests that prioritisation of children's best interests falls out of focus when children commit crime. There are also indications that the tough youth justice measures in place in England put the welfare of society above children's welfare and that 'they risk breaching the spirit, if not the letter, of the UNCRC' (Henricson and Bainham, 2005).

The Committee on the Rights of the Child have raised deep concerns about the situation of children in conflict with the law in the UK and identified that the situation has *worsened* over time (CO United Kingdom, 2002, para 59). They expressed concern about the abolition of *doli incapax* and the low age of criminal responsibility in England (10 years old). Under the Crime and Disorder Act 1998 a number of non-criminal orders, including anti-social behaviour orders and child curfews were introduced to enable early intervention even if no criminal act had been committed. Breach of such orders could lead to more stringent and harsher sanctions that those under the Criminal Justice and Public Order Act 1994. A detention and training order was also introduced (a custodial sentence for young people aged 12-17 imposed for offences which would be punishable with imprisonment when committed by adults).

Critical commentaries of the Act described it as 'institutionalised intolerance' (Muncie, 1999) and as 'misguided and misconceived' (Gelsthorpe and Morris, 1999, p.209). It is noteworthy that the Bulger case[11] and media portrayals of youth as 'anti-social, deviant, irresponsible and in need of firm social control' informed policy developments in the 1990s (Franklin, 2002, p.28). In respect of youth justice the Government has remained unresponsive to Committee recommendations and tensions between the principles of the child welfare system and youth justice persist. However, it is noteworthy that government inaction has come under scrutiny at the national level and the Joint Committee on Human Rights has called ministers to respond to a number of issues raised by the Committee. That said, in its latest report the Government simply state that they are 'concerned about 10 and 11 year olds being drawn to offending behaviour and believe that commencing criminal responsibility

11 James Bulger was a two year old toddler who was murdered by two ten year old boys in 1993.

from the age of 10 helps children develop a sense of responsibility for their behaviour' (UK Government, 2007, para. 55).

PARTICIPATORY RIGHTS

Debates relating to the role, purpose and potential of the UNCRC from promoters and opponents of it, connect to ongoing discussions and tensions about the conception of childhood, citizenship, the family, rights and responsibilities and the role of the State (see for discussion, Fox-Harding, 1996; Freeman, 1992; Prout, 2001; Roche, 1999; Such and Walker, 2005). Participatory rights have been of particular concern to some pressure groups in the United States who are resistant to the UNCRC (Rutkow and Lozman, 2006). The 'Christian Right' have asserted that the UNCRC is a danger to their pro-family agenda. The information presented by them (see for example, Concerned Women for America, http://www. cwfa.org /main.asp) has been used to argue that the UNCRC 'seeks to upsurp parents' rights to control the educational, religious and moral development of children' (Butler, 2000, p.362). Although their assertions are misleading[12] they do reveal a fear of intrusion into family life (Kilbourne, 1998). Those jurisdictions traditionally in favour of minimal state intervention and that strongly endorse the privacy of family life may be more reluctant to embrace the principles of the UNCRC[13]. Lansdown (1995) makes the important point that participation does not imply that adults abdicate all responsibility and leave children to make decisions alone.

Defences linked to the right to family life sometimes fail to adequately acknowledge that some family environments are neglectful and abusive. Sanders and Mace (2006) identify a number of dilemmas that child protection professionals face as they seek to safeguard children from harm. These include: potential conflicts between the need to protect a child's best interests and the child having a voice; balancing the needs and rights of the parent(s) and child; and the unequal distribution of power between different parties.

Policy developments in England indicate that the legacy that children are not capable of participating in decisions affecting their lives, or that they should not be burdened with this responsibility, are slowly changing. Recognition of this does vary in different settings, for example, parents' rights continue to be a dominant influence in the education arena (Henricson and Bainham, 2005), whilst increasingly, steps are being taken to increase children and young people's involvement in policy making. The *Children and Young People's Plan (England) Regulations 2005* placed a duty on authorities to produce a strategic overarching plan for all services affecting children and young people. The regulations explicitly state that during the preparation of the plan the authority shall consult 'such children, relevant young persons and families… as the authority consider appropriate' (sec 7(1a)). Analysis of 75 Children and Young People's Plans (CYPPs) revealed that they all indicated that the views of children and young people had informed the development of their plan (Lord et al., 2006). A number of local authorities have also used the *Hear By Right*

---

12 The UNCRC recognises 'that the family, as the fundamental group of society and the natural environment for the growth and well-being of all its members and particularly children , should be afforded the necessary protection and assistance so that it can fully assume its responsibilities within the community (UN Convention on the Rights of the Child, Preamble).

13 This is one reason cited for the United States failure to ratify the UNCRC. It can however be a barrier to effective implementation in countries that have ratified the Convention.

(Local Government Association, 2001) standards framework to assess and improve practice and policy on the active involvement of children and young people. The intention is that young people's involvement is built into the organisation.

Evidently, consultation with children and young people has expanded significantly in recent years. What is less clear, is the level of participation. Kirby and colleagues (2003) suggests that participation is a multi-layered concept and a *process*, rather than an isolated one-off participation activity or event (p.3). They identify the following levels of participation: children and young people's views taken into account (one source, amongst others that adults use to make decisions); children and young people involved in decision-making (involvement at the point a decision is made, children and adults share views and discuss issues); children and young people share power and responsibility for decision-making with adults (by negotiation, consensus or voting); children and young people making autonomous decisions (often implementation will require input from adults and is dependent on adult structures, responsibility and power) (p.22-23).

Lord and colleagues (2006) found interchangeable use of terms to describe activities with young people to inform the development of CYPPs. These included consulting, involvement, participation, engagement, listening and hearing children's thoughts and views. This may be indicative of confusion about what is expected and the differences between activities. The purpose of asking children and young people for their views differed between local authorities. In some authorities children were asked whether the CYPP reflected their views; others were asked about issues that affected them. Elsewhere, activities moved beyond this and children were asked to identify and/or agree priorities and targets (Lord et al., 2006). At governmental level there is some evidence of greater willingness to move beyond simply asking children and young people for their views and increasing their power in the process. For example, under recently announced plans, as part of a ten year youth strategy, the government has announced the intention to devolve up to five percent of youth services budgets to young people by 2010/11, rising to 25 percent by 2018 (HM Treasury, 2007).

Although there has been a drive to increase all children and young people's participation, there are indications that particular groups may be afforded more opportunities to have their views heard in relation to policy developments. These groups include, looked after children, children with disabilities, care leavers and black and minority ethnic groups. A broader range of participatory rights are also afforded to some groups. In the court arena, children in public care have a right for their ascertainable wishes and feelings to be taken into account in matters affecting them (in accordance with their age and understanding (Children Act 1989, sec 22(4)). More recently, this entitlement has been extended to children in need (Children Act 2004, sec. 53). Ironically, while these groups may have greater opportunity for involvement in decisions, in practice there may be additional barriers to effective delivery of these rights. Winter (2006) suggests that there is an inclination to focus on protection and provision when children are in care and this can undermine their participatory rights. Although there may be some way to go in social work practice to ensure that the voices of children and young people in public care are heard in practice (see among others, Leeson, 2007; Winter, 2006), looked after children may still be involved in broader range of decisions than their peers living at home.

Walker (personal communication) identifies three types of decision: day-to-day decisions, life event decisions and life decisions. Day to day decisions include decisions about pocket money or staying over night at a friend's house. Life event decisions are less frequent and take place at specific points, for example, choice of school at the point of transition from junior to secondary school. Both these types of decision are common to all children. However, life decisions cover a issues that most children living in the community generally do not have to consider, for example, where, and with whom, the child will live or whether to maintain contact with certain family members. At the same time, it has been argued that the judiciary have continued to err towards paternalistic assumptions of children's incompetence and need for protection (Freeman, 2002; Roche, 2002).

Implementation of policies is very different from seeing substantive change and progress. The need to raise awareness of children's rights and the UNCRC should not be underestimated, as lack of knowledge and awareness of the principles and purpose of it is widespread amongst the general public, professionals and children and young people in England (Willow et al., 2007). The role of the Children's Commissioner is therefore important. In 2005, the first Children's Commissioner (for England), Professor Sir Albert Aynsley-Green, was appointed. His function is promoting awareness of the views and interests of children (Children Act 2004, sec. 2(1)). The establishment of the post was recommended by the Committee on the Rights of the Child in 1995, but despite the recommendations of Select Committees and statutory and voluntary bodies, the government argued that there were already sufficient channels and mechanisms to ensure children's views were heard (for fuller discussion see Lansdown, 2002). Elsewhere in the UK, progress has been faster and Wales, Scotland and Northern Ireland established Commissioner's earlier than England.

CONCLUSION

Internationally, despite wide ranging differences in social, political and economic situations 192 countries signed up to acknowledge that children have rights, not only to 'basic physical sustenance but also, crucially, emotional nurturing, social support, health and education, the provision of information and respect for their views' (Waterston and Davies, 2006, p.635). Ratification can be seen as the 'beginning of a shift that is to take some time to become part and parcel of the world's understanding of itself' (Kennedy, 2004). A complex inter-play of factors will influence the extent to which progress is made and desired results are achieved. Hathaway (2002) notes that:

> external pressure on countries to demonstrate a commitment to human rights norms creates strong incentives for countries to engage in favourable expressive behaviour by ratifying human rights treaties. But because human treaties are generally only minimally monitored and enforced, there is little incentive for ratifying countries to make costly changes in actual policy
> (p.2020).

Indeed, it has been suggested that in the UK an 'aura of complacency' greeted the ratification of the UNCRC (Freeman, 1992). Since then progress has undoubtedly been made, although it is rather less clear that policy initiatives have been driven by a commitment to children's rights.

There are indications that the Government has been far more willing to take responsibility and to act as a 'corporate parent' to 'deserving' children and young people. Although policy developments have not necessarily been implemented with the promotion of children's rights in mind, they have generally served to improve service provision for specific groups of children and young people, including looked after children and care leavers. Arguably, children and young people identified as 'undeserving' have fared less well and there has been greater reticence on the government's part to take on the role of the 'corporate parent' for these young people. The losers in policy development and human rights terms have therefore included young offenders and asylum seeking children. This reveals how societal concerns and prevailing values and beliefs can militate against enhanced rights and entitlements for certain groups.

Variations in the provisional, protective and participatory rights afforded to different groups play out public and political tensions of children on one hand as vulnerable and needy and on the other disruptive and dangerous. Daniel and Ivatts (1998) distinguish between children and victims, children as threats and children as investments and Green (2006) identifies how:

> Conceptions of children – as good or evil, as competent or incompetent, as needing care or control, or unconsciously and uncritically played out throughout society with children (p.82).

The balance between the rights and interests of society, the family and the individual child are not consistent and shift, influenced by these classifications and political agendas and public concerns. Notwithstanding these contradictions, patchy progress and the fact that changes have not necessarily been motivated by a desire to promote children's rights, positive developments have taken place. Retrospectively, legislative and policy changes are now examined to determine how they measure up to the UNCRC. A Children's Commissioner has been appointed and investment and policy developments signify a commitment to reducing social exclusion. This should enhance children's provisional and protective rights. Children in need and in care have also seen an expansion in the opportunities they are given to express their views. The tide is perhaps turning, and the UNCRC is a useful benchmark that individuals, national and international groups can use to monitor government compliance and highlight areas of weakness.

REFERENCES

Aynsley-Green, A. (2006). Memorandum from the Office for the Children's Commissioner to the Joint Committee on Human Rights on the Treatment of Asylum Seekers. 29 September 2006.

Ben-Arieh, A. and Boyer, Y. (2005). Citizenship and Childhood: The state of affairs in Israel. *Childhood*. 12 (1), 33-53.

Bercow J., Lord Dubs and Harris, E. (2006). Alternatives to immigration detention of families and children, A discussion paper for the All Party Parliamentary Groups on Children and Refugees, Supported by the No Place for a Child Coalition, July 2006. Available at http://www.biduk.org/pdf/res_reports/alternatives_to_detention_july_2006.pdf

Biehal, N., Clayden, J., Stein, M. and Wade, J. (1995). *Moving On: Young People and Leaving Care Schemes*. London: HMSO.

Bradbury, B. and Jantti, M. (1999). *Child Poverty Across Industrialised Nations. Innocenti Occasional Papers, Economic and Social Policy Series no. 71.* Available at http://www.unicef-icdc.org/publications/pdf/eps71.pdf

Bradshaw, J. (2005). Child poverty and deprivation. In: J. Bradshaw and E. Mayhew (Eds.) The Well-being of Children in the UK (2nd edition, pp.35-64). London: Save the Children.

Butler, J. (2000). The Christian right coalition and the UN special session on children: Prospects and strategies. *The International Journal of Children's Rights,* 8, 351-371.

Cabinet Office (2007). Reaching Out: Think Family: Analysis and themes from the families at risk review. Available at http://www.cabinetoffice.gov.uk /social_exclusion_task_force/documents/think_families/think_families.pdf

Cemlyn, S. and Briskman, L. (2003). Asylum, children's rights and social work. *Child and Family Social Work*, 8, 163-178.

Children Act 1989 (1989). London: HMSO.

Children Act 2004 (2004). London: The Stationery Office.

Children (Leaving Care) Act 2000 (2000). London: The Stationery Office.

CO United Kingdom of Great Britain and Northern Ireland (2002). *Concluding Observation: United Kingdom of Great Britain and Northern Ireland,* CRC/C/15/Add.188, 9th October 2002.

Crawley, H. (2007). *When is a child not a child? Asylum age disputes and the process of age assessment.* Swansea University for the Immigration Law Practitioners' Association (ILPA) (www.ilpa.org.uk).

Cummings, C., Dyson, A., Papps, I., Pearson, D., Raffo, C., Tiplady, L. and Todd, L. (2006). Evaluation of the Full Service Extended Schools initiative, second year: Thematic papers. London: Department for Education and Skills.

Daniel, P. and Ivatts, J. (1998). *Children and Social Policy*. Basingstoke: Macmillan

Dennis, J. (2002). A case for change: How refugee children in England are missing out. London: Children's Society/Save the Children/Refugee Council.

Department for Education and Skills (2006a). *National Statistics: Children Looked After in England (including adoptions and care leavers), 2005-2006.* London: DfES.

Department for Education and Skills (2006b). *National Statistics: National Curriculum Assessment, GCSE and Equivalent Attainment and Post-16 Attainment by Pupil Characteristics in England 2005/06).* London: DfES.

Department for Work and Pensions (2006). *Opportunity for all. Eight annual report 2006, strategy document.* London: Department for Work and Pensions.

Department of Health (1998). *Modernising Health and Social Services: National Priorities Guidance 1999/00-2001/2*. London: Department of Health.

Dobrowolsky, A. (2002). Rhetoric versus reality: the figure of the child and New Labour's strategic "social investment state". *Studies in Political Economy,* Autumn, 43-73.

Dolowitz, D. with Hulme, R. Nellis, M. and O'Neal, F. (2000). *Policy Transfer and British Social Policy*. Buckingham: Open University Press.

Fawcett, B., Featherstone, B. and Goddard, J. (2003). *From the Womb to the Workplace: Child Welfare under New Labour.* Paper resented to the *Annual Conference of the Social Policy Association*, 15 July, Middlesbrough: University of Teeside.

Franklin, B. (2002). Children's rights and media wrongs: Changing representations of children and the developing rights agenda. In: B. Franklin (Ed.), *The New Handbook of Children's Rights. Comparative policy and practice* (pp.15-42). Abingdon, Oxon: Routledge.

Freeman, M. (1992). Taking children's rights more seriously. In: P. Alston, S. Parker, and J. Seymour. (Eds.), *Children, Rights and the Law* (pp.52-71). Oxford: Clarendon Press.

Freeman, M. (2002). Children's rights ten years after ratification. In: B. Franklin (Ed.), *The New Handbook of Children's Rights. Comparative policy and practice* (pp.97-118). Abingdon, Oxon: Routledge.

Fortin, J. (1998). *Children's Rights and the Developing Law.* London: Butterworths.

Fox-Harding, L. (1996). *Family, State and Social Policy.* London: Macmillan.

Gelsthorpe, L. and Morris, A. (1999). Much Ado About Nothing - a critical comment on key provisions relating to children in the Crime and Disorder Act 1998. *Child and Family Law,* 11 (3), 209-221.

Goldthorpe, L. (2004). Every Child Matters: A legal perspective. *Child Abuse Review,* 13, 115-136.

Green, L. (2006). An overwhelming sense of injustice? An exploration of child sexual abuse in relation to the concept of justice. *Critical Social Policy,* 26 (1), 74-100.

Hammarberg, T. (1990). The U.N. Convention on the Rights of the Child – And How to Make it Work. *Human Rights Quarterly,* 12, 97-105.

Hathaway, O. A. (2002). Do Human Rights Treaties make a difference? *Yale Law Journal,* 111, 1935-2042.

Henricson, C. and Bainham, A. (2005). *The Child and Family Policy Divide – tensions, convergence and rights.* Joseph Rowntree Foundation, York.
Available at http://www.jrf.org.uk/Knowledge/findings/socialpolicy/0255.asp.

HM Treasury (2007). *Aiming high for young people: A ten year strategy for positive activities.* London: HM treasury. Available at
http://www.hm-treasury.gov.uk/media/2/8/cyp_tenyearstrategy_260707.pdf.

HM Government (2003). *Every Child Matters.* Norwich: The Stationery Office. Available at
http://www.everychildmatters.gov.uk/_files/EBE7EEAC90382663E0D5BBF24C99A7AC.pdf.

HM Government (2007a). *Reaching Out: An Action Plan on Social Exclusion.* London: The Cabinet Office, Social Exclusion Task Force. Available at http://www.cabinetoffice.gov.uk/social_exclusion_task_force/publications/reaching_out/

HM Government (2007b). *Care Matters: Time for Change.* London: The Stationery Office.

House of Commons Hansard debates for 13 September 2004.

Howard-Hassmann, R. E. (2005). The second great transformation: Human rights leapfrogging in the global era of globalization. *Human Rights Quarterly,* 27 (1), 1-40.

Hudson, J. and Lowe, S. (2004). *Understanding the policy process: Analysing welfare policy and practice.* Bristol: Policy Press.

Human Rights Act 1998 (1998). London: The Stationery Office.

Instituto degli Innocenti (2006). *Survey on the CRC Committee's concluding observations on the last EU Countries' reports.* Firenze: Instituto degli Innocenti.

Kennedy, T. I. (2004). *Children and the CRC.* Paper presented at the 46th International FICE Congress, September 2004. Available at
http://www.sircc.strath.ac.uk/fice2004/presentations/Children%20and%20the%20CRC.pdf

Kilbourne, S. (1998). The wayward Americans – Why the USA has not ratified the UN Convention on the Rights of the Child. *International Family Law*, 104-112.

Kirby, P. Lanyon, C., Cronin, K. and Sinclair, R. (2003). *Building a culture of participation. Involving children and young people in policy, service planning, delivery and evaluation. Research report.* London: Department for Education and Skills.

Laming, Lord (2003). The Victoria Climbié Inquiry Report. London: TSO.

Lansdown, G. (1995). *Taking Part: Children's Participation in Decision Making.* London: Institute for Public Policy Research.

Lansdown, G. (2002). Children's Rights Commissioners for the UK. In B. Franklin (Ed.), *The New Handbook of Children's Rights: Comparative policy and practice.* (pp. 285-297). Oxford: Routledge.

Lansdown, G. and Karkara, R. (2006). Children's right to express views and have them taken seriously. *The Lancet*, 367 (February 25), 690-691.

Leeson, C. (2007). My life in care: Experiences of non-participation in decision-making processes. *Child and Family Social Work*, 12 (3), 268-277.

Lister, R. (2003). Investing in the Citizen-workers of the Future: Transformations in Citizenship and the State under New Labour. *Social Policy and Administration 37*, 5, 427-443.

Lister, R. (2006). Children (but not women) first: New labour, child welfare and gender. *Critical Social Policy*, 26, 315-335.

Local Government Association (2001). *Hear by right: setting standards for the active involvement of young people in democracy.* Local Government Association (in partnership with the National Youth Agency. Available at http://www.lga.gov.uk/lga/blg/HearbyRight.pdf

Lord, P., Wilkin, A., Kinder, K., Murfield, J., Jones, M., Chamberlain, T., Easton, C., Martin, K., Gulliver, K., Paterson, K., Ries, J., Moor, H., Stott, A., Wilkin, C. and Stoney, S. (2006). *Analysis of Children and Young People's Plans 2006.* Slough: NFER.

Lyon, C. (2007). Children's Rights and the UNCRC and ECHR: Interrogating the concentration on the UNCRC instead of the ECHR. *Children and Society*, 21 (1), 221-229.

McDonald, A. (2007). The impact of the UK Human Rights Act 1998 on Decision Making in Adult Social Care in England and Wales. *Ethics and Social Welfare*, 1 (1), 76-94.

Minoff, E. (2006). *The UK Commitment: Ending Child Poverty by 2020.* Washington: Center for Law and Social Policy. (www.clasp.org).

Muncie, J. (1999). Institutionalized intolerance: Youth justice and the 1998 Crime and Disorder Act. *Critical Social Policy*, 19 (2), 147-175.

Munro, E. (2007). Confidentiality in a preventative child welfare system. *Ethics and Social Welfare*, 1 (1), 41-55.

O'Brien, M., Bachmann, M. Husbands, C., Shreeve, A. Jones., N., Watson, J. and Shemilt, I. (2006). Integrating Children's Services to Promote Children's Welfare: Early Findings from the Implementation of Children's Trusts in England. *Child Abuse Review*, 15, 377-395.

Pais, M. S. and Bissell, S. (2006). Overview and implementation of the UN Convention on the Rights of the Child. *The Lancet*, 367 (February 25), 689-90.

Parton, N. (2006). 'Every Child Matters': The shift to prevention whilst strengthening protection in children's services in England. *Children and Youth Services Review*, 28, 976-992.

Payne, L. (2003). So how are we doing? A review of the concluding observations of the UN committee on the rights of the child: UK. *Children and Society*, 17 (1), 71-74.

Pinheiro, P. S. (2007). *World Report on Violence Against Children*. Geneva: United Nations Secretary-General's Study on Violence against Children. Available at http://www.violencestudy.org/IMG/pdf/I._World_Report_on_Violence_against_Chidren.pdf.

Prout, A. (2001). Representing children: reflections on the children 5-16 programme. *Children and Society*, 15, 193-201.

Roche, J. (1999). Children: Rights, participation and citizenship. *Childhood*, 6 (4), 475-493.

Roche, J. (2002). The Children Act 1989 and children's rights. A critical reassessment. In B. Franklin (Ed.), *The New Handbook of Children's Rights: Comparative Policy and Practice* (pp. 60-80). Abingdon: Routledge.

Rutkow. L. and Lozman, J. T. (2006). Suffer the children?: A call for United States ratification of the United Nations Convention on the Rights of the Child. *Harvard Human Rights Journal*, 19, 123-160.

Sanders, R. and Mace, S. (2006). Agency policy and the participation of children and young people in the child protection process. *Child Abuse Review*, 15 (2), 89-109.

Skevik, A. (2003). Children in the welfare state: Individuals with entitlements, or hidden in the family? *Journal of Social Policy*, 32 (3), 423-440.

Smith, R. (2003). *Youth Justice: Ideas, Policy and Practice*. Cullompton: Willan.

Stein, M. (2004). *What Works for Young People Leaving Care?* Barkingside: Barnardos.

Such, E. and Walker, R. (2005). Young citizens or policy objects? Children in the 'rights and responsibilities' debate. *Journal of Social Policy*, 34 (1) 39-57.

UK Government. (2007). *The Consolidated 3rd and 4th Periodic Report to UN Committee on the Rights of the Child*. Available at http://www.everychildmatters.gov.uk /_ files /09796A5425218FB5DB5FEEE49AC9E858.pdf.

UNICEF (1998). *Implementation Handbook for the Convention on the Rights of the Child*. New York: UNICEF.

UNICEF (2005). *Changing a harmful social convention: female genital mutilation/cutting. Innocenti Digest*. Florence: UNICEF Innocenti Research Centre.

UNICEF (2007a). *Child poverty in perspective: An overview of child well-being in rich countries, Innocenti Report Card 7, 2007*. Florence: UNICEF Innocenti Research Centre.

UNICEF (2007b). United Kingdom's 3rd Quinquennial report to the UN Committee on the Rights of the Child. Submission from UNICEF UK. Available at http://www.unicef.org.uk/aboutus/ukdfes.doc.

United Nations (2000). General Assembly. *Millennium Declaration*. New York.

United Nations (2002). General Assembly. *A World Fit for Children*. New York.

Wade, J. and Munro, E. R. (2008). Leaving Care in the United Kingdom. In: M. Stein and E.R. Munro (Eds.), *Young People's Transitions from Care to Adulthood: International Research and Practice*. London: Jessica Kingsley Publishers.

Walker, S. (personal communication). Unpublished MA thesis on looked after children's perceptions and experiences of decision making. University of East Anglia.

Ward, H. and Munro, E. R. (2005). *Legal frameworks and administrative structures.* Briefing paper presented at an international seminar on 'Transitions to Adulthood of Care leavers' November. Queen's University: Belfast.

Waterston, T. and Davies, R. (2006) The Convention on the Rights of the Child. *The Lancet,* 367 (February 25), 635.

WHO (2003). *Hope for 11 million children facing death from illnesses.* News Release: http://www.who.int/mediacentre/news/releases/2003/prwha5/en/index.html

WHO (2006a). *Global Estimates of Health Consequences Due to Violence Against Children.* Background Paper to the UN Secretary-General's Study on Violence against Children. Geneva: World Health Organisation.

WHO (2006b). *Global Estimates of Health Consequences Due to Violence Against Children.* Background Paper to the UN Secretary-General's Study on Violence against Children. Geneva: World Health Organisation. Based on estimates by Andrews, G. et al. (2004) Child Sexual Abuse. Ch. 23. In M. Ezzati et al. (2004) *Comparative Quantification of Health Risks: Global and Regional Burden of Disease Attributable to Selected Major Risk Factors.* (Vol 2, pp. 1851-1940), Geneva: WHO, and using UN population division data for the population under 18 years.

Williams, F. (2004). 'What matters is who works: Why every child matters to New Labour. Commentary on the DfES Green Paper "Every Child Matters."' *Critical Social Policy,* 24 (3), 406-427.

Willow, C., Franklin, A. and Shaw, C. (2007). *Meeting the obligations of the Convention on the Rights of the Child. Children and young people's messages to Government.* Children's Rights Alliance for England, National Children's Bureau, UNICEF and Save the Children, commissioned by Department for Education and Skills. Available at http://www.nspcc.org.uk/Inform/policyandpublicaffairs/CYP_Msg_to_Govt_wdf48658.p df.

Winter, K. (2006). The participation rights of looked after children in their health care: A critical review of the research. *International Journal of Children's Rights*, 14, 77-95.

Wintersberger, H. (1999). Developments in International Law and European Policies. In B. Riepl and H. Wintersberg (Eds.), *Political Participation of Youth Below Voting Age* (pp.14-39). Vienna: European Centre for Social Welfare Policy and Research.

Wringe, C. (1995). Children's welfare rights: a philosopher's view. In: M. John (Ed.) *Children in Our Charge: The Child's Right to Resources.* London: Jessica Kingsley Publishers.

In: Human Rights Issues in the 21st Century ISBN 978-1-60456-119-7
Editors: M.S. Becker and J.N. Schneider, pp. 151-166

Chapter 7

EXPLAINING OPPOSITION TO RIGHTS FOR INDIVIDUALS WITH DISABILITIES: THE ROLES OF CULTURAL CONSERVATISM, RELIGIOUS OPENNESS (VERSUS CLOSED-NESS), AND DANGEROUS WORLD BELIEFS

H. Michael Crowson[1] and Joyce A. Brandes
The University of Oklahoma, USA

ABSTRACT

This chapter describes a test of a path model in which attitudes toward disability rights were predicted by religious fundamentalism, quest (religious) orientation, cultural conservatism, and belief in a dangerous world. Within the proposed model, dangerous world beliefs were expected to indirectly predict opposition to disability rights through several mediating variables: religious fundamentalism, quest orientation, and cultural conservatism. Additionally, the effects of fundamentalism and quest orientation on opposition to disability rights were expected to be mediated through cultural conservatism. Although quest orientation failed to mediate the relationship between dangerous world beliefs and cultural conservatism (or even to add incremental validity to the prediction of cultural conservatism) in our study, the remaining proposed relationships were supported by the data. Following re-specification of our path model, religious fundamentalism was found to exert an indirect positive effect on opposition to disability rights through cultural conservatism while also exerting a negative direct effect on disability rights opposition.

[1] Correspondence regarding this chapter should be addressed to the first author: Mike Crowson, Ph.D. Department of Educational Psychology, The University of Oklahoma, 820 Van Vleet Oval, Norman, OK 73019-2041,Phone: (405) 325-8795, Fax: (405) 325-6655, email: mcrowson@ou.edu.

INTRODUCTION

A well-documented finding within social and political psychology is that persons who hold culturally conservative views and/or are fundamentalist in their religious beliefs are more likely to exhibit prejudicial attitudes toward societal outgroups than those with less conservative or fundamentalist views. Empirically, measures incorporating a strong cultural conservatism[2] component have been shown to be related to prejudice toward a variety of ethnic-racial groups (Altemeyer, 1996; Cornelis and Van Hiel, 2006; Heaven and St. Quintin, 2003; Van Hiel and Mervielde, 2002; Van Hiel, Pandalaere, and Duriez, 2004), as well as women (Bäckström and Björklund, 2007; Whitley and Ǽgisdóttir, 2000) and non-normative groups such as homosexuals (Hunsberger, 1996; Whitley, 1999), rock stars, and feminists (Duckitt, 2006). These measures also appear to be positively related to support for restricting human rights and civil liberties (Cohrs, Kielmann, Maes, Moschner, 2005; Crowson, in press; Crowson, DeBacker, and Thoma, 2005, 2006; McFarland and Matthews, 2005; Moghaddam and Vuksanovic, 1990) and the use of aggression against groups believed to pose threats to in-groups (Cohrs, Moschner, Maes, and Kielmann, 2005; McFarland, 2005).

Individuals who hold fundamentalist attitudes have also been shown to exhibit greater levels of ethnic-racial prejudice, religious ethnocentrism, and prejudice against homosexuals (Altemeyer, 2004, 2007; Altemeyer and Hunsberger, 1992; Laythe, Finkel, and Kirckpatrick, 2001; Rowatt, Tsang, Kelly, LaMartina, McCullers, and McKinley, 2006) and to be less willing to grant civil liberties or support human rights for unpopular groups in society (McFarland and Matthews, 2005; Reimer and Park, 2001). In general, the existing research literature paints a picture of cultural conservatives and religious fundamentalists as "equal-opportunity bigots" (Altemeyer, 1998) who react negatively against a variety of perceived societal outgroups.

Despite these findings, there appears to be little research available on the relationships between cultural conservatism and fundamentalism and attitudes related to individuals with disabilities. Furthermore, there seems to be little available research linking more general beliefs and perceptions about the social world (i.e., in terms of dangerousness) and religious openness to attitudes related to persons with disabilities. In the current study, we reasoned that individuals who believe that the world is a dangerous place may be less inclined to react favorably to granting rights to persons with disabilities, while those who are more open to diverse religious experiences may react more positively to granting those same rights. This chapter describes our test of a path model (see Figure 1) in which attitudes toward disability rights are predicted by religious fundamentalism, quest (religious) orientation, cultural conservatism, and belief in a dangerous world. We hypothesized that the effects of belief in a dangerous world on opposition to disability rights would be mediated through religious

[2] Within the fields of social and political psychology, there has been a longstanding debate (e.g., Crowson, Thoma, & Hestevold, 2005; Ray, 1985; Van Hiel, Cornelis, Roets, & De Clercq, 2007) about the conceptual and empirical distinctiveness of conservative ideology and a related variable, right-wing authoritarianism (RWA). Conceptually, one of the three attitudinal clusters that make up RWA is conventionalism, and many of the items embedded within the RWA scale could also serve as indicators of cultural conservatism (Feldman, 2003). Additionally, cultural conservatism has been postulated by Duckitt (2001) to represent one of two (the other being economic conservatism) dimensions of social attitudes – a dimension within which RWA appears to be located (see review in Van Hiel, Cornelis, & Roets, 2007 for further detail). For these reasons, we refer to the literatures addressing RWA and/or cultural conservatism when discussing relationships between cultural conservatism and prejudice in this chapter.

fundamentalism, quest orientation, and cultural conservatism, whereas the effects of fundamentalism and quest orientation on those rights would be mediated (at least partially) through cultural conservatism. Below, we provide our reasoning behind the proposed path model.

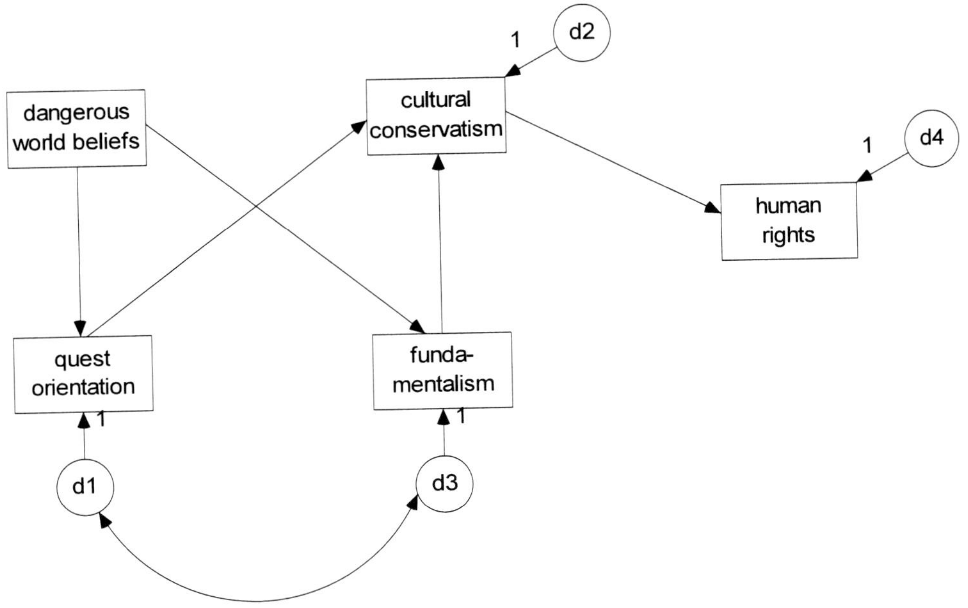

Figure 1. Hypothesized model.

Dangerous World Beliefs: An Indirect Predictor of Disability Rights?

Dangerous world beliefs (DWB) refer to a worldview characterized by the belief that the social world is constantly teetering on the edge of chaos and social disorder. According to models proposed by Duckitt and colleagues (Duckitt, 2001; Duckitt, Wagner, du Plessis, and Birum, 2002; Duckitt, 2006), these beliefs arise as a function of an enduring need for social conformity that is situated in one's personality organization, as well as situational or social contexts that activate concerns about the social world. Presumably, these beliefs influence behavior through the mediating function of social attitudes that are, themselves, oriented toward establishing societal security, stability, and order (Duckitt, 2006). In effect, one of the primary outcomes of DWB seems to be a rigid, conventional, and authoritarian style of relating to the world – manifested in the adoption of conservative and fundamentalist social ideologies (Duckitt et al., 2002).

As noted previously, in generating our path model we reasoned that individuals who perceive the social world as a dangerous and threatening place may be more likely to oppose rights for persons with disabilities than those who do not hold this view. This was based on two considerations. First, assuming that individuals high in DWB tend to view society as under constant threat of disintegrating into chaos, we reasoned that the need to maintain tight social control could translate into a form of prejudice that generalizes to all perceived outgroups in society – including persons who have disabilities. Although there has been little direct empirical study of the association between DWB and generalized outgroup prejudice, the evidence from several studies provides indirect support this contention. For example, an examination of the correlation matrices presented by Duckitt et al. (2002) indicates that DWB was a statistically significant positive correlate of generalized outgroup prejudice in their American sample (Study 1) and prejudice against two racial outgroups and a preference for the majority racial in-group in a South African sample (Study 2).

The second consideration was based the possibility that *any* group proposing societal changes that might require overriding established norms may be perceived by those holding DWB less favorably. Indeed, even if individuals with disabilities are not considered as constituting an outgroup per se, the assertion by these individuals or advocates that "special rights" or "privileges" are needed in society in order to gain greater access could be perceived by those high in DWB as consistent with the view that the foundations upon which society are built are crumbling.

Dangerous World Beliefs: A Direct Predictor of Religious Orientations?

In our hypothesized model, we expected that those individuals scoring higher on DWB would also exhibit greater levels of religious fundamentalism and lower levels of quest-orientated religiosity. With respect to fundamentalism, Altemeyer and Hunsberger (1992) defined this construct as "the belief that there is one set of religious teachings that clearly contains the fundamental, basic, intrinsic, essential, inerrant truth about humanity and deity", that this truth is under constant attack by forces of evil and "must be vigorously fought", and that one has a "special relationship with the deity" (p. 118). Conceptually, fundamentalism differs from religious orthodoxy since it primarily refers to the *ways* in which one's beliefs are held (Altemeyer, 1996, 2007), whereas orthodoxy refers to the degree of congruence between one's beliefs and a set of orthodox teachings and/or credos (Fullerton and Hunsberger, 1982). Based on this distinction, a person can hold orthodox beliefs without necessarily holding the view that those beliefs contain inerrant truths that are under constant threat from the outside. Furthermore, this conceptual distinction suggests that individuals maintaining a fundamentalist outlook may be more likely to hold prejudicial attitudes than those who simply hold orthodox beliefs.

Quest, on the other hand, refers to an open-ended approach to religion (Klaassen and McDonald, 2002) that is not a matter of "agnosticism, of anti-orthodoxy, of sophomoric religious doubt, or of religious conflict" (Batson and Schoenrade, 1991b). In effect, quest "involves honestly facing existential questions in their complexity, while at the same time resisting clear cut, pat answers" (p. 417). This definition suggests that the beliefs that quest-oriented individuals hold are considerably more fluid and open than those held by fundamentalists. One may question whether fundamentalism and quest orientation are really two-sides of the same conceptual coin – openness versus closed-ness of religious beliefs, respectively. Empirical evidence, however, suggests that they are not, with measures of these constructs exhibiting a fair amount of discriminant validity – "digging away" at their own particular aspect of religiosity[3] (Altemeyer and Husberger, 1992).

The reasoning behind the proposed predictive relationship between DWB and fundamentalism stems from the observation that fundamentalism is inherently about rigidity that is reflected in an intolerance of worldviews that contradict one's religious beliefs. If the belief that the world is a dangerous place motivates individuals towards holding beliefs in a manner that provides greater security, stability, and order, then fundamentalism would appear a reasonable candidate for meeting that need. This contention is supported by a recently obtained correlation between DWB and fundamentalism of .47 (p.>001) in a sample of 149 community adults (Crowson, unpublished data).

On the other hand, one can reason that the openness to religious doubts and questioning inherent in those who are more quest-oriented must be driven by different, or at least opposing, motives than those found with persons who score high on fundamentalism. Indeed, if high levels of DWB lead individuals to adopt more rigid and authoritarian belief systems, then it seems reasonable to assume that persons scoring lower on DWB will tend to be more open regarding their religious beliefs, presumably due to the lack of perceived need to establish absolute control over their social environments. This assertion is also supported by recent data in which quest orientation correlated with DWB at -.39 ($p<.001$) in a sample of community adults (Crowson, unpublished data).

Fundamentalism and Quest Orientation: Direct Predictors of Cultural Conservatism?

In addition to the abovementioned predictive relationships, we also reasoned that religious fundamentalism and quest orientation would emerge as statistically significant predictors of cultural conservatism. Cultural conservatism can be described as a set of beliefs and values that are oriented towards conforming to traditional social norms, as well as respect for conventional authorities (Van Hiel, Cornelis, Roets, and De Clerq, 2007) who support those norms. This is reflected in attitudes that encompass opposition to homosexuality, pre-marital sex, feminism, and the "right-to-die", as well as support for more authoritarian forms of parenting (Feldman, 2003). Additional contents seem to include the Protestant Work Ethic that incorporates beliefs about human value based on their willingness and capacity to work (Cokley, Kommaraju, Pickett, Shen, Patel, et al., 2007).

Given that many of the socio-political attitudes people express appear to flow from their religious (as well as other moral systems), we expected that fundamentalism and quest would emerge as significant predictors of cultural conservatism in our model. This was based on the reasoning that religious close-mindedness (i.e., fundamentalism) should direct individuals to adopt and maintain socio-political attitudes and beliefs that are (a) consistent with literal interpretations of religious dogma and (b) that are held with absolute certainty. Generally, individuals holding more culturally conservative socio-political attitudes also score higher on fundamentalism (Altemeyer, 1996). Religious openness, reflected in quest orientation, should have a contrary effect on the adoption of culturally conservative attitudes. Based on our

[3] Although empirically these variables appear distinct, we reasoned that they share enough conceptual overlap to justify correlating these factors in our path model (see Figure 1).

reasoning, we expected that persons scoring higher on fundamentalism and lower on quest orientation would score higher on cultural conservatism.

Cultural Conservatism and Opposition to Disability Rights

As discussed earlier, scales explicitly incorporating aspects of cultural conservatism have consistently been linked to prejudice and discrimination against societal outgroups within the empirical literature. In the current study, we reasoned that this finding may generalize to attitudes reflecting opposition to rights for persons with disabilities. Two possibilities guided our reasoning.

First, the strong valuing of social conformity, tradition, and security among individuals endorsing culturally conservative attitudes logically reflects the influence of DWB on ideological orientation. To the degree that the influence of DWB is "transmitted" through the mediating variables, quest and fundamentalism, one would expect cultural conservatives to fear societal changes that could arise by bestowing "new" rights. In other words, even if individuals with disabilities do not constitute a well-defined societal "outgroup", cultural conservatives may oppose increasing rights for these individuals out of fear of the changes that may take place.

On the other hand, the ideology of cultural conservatism could embody propositions that may, in theory, result in explicit categorization of persons with disabilities as outgroup members. This may have the effect of reducing support for human rights if these are perceived as providing accommodations for deficiencies that are either (a) deserved or (b) to be overcome. In our model, religious fundamentalism is assumed to function as a positive predictor of cultural conservatism. Beliefs that fundamentalists may hold include the belief that personal misfortune arises from one's own misdeeds or those of others – as reflected in the notion that "the sins of the father are visited down upon the son" – and/or that people become stronger as they struggle with life's misfortunes – as reflected in struggles encountered by Job (Weisel and Zaidman, 2003). In both cases, expanding rights for persons who have disabilities could be viewed as challenging God's will as He teaches individuals and families to be more faithful servants.

One other aspect of cultural conservatism that may bear on its proposed association with disability rights is the Protestant Work Ethic (PWE). According to Cokley, Kommaraju, Pickett, Shen, Patel, et al. (2007), the PWE is "a value system that stresses the moral value of work, self-discipline, and individual responsibility in forming a way to improve one's economic well-being" and whose central feature is the "notion that the success of an individual reflects his or her inner virtue" (p. 76). At its core, this value system suggests that individual worth is not to be bestowed or given by others, but rather earned by the individual him/herself. Assuming that the expansion of human rights in society is something that is given by others, we reasoned that persons scoring high on cultural conservatism would be more likely to oppose these rights than those scoring low on this factor.

METHODS

Participants

Our sample was comprised of 236 participants [males (n = 113), females (n = 121); 2 did not report gender] from the Mid-western United States who were sampled during the spring of 2007. Participants' ages ranged from 17 to 75 (Mean = 35.65, SD = 12.05), with 70% of the sample identifying themselves as White, 9% as African American, 4.2% as American Indian or Alaska Native, 5.1% as Asian, and 4.2% as multiracial or multiethnic. Six percent of our sample had only completed high school, while 31% reported attending some college (which includes community college). Of the remaining participants, 25% reported graduating college, 11% reported some graduate school experience, 23% reported graduating with a master's degree or equivalent, and 4% reported graduating with a doctorate or equivalent.

Measures

Participants responded to all measures in this study using a response format ranging from 1 (strongly disagree) to 7 (strongly agree). Cronbach's alphas for the measures are presented in Table 1.

Table 1. Descriptive Statistics

Variable	Description	Mean	SD	Cronbach's α
1. DWB	Dangerous world beliefs	3.871	.910	.76
2. Funda	Religious fundamentalism	4.098	1.606	.93
3. Quest	Quest orientation	3.704	1.113	.83
4. HR	Opposition to disability rights	2.508	.997	.83
5. CC	Cultural conservatism	3.694	.987	.77

Cultural Conservatism Scale (De Witte, 1990; translated for English use by I. Cornelis and A. Van Hiel). This 12-item scale measures various facets of culturally conservative attitudes and beliefs. Although this scale has not been utilized in previous research within English language samples, this scale has routinely been shown to demonstrate good construct validity in Flemish speaking samples, correlating predictably with measures of authoritarianism and racism (e.g., Cornelis and Van Hiel, 2006; Van Hiel et al., 2007; Van Hiel et al., 2004). In terms of content validity, items on the measure demonstrate considerable overlap with characteristics identified by Feldman (2003) as reflective of culturally conservative beliefs. Items from the scale include "Abortion should remain illegal under all circumstances", "Working hard makes you a better person", "It is best for parents to be strict when raising their children".

Revised Religious Fundamentalism Scale (Altemeyer and Hunsberger, 2004). This scale was a shortened form of a measure originally developed by Altemeyer and Hunsberger in 1992. This scale contains twelve items measuring the belief that there is only one set of true teachings regarding "humanity and deity" that are at under constant attack by evil forces and that must be vigorously defended. Items include "God has given humanity a complete and unfailing guide to happiness and salvation, which must be totally followed", "The basic cause of evil in this world is Satan, who is still constantly and ferociously fighting against God", and It is more important to be a good person than to believe in God and the right religion" (reverse scored).

Quest Scale (Batson, and Schoenrade, 1991a). This twelve item scale was designed to measure an approach to religion such that one "recognizes he or she does not know, and probably never will know, the final truth about...[existential] matters" (Batson, and Schoenrade, 1991b, p. 418). Items from the scale include "It might be said that I value my religious doubts and uncertainties", "For me, doubting is an important part of what it means to be religious", and "There are many religious issues on which my views are still changing".

Dangerous World Beliefs Scale (Duckitt et al., 2002). This ten item scale – eight of which were drawn from Altemeyer's (1988) Belief in a Dangerous World Scale – measures the belief that the social world is a dangerous and threatening place, one that teeters on the edge of chaos and social disorder. Example items from the scale include "Any day now chaos and anarchy could erupt around us. All the signs are pointing to it", "If a person takes a few sensible precautions, nothing bad is likely to happen to him or her" (reverse scored), and "It seems that every year there are fewer and fewer truly respectable people, and more and more persons with no morals at all who threaten everyone else".

Opposition to Human Rights – D Scale. This twelve item scale was formulated specifically for the purposes of the present study in order to measure opposition to human rights for persons with disabilities. Example items include "It is unreasonable to expect that an individual with a disability should have the same employment opportunities as a person who does not have a disability", "The challenges that students with disabilities face far outweigh the value of educating them in the public schools", "People who have disabilities should not be allowed to have children", and "Disability-rights advocates help to strengthen our society" (reverse scored).

Procedures

Adult participants were recruited by graduate students enrolled in statistics courses taught by the first author. Students were asked to seek out approximately equal numbers of males and females and to enlist only those whom they believed would provide thoughtful answers to questionnaires. Those individuals agreeing to participate in the study were administered a packet containing a copy of a questionnaire and a letter from the first author describing the research project. Upon completing their packets, participants returned them to the graduate student researcher who recruited them.

RESULTS

Descriptive Statistics

Descriptive statistics are provided in Table 1. In general, participants scored at the scale midpoint on fundamentalism, while scoring slightly below the scale midpoint on DWB, quest orientation, and cultural conservatism. The average score for opposition to disability rights was the lowest of all the measures.

Correlation Analysis

Table 2 contains the correlations among the variables in this study. Consistent with expectations, DWB were positively correlated with fundamentalism and cultural conservatism and negatively correlated with quest orientation. Also as expected, DWB was positively correlated with opposition to human rights for persons with disabilities, although this correlation was small. Fundamentalism exhibited a strong positive correlation with cultural conservatism, while demonstrating a fairly strong negative correlation with quest orientation. Unexpectedly, fundamentalism and quest orientation were both unrelated to opposition to disability rights. Finally, consistent with expectations quest orientation was negatively correlated with cultural conservatism.

Table 2. Correlation coefficients

	1	2	3	4	5
1. DWB	-	.358***	-.207**	.156*	.219**
2. Funda		-	-.450***	.033	.540***
3. Quest			-	-.094	-.291***
4. HR				-	.304***
5. CC					-

Note. *$p<.05$, **$p<.01$, ***$p\leq.001$.

Path Analysis

We tested the fit of our hypothesized model using AMOS 6.0. Missing data were treated using full-information maximum likelihood (FIML) estimation that comes standard in the AMOS program. The overall model fit for our model was assessed by consulting three primary fit indices: χ^2/df ratio, Root-mean square error of approximation (RMSEA), and Comparative fit index (CFI). The χ^2/df ratio functions as an index of absolute model fit with values close to 1 indicating greater overall fit. According to Schumacker and Lomax (2004), values less than 5 indicate reasonable model fit. The RMSEA also serves as an index of absolute fit, yet also incorporates a penalty for less parsimonious models. Values falling at .06 or below are generally considered indicating of well-fitting models, whereas values falling between .06 and .08 are generally considered "acceptable" (Kline, 2005). The CFI indexes the degree of improvement of a hypothesized model over a null model (i.e., variables are considered to be uncorrelated). Values falling around .95 are considered to indicate optimal model fit (Hu and Bentler, 1999).

Table 3 contains the fit indices associated with the test of our hypothesized model. Both the chi-square degrees of freedom ratio and CFI values indicated that the hypothesized model fit the data well. Additionally, although the RMSEA value was slightly higher than typically preferred, it nevertheless was non-significant (p=.158) when subjected to a test of close fit. An evaluation of the path coefficients revealed that only one path coefficient was not statistically significant [b = -.052, SE = .056, β = -.095, p = .352] in the model – that running from quest orientation to cultural conservatism. In the model, DWB accounted for statistically significant [b = .634, SE = .110, β = .359, p<.001] variation in fundamentalism scores, while fundamentalism accounted for statistically significant variation in cultural conservatism [b = .315, SE = .039, β = .512, p<.001]. Dangerous world beliefs was a significant [b = -.255, SE = .080, β = -.209, p = .001] predictor of quest orientation, while cultural conservatism significantly [b = .311, SE = .064, β = .307, p < .001] predicted opposition to human rights for persons with disabilities. Each of the aforementioned path coefficients fell in the expected direction.

Table 3. Fit statistics for path analysis models

	Df	χ^2	χ^2/df	RMSEA	CFI
Null model	15	187.545***	12.503	.221***	.000
Hypothesized model	4	10.307*	2.577	.082 (ns)	.963
Re-specified model 1	5	11.154*	2.231	.072 (ns)	.964
Final model	4	6.461 (ns)	1.615	.051 (ns)	.986

Note. RMSEA values are accompanied by information regarding test of close fit. *p<.05, ***p<.001. (ns) = p > .10.

Although the overall fit of our hypothesized model was rather strong, we were interested in determining if we could improve its fit to the data while also minimizing non-significant path coefficients. In a second model (Re-specified model 1), we deleted the non-significant path from quest orientation to cultural conservatism, which resulted in a slight improvement in model fit, as evidenced by the reduction in RMSEA from .082 to .072. In a final modification to the model (Re-specified model 2), we added a direct path from fundamentalism to opposition to human rights based on the reasoning that the influence of fundamentalism on human rights attitudes might not be fully mediated by conservatism. The resulting model was clearly an improvement over the previous two models (see Table 3).

In the final model (see Figure 2 for path coefficients) all of the path coefficients remained the same (from Re-specified model 2) except for the path running from cultural conservatism to opposition to human rights. This path remained statistically significant [b = .404, SE = .075, β = .400, $p < .001$] in the new model, while also appearing stronger than in the previous two models. Also, in an unexpected turn, fundamentalism exhibited a statistically significant *negative* [b = -.101, SE = .047, β = -.163, p = .030] relationship with opposition to human rights, in contrast to the expected positive relationship. In other words, individuals scoring higher on cultural conservatism were more likely to support opposition to human rights for persons with disabilities while those scoring higher on fundamentalism were less likely to endorse opposition.

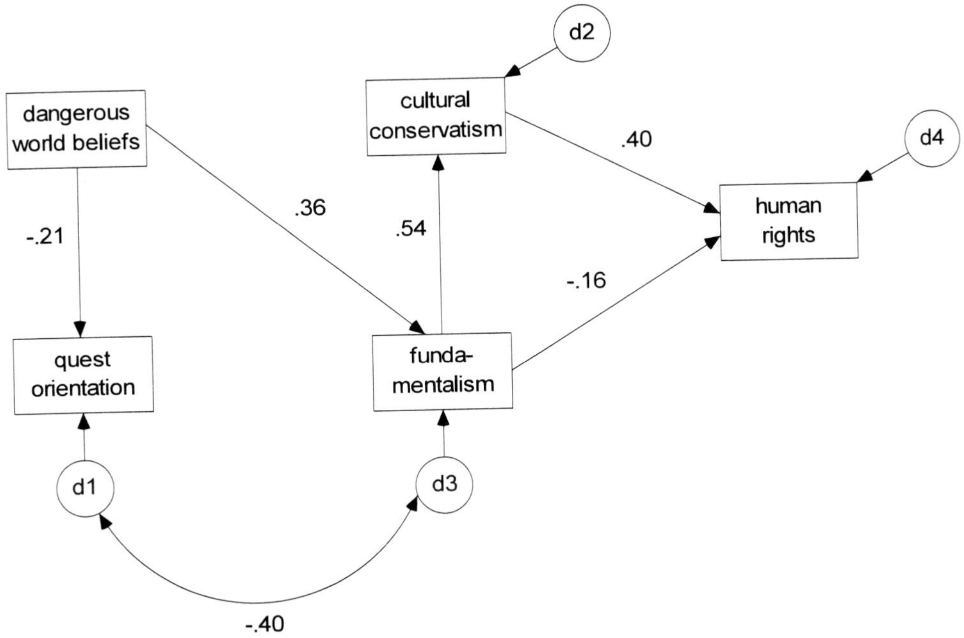

Note. All paths statistically significant at $p < .05$.

Figure 2. Standardized path coefficients for final re-specified model.

Assessment of Mediated Effects

We tested our speculation of mediated effects in our final model by conducting Sobel tests for each simple mediated relationship. Computations were performed via an interactive calculator made available by Preacher and Leonardelli at http://www.psych.ku. edu/ preacher/sobel/sobel.htm. The indirect path from DWB to cultural conservatism via fundamentalism was statistically significant ($p < .001$), as was the indirect path from fundamentalism to opposition to human rights via cultural conservatism ($p < .001$). Finally, the simple indirect relationship between DWB to opposition to human rights via fundamentalism was statistically significant (p = .04) in the model. See Table 4 for coefficients for direct and indirect effects.

Table 4. Unstandardized and standardized indirect effects

	Unstandardized effects	Standardized effects
DWB→Funda→CC	.208	.194
DWB→Funda→HR	-.063	-.058
Funda→CC→HR	.132	.216
DWB→Funda→CC→HR	.083	.078

Conclusion

The results from our data analyses provided reasonable support for many of the proposed relationships in our hypothesized model. Fit indices for the hypothesized model suggested a reasonably well-fitting model, consistent with the causal ordering laid out in our hypotheses. Within that model, dangerous world beliefs emerged as a significant predictor of both quest orientation and fundamentalism, while fundamentalism emerged as a significant predictor of cultural conservatism. Also consistent with expectations was the fact that cultural conservatism explained significant variation in opposition to human rights for persons with disabilities.

Contrary to expectations, quest orientation did not explain significant variation in cultural conservatism when pitted against fundamentalism in the model. An examination of the zero-order correlations reveals that quest orientation and fundamentalism shared a large amount of variation, while fundamentalism was more strongly related to cultural conservatism than quest. As such, it is no surprise that fundamentalism predicted human rights attitudes, while quest orientation did not.

In order to see if we could improve upon the fit of the hypothesized model, the non-significant path from quest orientation to cultural conservatism from the initial model was removed (in an initial re-specification) and a path from fundamentalism to human rights attitudes was added (in a second re-specification). These two modifications yielded a model that was a considerable improvement over the initial hypothesized model in terms of global fit. Once again, dangerous world beliefs significantly predicted quest orientation and fundamentalism, while fundamentalism significantly predicted both cultural conservatism *and* human rights attitudes.

An examination of the indirect effects in the final model revealed that dangerous world beliefs was a significant positive predictor of cultural conservatism and a significant negative predictor of human rights through the mediator, religious fundamentalism. With respect to the indirect relationship between fundamentalism and human rights attitudes, we found that it was significantly mediated through cultural conservatism.

Briefly, we note that the direct path leading from fundamentalism to opposition to human rights was negative, whereas the indirect path running through cultural conservatism was strongly positive – indicating that fundamentalism was exerting opposing influences on human rights attitudes. This seems to explain why the zero-order correlation between fundamentalism and human rights attitudes was not statistically significant during our correlation analyses.

In laying out our argument for the hypothesized model, two possibilities guided our assumption that cultural conservatism would predict human rights attitudes toward persons with disabilities: (a) The fear of societal degeneration associated with cultural conservatism may translate into a rejection of *any group* arguing for special rights or privileges in order to gain better access to the social, educational, and work worlds; (b) Aspects of culturally conservative ideology could contribute to designation of persons with disabilities as explicit outgroup members, thereby leading to prejudiced attitudes in the form of opposition to human rights. Although our model does not provide an explicit test of these competing explanations per se, we were able to deduce from our data the degree to which each of these explanations reasonably explain the observed covariation between conservatism and human rights attitudes.

Assuming the former explanation accurately depicts the relationship, one would expect cultural conservatism to fully mediate the effects of DWB (and fundamentalism) on human rights attitudes in our models. According to this assumption, the tendency for persons high in DWB to perceive societal change as threatening – and not the ideological component of cultural conservatism – will contribute to overlapping variation between cultural conservatism and human rights attitudes. Assuming the second explanation is a better depiction of the relationship, cultural conservatism would be expected to completely fail as a mediator of the relationship between DWB and human rights, although cultural conservatism would still function as a significant predictor. According to this assumption, the ideological content of cultural conservatism will contribute to the observed covariation of cultural conservatism with human rights attitudes, whereas generalized threat perceptions that are embodied in the DWB construct will not.

In our model, we found some evidence of a mediated relationship between DWB and human rights via fundamentalism and cultural conservatism; however, when one looks at the total effect of DWB [using the product of all standardized indirect effects; (.36)(.54)(.40)] – that is, .078 – on human rights attitudes through cultural conservatism (and fundamentalism) relative to the total effect of cultural conservatism – that is, .40 – it becomes readily apparent that the ideological component of cultural conservatism is the stronger driving force between the human rights-cultural conservatism association than DWB.

Limitations of Research

The correlational nature of our study prevents us from being able to make strong statements about causal relationships postulated in our models, as well as the overall fit of our models – at least in comparison to unexplored alternatives. It is well known that the strongest case for causality can be made by systematically manipulating one variable and then observing changes in another. The fact that this was not a feature of our study means that certain predicted causal associations may be (a) reversed in reality or (b) could reflect spurious associations with a third-variable. An additional impact of our design is that other path models could, in theory, fit the data as well or better than ours – whether or not they adequately reflect the true causal ordering among variables. Thus, we caution the reader that, although the current models were not falsified in light of the data, other models could potentially better represent the true relationships among the variables under study.

Final Thoughts

The study presented in this chapter represents, what appears to us, to be a fairly new way of looking at relationships between individual difference factors related to social perceivers and attitudes related to disability rights. Although a number of studies have documented empirical relationships among cultural conservatism and fundamentalism and prejudice, there appears to be little prior research on the relationships between these factors and attitudes toward disability rights. The current study, thus, was designed in order to begin filling this gap in the empirical literature.

It is also noteworthy that the predictive relationship between DWB and cultural conservatism has been studied in previous research. However, no research to date has attempted to model relationships among DWB, religious open- versus closed-ness, and conservatism – let alone opposition to human rights. In this way, the model builds upon research begun by Duckitt and colleagues (Duckitt, 2001; Duckitt et al., 2002) by incorporating potential mediators of the DWB and cultural conservatism relationship.

REFERENCES

Altemeyer, B. (1988). *Enemies of freedom: Understanding right-wing authoritarianism.* San Francisco: Jossey-Bass Altemeyer, B. (1996). *The authoritarian specter.* Cambridge, MA: Harvard University Press.

Altemeyer, B. (1998). The other "authoritarian personality." In M.P. Zanna (Ed.), *Advances in Experimental Social Psychology*, (Vol. 30, pp. 47-92). San Diego, Academic Press.

Altemeyer, B. (2004). Why do religious fundamentalists tend to be prejudiced? *The International Journal for the Psychology of Religion, 13,* 17-28.

Altemeyer, B. (2006). *The authoritarians.* Book published online at http://home. cc. umanitoba.ca/~altemey/.

Altemeyer, B., and Hunsberger, B. (1992). Authoritarianism, religious fundamentalism, quest, and prejudice. *The International Journal for the Psychology of Religion, 2,* 113-133.

Altmeyer, B., and Hunsberger, B. (2004). A revised Religious Fundamentalism Scale: The short and sweet of it. *The International Journal for the Psychology of Religion, 14,* 47-54.

Bäckström, M. and Björklund, F. (2007). Structural modeling of generalized prejudice: The role of social dominance, authoritarianism, and empathy. *Journal of Individual Differences, 28,* 10-17.

Batson, C.D., and Schoenrade, P.A. (1991a). Measuring religion as quest: Reliability concerns. *Journal for the Scientific Study of Religion, 30,* 430-447.

Batson, C.D., and Schoenrade, P.A. (1991b). Measuring religion as quest: Validity concerns. *Journal for the Scientific Study of Religion, 30,* 416-429.

Cohrs, J.C., Kielmann, S., Maes, J., and Moschner, B. (2005). Effects of right-wing authoritarianism and threat from terrorism on restriction of civil liberties. *Analysis of Social Issues and Public Policy, 5,* 263-276.

Cokley, K., Kommaraju, M., Pickett, R., Shen, F., Patel, N., Belur, V., and Rosales, R. (2007). Ethnic differences in endorsement of the Protestant Work Ethic: The role of identity and and perceptions of social class. *Journal of Social Psychology, 147,* 75-89.

Cornelis, I., and Van Hiel, A. (2006). The impact of cognitive styles on authoritarianism based conservatism and racism. *Basic and Applied Social Psychology, 28,* 37-50.

Crowson, H.M. (2007). Authoritarianism and human rights attitudes in U.S. law students: A brief look. *Individual Differences Research, 5,* 260-266.

Crowson, H.M., DeBacker, T.K., and Thoma, S.J. (2005). Does authoritarianism predict post-9/11 attitudes? *Personality and Individual Differences, 39,* 1273-1283.

Crowson, H.M., DeBacker, T.K., and Thoma, S.J. (2006). The role of authoritarianism, perceived threat, and need for structure in predicting post-9/11 attitudes and beliefs. *Journal of Social Psychology,* 146, 733-750.

Crowson, H.M., Thoma, S.J., and Hestevold, N. (2005). Is political conservatism synonymous with authoritarianism? *Journal of Social Psychology, 145,* 571-592.

De Witte, H. (1990). Conformisme, radicalisme en machteloosheid: Een onderzoek naar de sociaal-culturele en sociaal-economische opvattingen van arbeiders in Vlaanderen [Conformism, radicalism and powerlessness: Examining Flemish workers' socio-cultural and socio-economical opinions]. Leuven, Belgium: HIVA, K.U. Leuven.

Duckitt, J. (2001). A dual-process cognitive-motivational theory of ideology and prejudice. In M.P. Zanna (Ed.), *Advances in Experimental Social Psychology,* (Vol. 33, pp. 41-113). San Diego: Academic Press.

Duckitt, J. (2006). Differential effects of right-wing authoritarianism and social dominance orientation on outgroup attitudes and their mediation by threat from competitiveness to outgroups. *Personality and Social Psychology Bulletin, 32,* 684-696.

Duckitt, J., Wagner, C., du Plessis, I., and Birum, I. (2002). The psychological bases of ideology and prejudice: Testing a dual process model. *Journal of Personality and Social Psychology, 83,* 75-93

Feldman, S. (2003). Enforcing social conformity: A theory of authoritarianism. *Political Psychology, 24,* 41-74.

Fullerton, T.J., and Hunsberger, B. (1982). A unidimensional measure of Christian orthodoxy. *Journal for the Scientific Study of Religion, 21,* 317-326.

Heaven, P.C.L., and St. Quintin, D. (2003). Personality factors predict prejudice. *Personality and Individual Differences, 34,* 625-634.

Hunsberger, B. (1996). Religious fundamentalism, right-wing authoritarianism, and hostility toward homosexuals in non-Christian religious groups. *International Journal for the Psychology of Religion, 6,* 39-49.

Klaassen, D.W., and McDonald, M.J. (2002). Quest and identity development: Re-examining pathways for existential search. *International Journal for the Psychology of Religion, 12,* 189-200.

Kline, R.B. (2005). *Principles and practice of structural equation modeling* (2nd ed.). New York: Guilford.

Laythe, B., Finkel, D., and Kirkpatrick, L.A. (2001). Predicting prejudice from religious fundamentalism and right-wing authoritarianism: A multiple-regression approach. *Journal for the Scientific Study of Religion, 40,* 1-10.

McFarland, S. (2005). On the eve of war: Authoritarianism, social dominance, and American students' attitudes toward attacking Iraq. *Personality and Social Psychology Bulletin, 31,* 360-367.

McFarland, S., and Matthews, M. (2005). Who cares about human rights? *Political Psychology, 26,* 365-385.

Moghaddam, F.M., and Vuksanonvic, M. (1990). Attitudes and behavior toward human rights across different contexts: The role of right-wing authoritarianism, political ideology, and religiosity. *International Journal of Psychology, 25,* 455-474.

Ray, J.J. (1985). Defective validity in the Altemeyer authoritarianism scale. *Journal of Social Psychology, 125,* 271-272.

Reimer, S., and Park, J.Z. (2001). Tolerant (in)civility? A longitudinal analysis of Protestants' willingness to grant civil liberties. *Journal for the Scientific Study of Religion, 40,* 735-745.

Rowatt, W.C., Tsang, J., Kelly, J., LaMartina, B., McCullers, M., and McKinley, A. (2006). Associations between religious personality dimensions and implicit homosexual prejudice. *Journal for the Scientific Study of Religion, 45,* 397-406.

Schumacker, R. E., and Lomax, R. G. (2004). *A beginner's guide to structural equation modeling* (2nd ed.). Mahwah, NJ: Erlbaum.

Van Hiel, A., Cornelis, I., and Roets, A. (2007). The intervening roles of social worldviews in the relationship between the five factor model of personality and social attitudes. *European Journal of Personality, 21,* 131-148.

Van Hiel, A., Cornelis, I., Roets, A., and De Clerq, B. (2007). A comparison of various authoritarianism scales in Belgian Flanders. *European Journal of Personality, 21,* 149-168.

Van Hiel, A. and Mervielde, I. (2002). Explaining conservative beliefs and political preferences: A comparison of social dominance orientation and authoritarianism. *Journal of Applied Social Psychology, 32,* 965-976.

Weisel, A., and Zaidman, A. (2003). Attitudes of secular and religious Israeli adolescents towards persons with disabilities: A multidimensional analysis. *International Journal of Disability, Development and Education, 50,* 309-323.

Whitley, B.E. (1999). Right-wing authoritarianism, social dominance orientation, and prejudice. *Journal of Personality and Social Psychology, 77,* 126-134.

Whitley, B.E., and Ǽgisdóttir, S. (2000). The gender belief system, authoritarianism, social dominance orientation, and heterosexuals' attitudes toward lesbians and gay men. *Sex Roles, 42,* 947-967.

In: Human Rights Issues in the 21st Century ISBN 978-1-60456-119-7
Editors: M.S. Becker and J.N. Schneider, pp. 167-187

Chapter 8

HUMAN RIGHTS DIMENSION IN THE GLOBAL COUNTERTERRORISM STRATEGY

Jean-Paul Laborde[1] and Danil Kerimi[2]
United Nations on Drugs and Crime[3]

I. INTRODUCTION

One of the most pressing human rights issue in the beginning of the 21st century is the security and human rights nexus. On the forefront of the discussion is the impact of the global effort to counter terrorism on human rights.

September 11, 2001 signalled a new era in the chapter of the humanity's action against terrorism. Although the immediate response was that of a military nature, it is widely recognized that a prolonged counter terrorism action will be on the criminal justice front. A number of governments around the world started reforming their criminal justice systems to bring them up to date to face the challenge of international terrorism.

Recent developments show that the nature of terrorism is changing. Terrorism became indiscriminate and global in nature. If before terrorists targeted heads of states and governments and other VIP, nowadays, common civilians are targeted to produce an atmosphere of fear and panic among the population. Moreover, the international terrorism highlighted the 'dark side' of globalization. Today a leader of a terrorist organization could be coming from a state A, be radicalized in his believes in a state B, recruit members of his organization in a state C, get financing from a state D, fight for a 'cause' in a state E, while finding safe haven in a state F. Terrorists pay as much respect to national borders as swarms of locusts. The nations of the world and their criminal justice systems were slow to adapt to this new global 'modus operandi'. In my lectures, I often use the metaphor that it looks like we are using our bicycles trying to chase criminals that are driving fast modern vehicles.

---

[1] Chief, Terrorism Prevention Branch, United Nations Office on Drugs and Crime
[2] Associate Crime Prevention Expert, Terrorism Prevention Branch, UN Office on Drugs and Crime
[3] The views expressed in this article are those of the authors and do not necessarily reflect the position of the United Nations Secretariat.

Recognizing this problem, former UN Secretary-General Mr. Annan highlighted that

> ... terrorism is *a threat to all states and to all peoples*, which can strike anytime, anywhere. It is a direct attack on the core values the United Nations stands for: the rule of law; the protection of civilians; mutual respect between people of different faiths and cultures; and peaceful resolution of conflict... the United Nations must be at the forefront in fighting against it, and first of all in proclaiming, loud and clear, that terrorism can never be accepted or justified, in any cause whatsoever.[4]

As the only truly global organization with the goals and means of preserving peace and security, the UN is naturally expected to be at the forefront of the global action against terrorism. Although having addressed terrorism prior to 9/11, the UN, because of the diversity of its membership, never had a comprehensive strategic approach how to fight it. On 8 September 2006, the UN General Assembly (GA), in unprecedented show of international solidarity agreed on the 'Global Counter-Terrorism Strategy'. The adoption of the United Nations Global Counter-Terrorism Strategy by the GA was a landmark event, as it was the first time that all countries agreed to a common strategic approach to fight terrorism. The Strategy forms the basis for a concrete plan of action, consisting of four key areas:

- Measures to address the conditions conducive to the spread of terrorism;
- Measures to prevent and combat terrorism;
- Measures to build the capacity of States and the United Nations to prevent and combat terrorism; and
- Measures to ensure respect for human rights for all and the rule of law as the fundamental basis of the fight against terrorism.[5]

As you see, promotion of human rights while countering terrorism is considered so important that it is developed into a separate part of the strategy. The present article tries to challenge a common misconception that there has to be a certain trade off between new proactive counter terrorism legislation, on the one hand, and human rights on the other. We believe that since terrorism is a direct assault on the basic human right to life, any effort directed at countering this evil is also aimed at promoting human rights. A smartly designed criminal justice strategy aimed at preventing terrorist acts will only contribute to and promote establishing the rule of law.

The article is organized as following. First of all, we will tract the developments that led to the adoption of the Strategy. Secondly, we will see what actors are working in the field. Thirdly, we will see what issues are involved in a Counter-terrorism (CT)-Human Rights (HR) nexus. And finally, we will outline the role of the United Nations Office on Drugs and Crime in the global effort against terrorism.

---

[4] Kofi Annan. Keynote address to the Closing Plenary of the International Summit on Democracy, Terrorism and Security. Accessible at: http://english.safe-democracy.org/keynotes/a-global-strategy-for-fighting-terrorism.html.

[5] http://www.un.org/terrorism/strategy-counter-terrorism.html.

II. UN ACTION AGAINST TERRORISM

2.1. The Blue Ribbon Panel

In 1945, one of the main tasks of the UN, as set forth in the preamble of the UN Charter, was

> to maintain international peace and security, and to that end: to take effective collective measures for the prevention and removal of threats to the peace, and for the suppression of acts of aggression or other breaches of the peace.

As we are often reminded, threats to international peace and security are constantly evolving. Threats we face today could not have been foreseen yesterday. In 1945, the main concern was an act of aggression by one state against another state. The system of collective security, therefore, was designed in a way to prevent and cope with these threats while 'leaving the door open' for the possibility to address other threats, should the need arise.

In November 2003, then the UN Secretary-General Mr. Kofi Annan announced the creation of the High-Level Panel on Threats, Challenges and Change, charged with the task of examining threats to international security in the rapidly changing world and the suitability of the existing UN-based international system of collective security in addressing these threats. Often referred to as the 'wise men panel' or "Blue Ribbon Panel", the initiative brought together 16 distinguished men and women in a joint effort to fulfill the G-S's expectations. Consisting of persons of the highest caliber,[6] the Panel was well suited for the job. According to the official terms of reference of the Panel, it has been created:

- to examine today's global threats and provide an analysis of future challenges to international peace and security;
- to consider the contribution that collective action can make in addressing these challenges;
- to recommend the changes necessary to ensure collective action, including but not limited to the principal organs of the United Nations and the relationship between them.[7]

At the end of its work period, the Panel produced the report *"A More Secure World: Our Shared Responsibility"*[8], in which it identified the gravest threats that we face today:

[6] The Panel members include the Secretary-General of the League of Arab States, former Prime Minister of the Russian Federation, former Vice Prime Minister and Minister for Foreign Affairs of PR China and the former United States National Security Adviser.

[7] Terms of reference of the Panel are available at http://www.un.org/News/dh/hlpanel/terms-of-reference-rehl-panel.pdf.

[8] A/59/565 and Corr. 1

6 clusters of threats identified by the 'Blue Ribbon Panel':

- Economic and social threats, including poverty, infectious disease and environmental degradation
- Inter-State conflict
- Internal conflict, including civil war, genocide and other large-scale atrocities
- Nuclear, radiological, chemical and biological weapons
- Terrorism
- Transnational organized crime[9]

Thus the Panel, in its report identified terrorism as one of the main challenges facing the international community. And indeed, as mentioned by the UN S-G on numerous occasions, terrorism as an assault on the principles of Rule of Law, human rights and the peaceful settlement of disputes, runs counter to the purposes and principles of the United Nations. As a main guarantor of the peace and security, the UN is naturally expected to come up with a comprehensive and effective strategy to meet this threat to the international community and organization itself. In its report, the Panel made also a proposal for working on a general definition of terrorism.

One of the elements of the general definition of terrorism proposed by the Panel:

"Any action, in addition to actions already specified by the existing conventions on aspects of terrorism, the Geneva Conventions and Security Council resolution 1566 (2004), that is intended to cause death or serious bodily harm to civilians or non-combatants, when the purpose of such an act, by its nature or context, is to intimidate a population, or to compel a Government or an international organization to do or to abstain from doing any act".

"A More Secure World: Our Shared Responsibility" was supposed to serve as a background paper to the Report of the S-G himself, in which he was expected to present his views on security in the modern world and the UN's current level of preparedness to face new as well as old challenges.

2.2. In Larger Freedom

The S-G's report called 'In Larger Freedom: Towards Development, Security and Human Rights for all'[10], was made public on the 21st of March 2005. As the title indicates, the report consists of three parts dealing with the three most import dimensions of the UN's work: security, development and human rights. The report based its analysis on the recommendations of two other reports. For the part on security, it relied extensively on the

---

[9] Accessible at: A more secure world: Our shared responsibility. p.23. Accessible at: http://www.un.org/secureworld/report3.pdf.

[10] The first part of the report's title was taken from the UN Charter while the second part stresses three most important dimensions of the Organization's work.

recommendations of the High-Level Panel in its report - 'A More Secure World'. For the chapter on development, the S-G used mainly the report, produced by a team of 250 experts headed by Jeffrey Sachs - 'Investing in Development: A Practical Plan to Achieve the Millennium Development Goals'[11]. This report evaluates the progress made by the international community in meeting the famous Millennium Development Goals.

The S-G's report, "In Larger Freedom", was intended to serve as a 'wake-up call' for the member-states to consider a broad spectrum of reforms prior to and during the anniversary session of the United Nation General Assembly that will be held in New York in September. The S-G presented the Report to the Member-States in March to give them enough time to consider and analyze it before the beginning of the anniversary session of the General Assembly in September.

The momentum was indeed too important to ignore. As the S-G highlighted it in his report "In Larger Freedom",

> Five years into the new millennium, we have it in our power to pass on to our children a brighter inheritance than that bequeathed to any previous generation... we can forge a set of updated international institutions to help humanity achieve these noble goals. If we act boldly — and if we act together — we can make people everywhere more secure, more prosperous and better able to enjoy their fundamental human rights. "[12]

2. 3. " 5 Ds "

In March 2005, at the Madrid Summit on Democracy, Terrorism and Security, the UN SG presented the United Nations strategy he had in mind in the form of "5 Ds":

"5 Ds" of the UN S-G:

- to dissuade disaffected groups from choosing terrorism as a tactic to achieve their goals;
- to deny terrorists the means to carry out their attacks;
- to deter states from supporting terrorists;
- to develop state capacity to prevent terrorism;
- to defend human rights in the struggle against terrorism.

The Secretary-General's strategy was based on the clear message that terrorism of any kind or form is unacceptable and will be condemned and punished by the international community. In the launch of the strategy, and in subsequent initiatives (such as those in the "In Larger Freedom" report), the Secretary-General stressed that agreement on a common definition of terrorism by Member States is important in underscoring this aim. He called on Member States to cut through the political debates and agree to complete a comprehensive convention outlawing terrorism in all its forms. At the September 2005 Summit, world

[11] Investing in Development: A Practical Plan to Achieve the Millennium Development Goals. Accessible at : http://www.unmillenniumproject.org/reports/index.htm

[12] In larger freedom: towards development, security and human rights for all. Report of the Secretary-General.p.3 Accessible at : http://www.un.org/largerfreedom/report-largerfreedom.pdf.

leaders agreed to make every effort to conclude negotiations on a comprehensive convention against terrorism in the year ahead.

The last D has a direct relevance to the issues discussed in the paper as it refers to the importance of respecting human rights and the rule of law in the fight against terrorism. In his Madrid Speech the SG strongly condemned any human rights abuses conducted in the name of the national security. He stressed that:

> "Human rights law makes ample provision for counter-terrorist action, even in the most exceptional circumstances. But compromising human rights cannot serve the struggle against terrorism. On the contrary, it facilitates achievement of the terrorist's objective – by ceding to him the moral high ground, and provoking tension, hatred and mistrust of government among precisely those parts of the population where he is most likely to find recruits."[13]

At that time the relationship between HR and CT was still considered to be a zero-sum game. It could be seen from the title of the last "D"- 'defending HR in the CT struggle'. This misconception later changed. It was recognized that CT efforts and HR rights go hand in hand. The international community started talking about 'promoting HR while countering terrorism'.

Nevertheless, the last 'D' laid down the foundation of many UN efforts in this field, led to the creation of several new programs and was later further developed into the fourth pillar of the Global CT Strategy.

2.4. The Summit Outcome Document

The 2005 World Summit brought together more heads of the states and governments to New York than any of the events in the past. The Summit produced a document entitled "2005 World Summit Outcome", adopted as a General Assembly resolution A/RES/60/1. In this document the world leaders made several references to the role of the UN in counter-terrorism.

At the World Summit, member states requested the S-G to produce a report to serve as a basis for the negotiations on the Global Counter Terrorism Strategy.

Extract from the "Outcome Document" :

- We strongly condemn terrorism in all its forms and manifestations, committed by whomever, wherever and for whatever purposes, as it constitutes one of the most serious threats to international peace and security;
- We welcome the Secretary-General's identification of elements of a counterterrorism Strategy;
- We stress the need to make every effort to reach an agreement on and conclude a comprehensive convention;
- We recognize that international cooperation to fight terrorism must be conducted

[13] "A Global Strategy for Fighting Terrorism", Keynote Address to the Closing Plenary of the International Summit on Democracy, Terrorism and Security, Madrid, 10 March 2004.

in conformity with international law, including the Charter and relevant international conventions and protocols;

- We acknowledge the important role played by the United Nations in combating terrorism;
- We urge the international community, including the United Nations, to assist States in building national and regional capacity to combat terrorism.

Source: GA Resolution A/RES/60/1. http://daccessdds.un.org/doc/UNDOC/GEN/N05/487/ 60/PDF /N0548760.pdf?OpenElement

2.5. "Uniting Against Terrorism: Recommendations for a Global Counter-Terrorism Strategy[14]

In his released in April 2006 report, the S-G has further developed his idea of "5 Ds" (to dissuade disaffected groups from choosing terrorism as a tactic to achieve their goals; to deny terrorists the means to carry out their attacks; to deter states from supporting terrorists; to develop state capacity to prevent terrorism; to defend human rights in the struggle against terrorism). He has also extensively outlined how the United Nations system is contributing to the global fight against terrorism. All Departments and Agencies of the United Nations were called to contribute to carrying out this comprehensive system-wide strategy. After making his strategy public, the S-G declared that he is planning to create an implementation task force, under the UN-Secretariat, which will meet regularly to review the handling of terrorism and related issues throughout the UN system, and make sure that all parts of it play their proper role.

2.6. The United Nations Global Counter Terrorism Strategy and the Counter-Terrorism Implementation Task Force (CTITF)[15]

On 8 September 2006 the General Assembly adopted a comprehensive UN CT strategy in the form of a resolution and annexed plan of action. For the first time, the diverse body agreed on a common comprehensive approach to fight it. The emphasis was put both on its prevention and combating the existing evil. Reiterating their strong condemnation of terrorism in all its forms and manifestations, committed by whomever, wherever and for whatever purposes, all 192 member states once again highlighted that terrorism constitutes one of the most serious threats to international peace and security. Furthermore, the resolution "reaffirmed that acts, methods and practices of terrorism in all its forms and manifestations are activities aimed at the destruction of human rights, fundamental freedoms and democracy.... "

---

[14] "Uniting against Terrorism: Recommendations for a global counter-terrorism Strategy". Report of the Secretary General (A/60/825). http://www.un.org /unitingagainstterrorism /contents.htm.

[15] This sub-chapter is adopted from a TPB/UNODC working document prepared as a background paper for the Symposium On "Advancing The Implementation Of The United Nations Global Counter-Terrorism Strategy", Vienna International Centre, 17-18 May 2007.

Since the adoption of the Strategy, much of the implementation work has been initiated by the UN system, under the leadership of the CTITF. The General Assembly welcomed the institutionalization of the Task Force, which brings together representatives of 24 actors - UN entities and other international organizations - active in the area of counter-terrorism, working in coordination under mandates from the General Assembly, the Security Council, and various specialized agencies, funds, and programmes. The work carried out by Task Force entities does not substitute actions taken by Member States, nor does it aim to supersede existing UN mechanisms, including the SC-related bodies, but to complement and support their work. The Task Force framework serves as an 'umbrella' for coordinating the individual actions of its entities into a common strategic effort as well as combining the expertise and capacity of various entities to pursue actions called for by the Strategy.

Table: Composition of the CTITF[16]

- The Counter-Terrorism Executive Directorate (CTED)
- The Department for Disarmament Affairs (DDA)
- The Department of Peacekeeping Operations (DPKO)
- The Department of Political Affairs (DPA)
- The Department of Public Information (DPI)
- The Department for Safety and Security (DSS)
- The Expert Staff of the 1540 Committee
- The International Atomic Energy Agency (IAEA)
- The International Civil Aviation Organization (ICAO)
- The International Maritime Organization (IMO)
- The International Monetary Fund (IMF)
- The International Criminal Police Organization (INTERPOL)
- The Monitoring Team of the 1267 Committee
- The Office of the High Commissioner of Human Rights (OHCHR)
- The Office of Legal Affairs (OLA)
- The Organization for the Prohibition of Chemical Weapons (OPCW)
- The Special Rapporteur on Promoting and Protection of Human Rights While Countering Terrorism
- The United Nations Development Program (UNDP)
- The United Nations Educational, Scientific and Cultural Organization (UNESCO)
- The United Nations Interregional Crime and Justice Research Institute (UNICRI)
- The United Nations Office on Drugs and Crime (UNODC)
- The World Customs Organization (WCO)
- The World Bank
- The World Health Organization (WHO)

Following the adoption of the Strategy, efforts by the CTITF were aimed at assisting Member States in implementing the Strategy. The Task Force has established several

[16] http://www.un.org/terrorism/cttaskforce.html

Working Groups and identified concrete areas in which the UN system could produce tangible results in the coming 6-12 months. These include:

- Assisting interested Member States in implementing the Strategy in an integrated manner;
- Providing a forum for addressing political and economic exclusion, in particular among youth;
- Enhancing technical assistance assessment, delivery, and follow-up;
- Improving UN coordination in planning the response to a terrorist attack that uses nuclear, chemical, biological or radiological materials;
- Bringing together stakeholders and partners to discuss the abuse of the Internet for terrorist purposes and identify innovative means to counter it;
- Finding ways to meet international standards for countering financing of terrorism;
- Establishing best practices on protecting vulnerable targets - including UN field staff -and creating a mechanism to share experience in this regard;
- Assisting countries in strengthening domestic legislation to protect human rights in order to comply with international standards; and
- Bringing together victims from around the world to identify their needs and possible government responses.

One of the most important technical assistance tools developed by the Secretariat to provide information on the work of the CTITF is the online handbook. The purpose of the website (http://www.un.org/terrorism/cthandbook/index.html) is to provide member states with the updated information on the activities of the UN on the counter terrorism front. The information is organized as following: by substantive issues, UN and other actors and entities involved in the CT efforts and the regions. The website also has an index to search (http://www.un.org/terrorism/cthandbook/keyword.html). The website is a timely and extremely useful tool for both the donor community and recipient states.

2.7. Human Rights Dimension in the Strategy

The human rights issues were considered so important that member states developed an entire part of the strategy solely devoted to them. The fourth pillar of the CT strategy is called "*Measures to ensure respect for human rights for all and the rule of law as the fundamental basis of the fight against terrorism*" and has 8 suggested areas of action.

- First of all, states reaffirmed that the GA resolution 60/158 (2005) should serve as a framework for any action in the field;
- Secondly, states highlighted the importance of human rights, refugee and humanitarian law in the fight against terrorism;
- Thirdly, states were encouraged to join the international instruments in the above mentioned legal fields;
- Fourthly, states were invited to developed proactive, effective criminal justice systems to protect the rule of law and to counter terrorism;

III. COUNTER TERRORISM AND HUMAN RIGHTS: ACTORS AND ISSUES

Table: overview of the main actors involved in promoting human rights while countering terrorism.

Global Level

Governmental	*Non-governmental*
UN: Department of Political Affairs (DPA) Department of Peacekeeping Operations (DPKO) Human Rights Council Special Rapporteur on Human Rights while Countering Terrorism Office of the High Commissioner of Human Rights (OHCHR) United Nations Development Programme (UNDP) United Nations Educational, Scientific and Cultural Organization United Nations Office of Drugs and Crime (UNODC) Non- UN: Commonwealth Secretariat L'Organisation internationale de la Francophonie Organization of Islamic Conference	Amnesty International International Commission of Jurists International Crisis Group Human Rights First Human Rights Watch

Regional and Sub-regional

Africa	*Americas*	*Asia and Pacific*	*Europe*
African Union Communauté Economique et Monétaire de l'Afrique Centrale (CEMAC) Intergovernmental Authority for Development (IGAD) Southern Africa Development Community (SADC) Union Economique et Monétaire Ouest Africaine (UEMOA)	Organization of American States	Association of South East Asian Nations Cooperation Council for the Arab States of the Gulf League of Arab States Pacific Islands Forum Secretariat South Asian Association for Regional Cooperation Shanghai Cooperation Organization	Black Sea Economic Cooperation Collective Security Treaty Organization Commonwealth of Independent States Council of Europe European Union Organization for Security and Cooperation in Europe

Table: Main issues involved in CT and HR[58]	
Humanitarian Law	A number of provisions in the *Geneva Convention* of 1949 and its *Additional Protocols* prohibit "measures of terrorism" and "acts of terrorism". For example, "collective penalties and likewise all measures of intimidation or of terrorism" are prohibited[59]. Acts or threats of violence intended to spread terror among the civilian population are prohibited in both international and non-international armed conflicts[60]. Article 4(d) of Additional Protocol II prohibits "acts of terrorism" against persons not or no longer taking part in hostilities, in the case of a non-international armed conflict[61]. International humanitarian law does not provide a specific definition of terrorism. The ICRC has noted that in situations of armed conflict, there is no legal significance in describing deliberate acts of violence against civilians or civilian objects as "terrorist" because such acts would already constitute war crimes[62].
Criminal Procedure	All persons are protected against the unlawful or arbitrary interference with their liberty.[63] This protection is applicable in the context of criminal proceedings, as well as other areas in which the State might affect the liberty of persons.[64] Counter-terrorism measures may impact upon the liberty of persons through: pre-trial procedures for terrorism offences, including provisions concerning bail and the remand of persons in custody awaiting trial; investigative detention (the detention of a person prior to the laying of a criminal charge against that person for the purpose of further investigating whether that person was involved in the commission, or assisted in the commission, of a terrorist offence); preventive detention (the detention of a person for the purpose of preventing

58 This part is adopted from another TPB/UNODC document titled 'Human Rights, Terrorism and Counter-Terrorism'.

59 Geneva Convention IV, art. 33.

60 Protocol (I) Additional to the Geneva Conventions of 12 August 1949 and Relating to the Protection of Victims of International Armed Conflicts (Protocol I), opened for signature 8 June 1977, 1125 UNTS 4 (entered into force 7 December 1978), Article 51(2); art. 13(2) Additional Protocol II.

61 The Sub-Commission Special Rapporteur on terrorism and human rights has listed further examples, including: physical mutilation and cutting off limbs; massive resort to detention and torture; extrajudicial killings and disappearances; attacks on whole villages; widespread and indiscriminate bombing; mass rape and gross violence against women; and the use of civilians as human shields. Sub-Commission Special Rapporteur on terrorism and human rights, Specific Human Rights Issues: New priorities, in particular terrorism and counter-terrorism, UN Doc E/CN.4/Sub.2/2004/40 (2004), paragraph 25.

62 See Official Statement of ICRC, 21.07.05 The Relevance of IHL in the context of terrorism.

63 See, for example, Article 9 of the *International Covenant on Civil and Political Rights* (n 23).

64 Human Rights Committee, *General Comment 8 (Article 9, Right to liberty and security of persons)*, UN Doc CCPR/C*** (1982), paragraphs 1 and 4.

	that person from committing, or assisting in the commission of, a terrorist offence); control orders (the imposition of conditions upon a person, short of detention, for the purpose of preventing that person from committing, or assisting in the commission of, a terrorist offence, including the detention of a person awaiting determination of immigration or refugee status); and compulsory hearings (the detention and compulsory questioning of a terrorist suspect, or non-suspect, for the gathering of intelligence about terrorist activities). Guaranteeing the right of terrorist suspects to a fair trial is critical for ensuring that anti-terrorism measures respect the rule of law. The human rights protections for all persons charged with criminal offences, including terrorism-related crimes, include the right to be presumed innocent, the right to a hearing with due guarantees and within a reasonable time, by a competent, independent and impartial tribunal, and a right to have a conviction and sentence reviewed by a higher tribunal satisfying the same standards.[65] International humanitarian law provides for largely identical protections for the trial of persons in the context of armed conflicts.[66]
Refugee law	In September 2001, the Security Council adopted resolution 1373, which obliges Member States to take a number of measures to prevent terrorist activities and to criminalize various forms of terrorist actions, as well as to take measures that assist and promote cooperation among countries including adherence to international counter-terrorism instruments. The implementation of this resolution has various implications related to immigration and refugee status. For example, States are required to prevent the movement of terrorists by implementing effective border controls and take measures to secure the integrity of identity papers and travel documents (para 2(g)). States also are called upon to take measures to ensure that refugee status is not granted to asylum-seekers that have planned, facilitated or participated in the commission of terrorist acts (para 3(f)), and to ensure that refugee status is not abused by perpetrators, organizers, or facilitators of terrorist acts (para 3(g)). The UN High Commissioner for Refugees has endorsed the position that those responsible for committing terrorist acts must not be permitted to manipulate refugee mechanisms in order to find safe haven or achieve impunity. The

65 See generally Human Rights Committee, General Comment 13 (Article 14), UN Doc ** (1984).

66 Independent expert on human rights and countering terrorism (n 56) paragraph 44.

	framework of international refugee law contains a number of provisions aimed at guarding against abuse and is thus able to respond to possible exploitation of refugee mechanisms by those responsible for terrorist acts.[67]
Other challenges	The freedom from torture is an absolute right, being a peremptory norm of customary international law and a treaty right that is non-derogable even in states of emergency threatening the life of the nation, also codified in the four *Geneva Conventions* and their *Additional Protocols* Since 11 September 2001, some States have reportedly extradited, expelled, deported, or otherwise transferred foreigners, some of them asylum-seekers, suspected of terrorism to their country of origin or to other countries where they allegedly face a risk of torture or ill-treatment, in disregard of the principle of *non-refoulement*. The principle of *non-refoulement*, set out in Article 33(1) of the *Convention relating to the Status of Refugees*, provides that States parties to that *Convention* cannot expel or return ('refouler') a refugee in any manner whatsoever to a territory where that person's life or freedom would be threatened by reason of his or her race, religion, nationality, membership of a particular social group or political opinion.[68] The use of indicator clusters to profile potential suspects is, in principle, a permissible means of investigation and law enforcement activity. Generally speaking, profiling is a filtering process involving a single or cluster of indicators that when grouped together present the characteristics of a high-risk person, passenger or consignment. When law enforcement agents use broad profiles that reflect unexamined generalizations, their practices may constitute disproportionate interferences with human rights. In particular, when one of the indicators on which profiling is based is a person's ethnic or national origin, this raises the question of the conformity of such profiling with the principle of non-discrimination. The Committee on the Elimination of Racial Discrimination has called on States to "ensure that any measures taken in the fight against terrorism do not discriminate, in purpose or effect, on the grounds of race, colour, descent, or national or ethnic origin and that non-citizens are not subjected to racial or ethnic profiling or stereotyping"[69] even in the case of measures designed to counter terrorism.[70]

67 See further the reports of the UN High Commissioner for Refugees: The Interface between Extradition and Asylum (Department of International Protection, PPLA/23003/05); and Note on Diplomatic Assurances and International Refugee Protection (Protection Operations and Legal Advice Section, August 2006).

68 Subsection 2 of that same article provides that this benefit cannot be "claimed by a refugee whom there are reasonable grounds for regarding as a danger to the security of the country in which he is, or who, having been convicted by final judgment of a particularly serious crime, constitutes a danger to the community of that country".

69 UN Committee on the Elimination of Racial Discrimination, General Recommendation No. 30: Discrimination against Non-Citizens (2004), UN Doc. CERD/C/64/Misc.11/rev.3, para. 10.

	The full impact of terrorism and counter-terrorism measures on human rights has yet to be measured. In particular, the potential impact of these measures on economic, social and cultural rights needs to be examined in greater detail. By way of example, what is the impact of counter-terrorism initiatives on resources normally allocated to international development assistance? What measures should be taken to address the underlying social and economic conditions, which may be conducive to exploitation by terrorists?[71] What is the impact of counter-terrorism measures on freedom of expression – for example, security measures that might curtail peaceful protests, the proscription of the incitement to terrorism, and the imposition of controls upon the media concerning the broadcasting or publication of matters concerning terrorist events, suspects, or others involved in countering terrorism. Other issues include the collection, sharing and transfer of information by counter-terrorism agencies, including the advance passenger screening of persons bound for international travel by air or by sea, which raise concerns about the privacy of individuals, and the security and potential use of the information collected. Advance passenger screening may also impact upon the right of persons to leave any country, including those fleeing persecution from their own State. Further challenges include issues related to judicial cooperation, such as questions related to the gathering of information by one State at the request of another; the transfer of information from one jurisdiction to another; judicial proceedings involving evidence gathered abroad; and the use of intelligence information in judicial proceedings. The human rights of victims of terrorist attacks is an issue of crucial importance, as reflected in the Global Counter-Terrorism Strategy recently adopted by the General Assembly[72]. Any counter-terrorism strategy should focus on the plight of victims of terrorism and of States' counter-terrorism measures. It must include the duty to

70 See "Statement on Racial Discrimination and Measures to Combat Terrorism", in Report of the Committee on the Elimination of Racial Discrimination, UN GAOR, 57th Sess of the UNGA, Supplement 18, 61st Sess of the CERD, UN Doc A/57/18, 107. See also the Committee's General Recommendation 30, Discrimination Against Non-Citizens, UN Doc CERD/C/64/Misc.11/rev.3 (2004), paragraph 10.

71 For example, the Special Rapporteur on Human Rights and Counter Terrorism has expressed the opinion that full respect for economic, social and cultural rights helps to eliminate the risk that individuals make the morally inexcusable decision to resort to acts of terrorism. See Report of the SR, Mission to Turkey, Conclusions and Recommendations.

72 See Global Counter Terrorism Strategy, GA. See also report of the Secretary-General, Uniting Against Terrorism: Recommendations for a Global Counter-terrorism Strategy, UN Doc A/60/825 (2006), paras 6, 13 to 17, and 22 to 27. Consider, for example, the Council of Europe, Guidelines on the Protection of Victims of Terrorist Acts (adopted by the Committee of Ministers at Strasbourg on 2 March 2005), DGII (2005) 6.

		investigate alleged terrorist activities as well as the possibilities of future terrorist acts to protect individuals from becoming victims, and to examine the rights of victims of terrorism to restitution and compensation, as well as other means of reparation. Finally, it must promote a definition of victims of terrorism to include individual victims of terrorist acts, and their families; as well as individual victims of States' counter-terrorism measures including through violation of economic, social and cultural rights

- Fifthly, they highlighted the UN role in CT efforts;
- Six, they supported the newly established Human Rights Council;
- Seven, they encouraged the Office of the United Nations High Commissioner for Human Rights to strenghten its operational capcity;
- And finally, states expressed their support to the Special Rapporteur on the promotion and protection of human rights and fundamental freedoms while countering terrorism.

Having seen the developments that led to the adoption of the Global Counter-Terrorism Strategy, we will now try to conceptualize the major issues and actors involved in the debate.

IV. Terrorism Prevention Branch of the United Nations Office on Drugs and Crime

The United Nations Office on Drugs and Crime, specialized office that belongs to the Secretariat of the UN, is stationed in Vienna and carriers out the work of the Secretariat on drugs, crime and terrorism. The General Assembly as well as Economic and Social Council (ECOSOC) and its Commissions on Narcotic Drugs (CND) and on Crime Prevention and Criminal Justice (CCPCJ) provide the relevant mandate to the office in the respective fields. The draft resolutions of the Crime Commission are either adopted by the commission or brought to the ECOSOC, which adopts them or approves those resolutions for adoption by the General Assembly. In recent years, in addition to its two original areas of work – drugs and crime, the UNODC has developed third pillar of its work- delivering legislative technical assistance on counter-terrorism.

4.1. Mandate

The mandate of the Terrorism Prevention Branch (TPB) within the Division for Treaty Affairs of the Office on Drugs and Crime (UNODC) is well defined as far as it concerns the provision of technical assistance and advisory services to countries in their fight against terrorism[1.] Drawing on the recommendations of the Symposium on *Combating International Terrorism: the contribution of the United Nations,* held in Vienna in June 2002, UNODC

[1] Mandates of the Terrorism Prevention Branch are contained in the following General Assembly and ECOSOC resolutions on:

Strengthening international cooperation and technical assistance in promoting the implementation of the universal conventions and protocols related to terrorism within the framework of the activities of the Centre for International Crime Prevention: A/RES/58/136;

Strengthening the UN Crime Prevention and Criminal Justice Programme: A/RES/58/140, A/RES/57/173, A/RES/56/123, A/RES/55/64, A/RES/54/131, A/RES/53/114, A/RES/52/90;

Vienna Declaration and Plans of Action: A/RES/57/170, A/RES/56/261, A/RES/55/59;

Measures to eliminate international terrorism: A/RES/58/81;

Questions relating to the programme budget: A/RES/57/292, A/RES/56/253 (Strengthening the Terrorism Prevention Branch), A/RES/52/220; and

Strengthening international cooperation and technical assistance within the framework of the activities of the Centre for International Crime Prevention in preventing and combating terrorism: ECOSOC 2002/19.

launched the *Global Programme against Terrorism* in October 2002. The Programme provides the framework for operational activities, which focus on *Strengthening the Legal Regime against Terrorism.* The overall aim of the *Global Programme* is to respond promptly and efficiently to requests for counter-terrorism assistance, in accordance with the priorities set by the Commission on Crime Prevention and Criminal Justice and the Security Council's Counter Terrorism Committee (CTC), through:

- Reviewing domestic legislation and providing advice on drafting new laws;
- Providing in-depth assistance on the ratification and implementation of new legislation against terrorism through a mentorship programme for follow-up action; and
- Facilitating and providing training to national criminal justice systems with regard to practical implementation of the universal instruments against terrorism.

The Global Strategy has given the TPB/UNODC more diversified work in its areas of expertise.

4.2. Activities Related to Reinforcing the Rule of Law and Human Rights[2]

For the past few years UNODC has focused its work on assisting national criminal justice systems to implement the universal instruments against terrorism (conventions and protocols):

- *First,* UNODC/TPB has assisted Member States to become party to the universal instruments against terrorism.
- *Second,* it has assisted States to incorporate in their national legislations the provisions of the instruments. It has also developed guidelines for steering such laws through national parliaments.
- *Third,* once these new laws have been put in place, UNODC has assisted States to train key criminal justice officials, especially prosecutors, attorneys general and judges.
- *Fourth,* UNODC has also assisted States to strengthen their ability to counter money laundering and terrorism financing.

In the future, and in response to the Strategy, UNODC will reinforce its work in the above areas. Moreover, it will strengthen its counter-terrorism technical assistance by taking new initiatives in relevant areas:

- *Fifth,* it will promote regional cooperation among criminal justice agencies (i.e. regarding mutual legal assistance and extradition), building on its anti-crime and anti-drugs expertise. The UNODC-sponsored Central Asian and Gulf Cooperation

[2] This part is based on a TPB working document 'putting into action the United Nations Global Counter-Terrorism Strategy: the Role of UNODC'.

Criminal Intelligence Centers could serve as models to build on the readiness of governments to address serious crimes at the regional level.

- *Sixth,* it will promote the use of "best" legal and criminal justice practices in counter-terrorism with countries that already have acceded to the international instruments but do not possess state-of-the-art terrorism prevention legislation and implementation capacity.
- *Seventh,* it will expand its current counter-terrorism legal research to include analysis of legislation, covering civil and common law, as well as developed and developing countries.
- *Eighth,* it will expand counter-terrorism specialized training to cover various areas of crime prevention and criminal justice administration.
- *Ninth,* it will promote academic training on counter-terrorism, in partnership with universities, for building up terrorism prevention expertise.
- *Tenth,* it will increase field level initiatives in areas of UNODC's counter-terrorism mandates, using the UNODC Field Offices around the world and benefiting from the operational advantages they offer, under the policy and substantive guidance from Headquarters. An important parallel objective will be to build up specialized counter-terrorism legal expertise at the field level.

In this context the following tools for the provision of legislative assistance have been developed:

- The UN Legislative Guide to the Universal Anti-Terrorism Conventions and Protocols;
- The Checklist of Offences and Jurisdiction contained in the twelve universal legal instruments, the Security Council resolution 1373 (2001); and
- The Technical Assistance Legislative Database, which includes model laws and examples of relevant national legislation.

4.3. Vienna and New York[3]

UNODC technical assistance activities have been conducted – and this will be stressed even more forcefully in the future – under the policy guidance of the CTC and in coordination with the work of the CTED. These bodies fulfil normative, policy, assessment, monitoring and coordination functions pertaining to Security Council resolution 1373 (2001). While they do not provide technical assistance directly to member states, they identify gaps in the ability of member states to counter terrorism. They have political and normative mandates that must precede everything and anything done by UNODC.

UNODC therefore operates downstream to both CTC and CTED. It provides legal and capacity-building technical assistance, focussed on areas of operation (country and/or theme) identified by CTC and CTED. As of today, the following working arrangements are in place:

[3] This part is based on a TPB working document 'putting into action the United Nations Global Counter-Terrorism Strategy: the Role of UNODC'.

(i) UNODC participates in CTC and CTED country visits, in accordance with Security Council resolution 1535 (2004);
(ii) CTC and CTED experts participate in UNODC national and regional activities and provide advice on priorities;
(iii) Information is shared in the planning of UNODC activities;
(iv) CTC and CTED provide guidance on the countries in need of assistance;
(v) UNODC helps Member States compile reports for submission to the CTC.

The provision of technical assistance by UNODC cannot take place in a vacuum: it has to be guided by the political priorities identified by the CTC and it must respect the operational requirements ascertained by CTED. Also, counter-terrorism assistance has to be offered in a context mindful of other criminal behaviors – especially those that can become breeding grounds for terrorist funding and logistics. Here UNODC has major comparative advantages and significant experience.

4.4. Contributing to the Counter-Terrorism Implementation Task Force[4]

To ensure that UNODC's counter-terrorism work is fully carried out in the broader context of and coordinated with the UN system-wide efforts, UNODC is a key participant in the Counter-Terrorism Implementation Task Force, established by the Secretary-General in June 2005. The Task Force, a coordinating and information-sharing body of an advisory nature, serves as a forum to discuss strategic issues and to develop policy recommendations. Chaired by the Office of the Secretary-General, it brings together 23 key actors of the UN system and its partners that can contribute to an effective coordinated fight against terrorism. The UN Global Counter-Terrorism Strategy welcomed the intention of the Secretary-General to institutionalize the Task Force. UNODC, as the lead UN entity for delivering counter-terrorism legal and related technical assistance, will continue to provide key contributions to the work of the Task Force.

4.5. Vienna Symposium on Advancing the Implementation of the United Nations Global Counter - Terrorism Strategy

In May 2007, UNODC had the honor of hosting a Global Symposium for the UN Member States, UN system entities, regional organizations and counter-terrorism experts. The main topic of discussions was how they can best work together on concrete measures required by the global strategy. The syposium was the first event of this kind since the adoption of the Strategy.

The symposium was an important coordinating event for all the UN and non-UN entities envolved in CT work. The results of the symposium is best seen from the conclusing remarks of the Chair, H.E. Thomas Stelzer, Permanent Representaitve of Austria to the UN, Vienna. [5]

---

[4] Ibid.

[5] Available at: http://www.unodc.org/pdf/ConcludingRemarks.pdf.

V. Conclusion

The UN is often criticized for its action (or more accurately, lack of action) on terrorism. "Lack of the definition" of terrorism, not addressing its "root causes", "victims", and other issues, are often cited by the critics to highlight UN impotence in dealing with this gravest manifestation of crime. Recently the main area of criticism evolved around human rights.

We, at the Terrorism Prevention Branch of the UNODC, are convinced that "the struggle against terrorism is not a zero-sum game. The misconception that effective anti-terrorism prevention and enforcement automatically diminish human rights protections under the rule of law should be avoided. A preventive, even aggressively proactive, anti-terrorism strategy can be based upon scrupulous observance of human rights, and can simultaneously enhance both the rule of law and the protective abilities of Member States.'[6] And we stand ready to provide any assistance needed in developing such a strategy.

References

"A Global Strategy for Fighting Terrorism", Keynote Address to the Closing Plenary of the International Summit on Democracy, Terrorism and Security, Madrid, 10 March 2004, <http://daccessdds.un.org/doc/UNDOC/GEN/N05/487/60/PDF/N0548760. pdf? Open Element>

"A More Secure World: Our Shared Responsibility". Report of the High-level Panel on Threats, Challenges and Change. <http://www.un.org/secureworld/brochure.pdf>

Annan, Kofi. "Keynote address to the Closing Plenary of the International Summit on Democracy, Terrorism and Security". <http://english.safe-democracy.org/keynotes/a-global-strategy-for-fighting-terrorism.html>

Boulden, Jane and Thomas G. Weiss. "Wither Terrorism and the United Nations", In: J. Boulden and Th. G. Weiss. *Terrorism and the UN: Before and after September 11.* Bloomington, Indiana University Press, 2004, p.22.

"Can the UN Battle Terrorism Effectively?" *USA Today Magazine,* January 2005.

Cortright, David. "A Critical Evaluation of the UN Counter- Terrorism Program: Accomplishments and Challenges". <http://www.tni.org/crime-docs/cortright.pdf>

Cortright, David, George A. Lopez, Alistair Millar, and Linda Gerbner. *An Action Agenda for Enhancing the United Nations Program on Counter-Terrorism.* Notre Dame, Indiana, Joan B. Kroc Institute for International Peace Studies, September 2004, p. 7, 9.

"Declaration on Measures to Eliminate International Terrorism", General Assembly resolution 49/60 of 9 December 1994. Annex; repr. In: *United Nations. International Instruments related to the Prevention and Suppression of International Terrorism.* New York, UN Office of Legal Affairs, 2001, p. 233.

de Jonge Oudraat, Chantal. "The Role of the Security Council". In: J. Boulden and Thomas G. Weiss (Eds.). *Terrorism and the UN. Before and after September 11.* Bloomington, Indiana University Press, 2004, p. 158.

---

[6] Preventing Terrorist Acts: A Criminal Justice Strategy Integrating Rule of Law Standards in Implementation of United Nations Anti-Terrorism Instruments. Terrorism Prevention Branch. Technical Assistance Working Paper.

Millar, Alistair, et al. "The Future of Multilateral Counter-Terrorism Policy Coordination, Monitoring, and Implementation" December 2005. <http://www.counter-terrorismcenter.org/pdf/future_mult_ct.pdf>

"Report of the High-Level Policy Working Group on the United Nations and Terrorism". New York, United Nations, 2002 (A/57/273;S/2002/875), pp. 1, 11.

Rosand, Eric. "The Security Council's Efforts to Monitor the Implementation of Al Qaeda/Taliban Sanctions". *The American Journal of International Law,* Vol. 98, p. 4.

Roush, Jim. "The United Nations, Terrorism, and Nations Building. World View Seminar on September 11 and its Aftermath", <http://www.unc.edu/world/united_nations.shtml>, 24/03/2004, p.1.

"Threats to international peace and security caused by terrorist acts". Joint briefing by the Chairs of three SC committees. Security Council. Sixty-first year. 5,446th meeting. Tuesday, 30 May 2006, 10 a.m. New York.

United Nations. "Combating international terrorism: The contribution of the United Nations". New York, UN, 2002.

"Uniting Against Terrorism: Recommendations for a global counter-terrorism strategy". Report of the Secretary-General. p. 24-25. <http://www.un.org/ unitingagainstterrorism /contents.htm>

White House, "Progress on the Global War on Terrorism", U.S. Department of State.

In: Human Rights Issues in the 21st Century
Editors: M.S. Becker and J.N. Schneider, pp. 189-195
ISBN 978-1-60456-119-7

Chapter 9

HUMAN RIGHTS AND PSYCHOLOGY ETHICS CODES IN ARGENTINA

Andrea Ferrero
National University of San Luis, Argentina

ABSTRACT

This work considers the importance of ethics in the practice of psychology. Within this general framework, this paper takes into account the central role that human rights take in the main professional ethic codes of psychology in Argentina, like in many other ethic codes from other countries. The particular inclusion of these topics in Argentinean ethic codes of psychology is analyzed in this case not only as the inclusion of general ethical principles that guarantee personal and community welfare. It is specially considered that the permanent direct or indirect reference to human rights in those Codes is related to the '70 dictatorial government that, as in many other Latin-American countries, established a terror system, in which personal and social rights were seriously damaged, causing a deep wound in society.

Keywords: psychology - ethic codes - human rights - Argentina.

Psychologist's scientific and professional community agree in the importance of ethics in the professional psychologist's training. It has also been stated that an ethical practice of psychology, as any other profession, must consider some general principles as *Beneficence* and *Nonmaleficence*, *Autonomy* and *Justice* (Childress, 1998). Upon these basic principles most ethics codes in psychology includes Fidelity and Social Responsibility, Integrity, and Respect for People's Rights and Dignity (Leach and Harbin, 1997; Lindsay, 1996; Loewy, 2003, Pettifor, 2004, Waring, Bore and Munro, 2003). All these professional commitments are referred to the expectations of an ethical practice of psychology (Graham, 2001; Lindsay, 1996; Pettifor and Horne, 2001, Ferrero, 2003).

In some Latin-American countries these principles take a particular relevance. As it is known, between 1970 and 1985, military forces overthrew democratic governments and established dictatorial governments in many Latin-American countries, characterized by the illegal capture, torture, and forced disappearance of thousands of people. In Argentina there was a *coup* on March 24th, 1976, that ended in October 1983, when democratic elections were held. There were about 30.000 missing people, mostly students, teachers, workers, members of any political party, and even priests and housewives. From all professional fields, psychologists had the higher number of missing colleagues (Comisión Nacional sobre la Desaparición de Personas [National Commission for Missing People], 1984).

Some of those missing people recovered their freedom and state their testimonies about the inhuman life conditions in clandestine detention centers, the frequent torture sessions -in many occasions supervised by medical doctors-, and the all kind of abuses they had to suffer. There also were over 300 babies born in those centers, whose mothers were killed after the birth and the babies were adopted, specially by families related to the military staff. Up to day 77 of those babies, young men and women, have recovered their real identity and met their biological families due to the praiseworthy work done by the *Abuelas de Plaza de Mayo*, which central goal is to recover their grandchildren, those who they could not knew because their pregnant daughters or daughters in law were kidnapped by military forces. As the *Madres de Plaza de Mayo*, the grandmothers lost their sons or daughters, but they still hope to recover their grandchildren (Comisión Nacional sobre la Desaparición de Personas [National Commission for Missing People], 1984). All this facts left a deep wound not only in those who have been directly involved themselves or their relatives, but in the whole society as well.

There is no doubt that respecting human rights is everybody's duty, as it is stated in the main Right's Declarations, beginning with the *Universal Declaration Of Human Rights* (United Nations, 1948). Since that moment, many new right's declarations, conforming the so called "generations", arose with the intention to protect any kind of individual and community's right. It is necessary to remark that rights also means duties, as everybody's rights imply some one's else duties (Tugendhat, 1997).

So everyone, both as person and part of a community, is obliged to respect these declarations, but in case of a professional relation, these duties take become even more relevant because of the asymmetrical relation between the parts, and that is why there are many right's declarations which function is to preserve people's rights, also within mental health field (United Nations, 1990; 1991; 1997). Due to this principles, any professional practice -including psychology in any field of application-, must consider the relation between rights and duties, relation that is expressed by professional ethics codes (Dobson and Breault, 1998; Ferrero, 2005; Knapp and VandeCreek, 2003; Leach and Harbin, 1997; Lindsay, 1996). Within these specific professional principles there are also ethical regulations specially referred to research with human beings, which main interest is to protect the autonomy and the welfare of the persons involved in medical treatment and research, as the *Helsinki Declaration* (World Medical Association, 1975/2000), the *Belmont Report* (National Commission for the Protection of Human Subjects of Biomedical and Behavioral Research, 1979), the *International Ethical Guidelines for Biomedical Research Involving Human Subjects* (Council for International Organizations of Medical Sciences (CIOMS), 2002), and the *International Code of Medical Ethics* (World Medical Association, 1949/ 1983)

In Argentina the practice of psychology is regulated by provincial federal laws all over the country. Each province has got its own Board of Psychologists leading to licensure and has developed local Ethics Codes with very few differences between them (Klappenbach, 2004). In this country there are two Psychology Ethics Codes with national application. One of them, is the National Ethics Code, stated in 1999 by the *Psychologists' Federation of the Argentine Republic* [Federación de Psicólogos de la República Argentina] (Federación de Psicólogos de la República Argentina [Psychologists' Federation of the Argentine Republic], 1999), and the other is a regional one called *Ethical Principles Framework for professional practice of psychology in the Mercosur and Associated Countries* [*Protocolo de Acuerdo Marco de Principios Éticos para Psicólogos del Mercosur y Países Asociados*] and involves not only Argentina but other countries of the *Mercosur* (Comité Coordinador de Psicólogos del Mercosur y Países Asociados [Psychologists' Committee of Mercosur and Associated Countries], 1997). The *Mercosur* is a socio-economic and cultural Union of the southeast countries of South America: Argentina, Brazil, Paraguay and Uruguay as full members, and Chile and Bolivia as associated countries.

Even though the *Psychologists' Committee of Mercosur and Associated Countries* has not reached the goals showed by the *European Federation of Psychologists' Associations*, whose Metha Code of ethics "provides a model of common principles or values" (Pettifor, 2004, p. 267), such Committee has also began the hard task of providing a framework for common training and practice standards in psychology, and also a common psychology Ethics Code for the countries of the Mercosur (Hermosilla, 2000).

The Ethics Code of the *Psychologists' Federation of the Argentine Republic* is considered the most important reference for psychologist's professional conduct in Argentina, and includes a Preamble, five Ethical General Principles and many Ethical Standards referred to deontological duties: informed consent, confidentiality, record keeping, education and training, research, publication, advertising and human relations with colleagues and clients (Federación de Psicólogos de la República Argentina [Psychologists' Federation of the Argentine Republic], 1999). The *Ethical Principles Framework for professional practice of psychology in the Mercosur and Associated Countries* is also a valuable reference, and its main interests are five Ethical General Principles, which are exactly the same of the mentioned National Code *Mercosur* (Comité Coordinador de Psicólogos del Mercosur y Países Asociados [Psychologists' Committee of Mercosur and Associated Countries], 1997).

The importance of human rights in psychology's Argentinean ethics codes can be firstly appreciate in the *Preambule* of the National Code, where this matter takes a relevant place:

> "(Psychologists)... promotes for both the person and the society the absolute validity of Human Rights, the defense of the democratic govern system, and the permanent looking for freedom, social justice and dignity, that will produce an active, critic and solidarity person and society"... "(Psychologists)... do not permit, nor even take part willingly of any kind of discriminatory action" (Federación de Psicólogos de la República Argentina [Psychologists' Federation of the Argentine Republic], 1999) (Translation is ours).

Both ideas of this *Preambule* of the National Ethics Code of Psychology are clear enough from the very beginning about the importance of human rights in this Code.

As we have already mentioned, both Ethics Codes, the psychologists' *Mercosur's Code* and the Argentinean one, include the same five General Principles: *Respect for People's*

Rights and Dignity, Professional Competence, Professional and Scientific Commitment, Integrity, and Social Responsibility (Comité Coordinador de Psicólogos del Mercosur y Países Asociados [Psychologists' Committee of Mercosur and Associated Countries], 1997; Federación de Psicólogos de la República Argentina [Psychologists' Federation of the Argentine Republic], 1999).

These principles do not differ much from the General Principles of the *Ethics Codes* of the American Psychological Association and the European Federation of Psychologist's Associations. In fact, the general principles of the American Psychological Association Ethics Code are: *Beneficence and Nonmaleficence, Fidelity and Responsability, Integrity, Justice, and Respect for People's Rights and Dignity.* And the general principles of the EPFA Metha Code are: *Respect for a Person's Rights and Dignity, Competence, Responsibility* and *Integrity* (APA, 2002; EFPA, 1995; Knapp and VandeCreek, 2003; Pettifor, 2004).

Human rights is a central topic in the North-American end European psychology ethics codes, and South-American countries are not an exception as all of them includes their commitment to this matter. Of course that all above-mentioned general principles share, directly or not, a relation with human rights, as they protect general people's welfare related to any psychological practice (Ferrero, 2002).

But in countries like Argentina, where human rights have been seriously defiled, this professional commitment acquires a very particular meaning. From this perspective the inclusion of human rights in psychological ethics codes in Argentina has a particular value, as it makes reference to a very painful past and promotes a reflection in a professional community that is part of a society that has been seriously injured.

That is why in this occasion we consider the relation between the same five General Principles of the Argentinean ethical codes and human rights, with the intention of analyzing the underlying links, some kind of silent and omnipresent role of human rights in all of these principles (Federación de Psicólogos de la República Argentina [Psychologists' Federation of the Argentine Republic], 1999; Comité Coordinador de Psicólogos del Mercosur y Países Asociados [Psychologists' Committee of Mercosur and Associated Countries], 1997).

The first mentioned General Principle of both Codes is specifically referred to human rights. It is called Respect for people's rights and dignity, and states:

> "Psychologists has a commitment with the principles stated by the Universal Declaration of Human Rights. They will respect fundamental rights, dignity and worth of all people, and will not take part in discriminatory actions. They will respect people's right to privacy, confidentiality, self-determination, and autonomy" (Federación de Psicólogos de la República Argentina [Psychologists' Federation of the Argentine Republic], 1999; Comité Coordinador de Psicólogos del Mercosur y Países Asociados [Psychologists' Committee of Mercosur and Associated Countries], 1997) (Translation is ours).

As we have already mentioned, the need to give priority to human rights in Argentinean psychology ethics codes can be appreciated in the other four General Principles, which are mainly focused to different aspects of an ethical practice of psychology. So the second point referred to *Competence*, remarks the importance of professional competence itself and states:

> "(Psychologists)... "Must consider that the competence required in the treatment, teaching or researching of communities, may vary according to the diversity of those communities" (Federación de Psicólogos de la República Argentina [Psychologists' Federation of the

> Argentine Republic], 1999; Comité Coordinador de Psicólogos del Mercosur y Países Asociados [Psychologists' Committee of Mercosur and Associated Countries], 1997) (Translation is ours).

This shows that psychologists must not only have to develop a high qualified intervention, but that this one must seriously consider the respect for the own characteristics of the community in which it is held, act that involves the respect of any kind of individual or cultural differences.

The next General Principle is referred to *Integrity*, and states:

> "Psychologists will be aware from using notions that might conclude in denigrating or discriminatory cualifications" and "In their scientific and professional role they will make clear the role of any of the parts involved and will act according to that" (Federación de Psicólogos de la República Argentina [Psychologists' Federation of the Argentine Republic], 1999; Comité Coordinador de Psicólogos del Mercosur y Países Asociados [Psychologists' Committee of Mercosur and Associated Countries], 1997) (Translation is ours).

Both ideas are referred to the fact that professional and scientific *Integrity* must take into account the respect for the person involved in the practice and the need of honesty to make a clear set up of that practice.

Finally, the General Principle referred to *Social Responsibility*, establishes:

> "Psychologists exert their social commitment through the study of reality and promote and/or help with the development of laws and social policies that, from their professional specificity, might contribute to the welfare and development of the person and the community" (Federación de Psicólogos de la República Argentina [Psychologists' Federation of the Argentine Republic], 1999; Comité Coordinador de Psicólogos del Mercosur y Países Asociados [Psychologists' Committee of Mercosur and Associated Countries], 1997) (Translation is ours).

This last General Principle points out that the practice of psychology is related to the possibility of being part of policies that could formally guarantee people's welfare, and personal and community development.

The analysis of the main psychology ethics codes in Argentina shows the importance that human rights had at the moment in which they have been stated. This fact has consequences regarding the local practice of psychology as it is regulated by these Codes, and points out that an ethical practice of psychology must always take into account not only ethical procedures themselves, but also their origins. The central role of human rights in Argentinean psychology Ethics Codes reveals part of the history of this country.

References

American Psychological Association (2002). Ethical Principles of Psychologists and Code of Conduct. *American Psychologist*, 57 (12), 1060–1073.

Childress, J. F. (1998). El lugar de la autonomía en la bioética. [The place of Authonomy in Bioethics]. In F. Luna and A. Salles (Eds.), *Bioética. Investigación, muerte, procreación y otros temas de ética aplicada.* [Bioethic. Research, death, procreation and other matters of applied ethics] (pp. 133-144). Buenos Aires: Sudamericana. (Original work published in 1990).

Comisión Nacional sobre la Desaparición de Personas (1984). *Nunca más. Informe de la Comisión Nacional sobre la desaparición de personas.* [Never again. Report of the National Commission for Missing People]. Buenos Aires: Eudeba.

Comité Coordinador de Psicólogos del Mercosur y Países Asociados [Psychologists Committee of Mercosur and Associated Countries] (1997). *Protocolo de acuerdo marco de principios éticos para el ejercicio profesional de los psicólogos en el Mercosur y Países Asociados.* [*Ethical Principles Framework for professional practice of psychology in the Mercosur and Associated Countries*]. In Conselho Federal de Psicologia [Federal Board of Psychology], *A psicologia no Mercosul* [*Psychology in the Mercosur*] (pp. 11-14). Brasilia, Brasil: Author.

Council for International Organizations of Medical Sciences (CIOMS) (2002). *International Ethical Guidelines for Biomedical Research Involving Human Subjects.* Author.

Dobson, K. S. and Breault, L. (1998). The Canadian Code of Ethics and the Regulation of Psychology. *Canadian Psychology, 39* (3), 212-218.

European Federation of Professional Psychologists Associations (1995). *Metha-Code of Ethics.* Brusels: Author.

Federación de Psicólogos de la República Argentina [Psychologists' Federation of the Argentine Republic] (1999). *Código de Etica. (Ethics Code).* Buenos Aires: Autor.

Ferrero, A. (2002). Importancia de los derechos humanos en los códigos deontológicos de psicología en la Argentina [The importance of human rights in psychology ethics codes]. *Revista Argentina de Psicología, 45*, 33-41.

Ferrero, A. (2003). Consecuencias sociales y psicológicas de la globalización en Argentina. Una mirada desde la ética profesional [Social and psychological globalization's effects. An ethical point of view]. *Revista Iberoamericana de Educación, Salud y Trabajo, 4*, 253-264.

Ferrero, A. (2005). El surgimiento de la deontología profesional en el campo de la psicología [The beginnings of professional deontology in psychology]. *Fundamentos en Humanidades, 6,* (10/11), 169-177.

Graham, J. (2001). Caring from Afar: Expanding our Concept of Care in the Professions. *Professional Ethics: a multidisciplinary Journal, 9* (1), 31-60.

Hermosilla, A. M. (2000). Psicología y Mercosur: la dimensión ética de la integración y antecedentes del debate en Argentina [Psychology and Mercosur: ethical perspective of integration and framework for the debate in Argentina]. *Fundamentos en Humanidades, 1*, 2, 63-76.

Klappenbach, H. (2004). Psychology in Argentina. In M. J. Strevens and D. Wedding (Eds.), *Handbook of International Psychology* (pp. 129-168). New York: Brunner-Routledge.

Knapp, S. and VandeCreek, L. (2003). An Overview of the Major Changes in the 2002 APA Ethics Code. *Professional Psychology: Research and Practice, 34* (3), 301-308.

Leach, M. M. and Harbin, J. J. (1997). Psychological Ethics Codes: a comparison of twenty-four countries. *International Journal of Psychology, 32* (3), 181-192.

Lindsay, G. (1996). Psychology as an Ethical Discipline and Profession. *European Psychologist, 1* (2), 79-88.

Loewy, E. (2003). Education, practice and bioethics: Growing barriers to ethical practice. *Health Care Analysis, (2),* 11, 171-179.

National Commission for the Protection of Human Subjects of Biomedical and Behavioral Research (1979) The Belmont Report Office of the Secretary. Ethical Principles and guidelines for the Protection of Human Subjects of Research. Author.

Pettifor, J. L. (2004). Proffesional Ethics accross National Boundaries. *European Psychologist, 9* (4), 264-272.

Pettifor, J. L. and Horne, K. (2001). Professional ethics: Social responsibility or the status quo? In R. Roth and S. Neill (Eds.), *A matter for life: Psychological theory, research and practice* (pp. 449–46). Berlin: Pabst.

Tugendhat, E. (1997) *Lecciones de ética*. Barcelona: Gedisa.

United Nations General Assembly (1948). *Universal Declaration Of Human Rights*. Author.

United Nations (1990). *Tallinn Guidelines For Action On Human Resources Development In The Field Of Disability*. Author.

United Nations (1991). Principles for the Protection of Persons with Mental Illnesses and the Improvement of Mental Health Care. Author

United Nations (1997). *Standard Rules on the Equalization of Opportunities for Persons with Disabilities*. Author.

Waring, T., Bore, M. and Munro, D. (2003). Ethics and the practice of psychology. Regulating, educating and selecting the ethical practitioner. *Australian Journal of Psychology, Supplement 2003*, 463-475.

World Medical Association (1975/2000). *Declaration of Helsinki: Ethical Principles for Medical Research Involving Human Subjects*. Author.

World Medical Association (1949/1983) *International Code of Medical Ethics*. Author.

INDEX

A

B

C

D

E

F

G

H

I

J

N

O

P

T

Y

Z